The Bible in the Public Square

Reading the Signs of the Times

Edited by Cynthia Briggs Kittredge,
Ellen Bradshaw Aitken,
and Jonathan A. Draper

FORTRESS PRESS

Minneapolis

THE BIBLE IN THE PUBLIC SQUARE
READING THE SIGNS OF THE TIMES

Cover image: Copyright © Martin Alipaz/EFE/Corbis. Used by permission.
Cover design: Brad Norr
Book design: Jessica A. Puckett

Library of Congress Cataloging-in-Publication Data
The Bible in the public square : reading the signs of the times / Cynthia Briggs Kittredge, Ellen Bradshaw Aitken, and Jonathan A. Draper, editors.
      p. cm.
   ISBN 978–0–8006–3859–7 (alk. paper)
   1. Christianity and politics—Biblical teaching. I. Kittredge, Cynthia Briggs. II. Aitken, Ellen Bradshaw, 1961- III. Draper, Jonathan A.
   BS680.P45B53 2008
   220.09'04—dc22   2007047972

The paper used in this publication meets the minimum requirements of American National Standard for Information Sciences—Permanence of Paper for Printed Library Materials, ANSI Z329.48-1984.

Manufactured in the U.S.A.

12   11   10   09   08   1   2   3   4   5   6   7   8   9   10

Contents

Part II: Questioning the *Ekklēsia* and the Academy

Part III: Prospects for Politically Engaged Biblical Studies

For Richard A. Horsley
scholar, catalyst, friend
for his encouragement, provocation, and high spirits

"The *basileia* of God is not coming with things that can be observed; nor will they say, 'Look, here it is!' or 'There it is!' For, behold, the *basileia* of God is among you." (Luke 17:20-21)

Introduction

"You know how to interpret the appearance of the sky,
but you cannot interpret the signs of the times." (Matt 16:3)

To read the Bible in the public square in these times is to take on a challenging task. Issues of hunger, poverty, and violence are urgent and call for our responses. For many, however, the Bible has lost its power to shape political and social imagination, while at the same time other forceful voices claim divine justification for their political positions by appeal to the Bible's authority.

The challenge is even more complicated for those whose educational privileges and institutional position gives them the ability to speak and to be heard. When they try to speak in the public arena, members of the academy who appear to have surrendered their commitment to a neutral objectivity risk losing their credibility and thus their potential influence, while those who stand detached from the social and ethical demands of our time are politically ineffective. The premise of this volume is that, because the Bible remains so powerfully influential in contemporary culture, interpreting it well remains an important responsibility. It follows that biblical scholars can and do have a role to play in the public square, an ecumenical, plural, democratic space that is neither the church sanctuary nor the university classroom. They carry out this obligation in different ways depending on what model they employ, their own location, their audience, and their area of expertise. For all of them, however, responsible biblical scholarship requires reading the signs of the times.

Reading the signs of the times requires taking seriously the political context in which we read the Bible. For scholars, it requires using their specialized knowledge of the Bible and its context to gain some kind of critical purchase or perspective on that political context. In the essays that follow, each author demonstrates how biblical scholarship contributes to the conversation between the Bible and the present historical times in which we live. For that engagement, these authors look to the Bible in various ways: as a positive resource, a source for criticism of culture; as a negative model to recognize and resist; as a powerful text with an ambiguous history; and, for yet others, as a means to understand the significance of contemporary events and, thus, to find a way forward.

A Shift in Paradigms

That biblical scholars can and should be engaged socially and politically represents a paradigm shift signaled by Elisabeth Schüssler Fiorenza in her 1987 Society of Biblical Literature presidential address. Schüssler Fiorenza argued for biblical scholars to understand themselves as engaged with and accountable to their social and political context.[1] As public intellectuals and members of a larger civic conversation broader than the professional guild, biblical scholars have a responsibility to take that context into their work and use their specialized knowledge for the good of the wider community. Krister Stendahl called this ethical concern the "public health" aspect of biblical studies.[2]

Few scholars have exemplified this commitment throughout their work as consistently as Richard A. Horsley. As a historian and biblical interpreter, Horsley has brought the Bible into the public square both directly and indirectly. He has critiqued the popular holiday of Christmas—which he describes as the American festival of consumption—from the perspective of the narrative of the birth of Jesus in Luke, a story of God's work among poor and ordinary people that fundamentally threatens the reign of Caesar.[3] More recently he has explicitly analyzed the "new world disorder" as parallel to the Roman Empire and modern Islamic resistance movements as analogous with ancient Judean groups.[4] Horsley's reading of Paul's letters and of the Gospel according to Mark within the context of Roman imperial propaganda proceeds from explicit comparisons between the Roman Empire and modern American political ideology and between the vision for the renewal of Israel of the earliest Christian communities and contemporary Christian movements.

Horsley's orientation to biblical studies as a practice with ethical dimensions stands in the spirit of the scholarship of Stendahl, for whom he wrote an eloquent appreciation in his introduction to *Paul and Politics*.[5] Though Horsley has not claimed for himself the title *socially engaged scholar* or claimed to be a political theologian or biblical preacher, in his role as historian of the ancient world and reader of biblical texts in their social context he has nevertheless made implicit claims about how Jesus, Paul, or other New Testament authors speak to contemporary issues of economic injustice, violence, or domination. His ethical concerns shape the questions he asks of the ancient sources. In his work, Horsley has sought to have an impact on a biblical studies guild that has, in the main, been highly ambivalent about entering the territory between the Bible and politics. How much he has succeeded in changing the discipline is a question that cannot yet be answered definitively. His scholarship, teaching, collaborative work, and encouragement have profoundly influenced many students and colleagues, however, and the voices of only some of those many, many friends are represented in these pages. These essays indicate how the socially engaged scholarship advocated by Elisabeth Schüssler Fiorenza and Krister Stendahl, and exemplified by Richard Horsley, among others, has been realized in fascinating and fruitful ways.

Reading at the Intersection of Politics and Religion

The guiding insight of much of Horsley's historical and interpretive work is the conviction that it has been an error for much of biblical scholarship to impose onto the ancient sources the modern separation between religion and politics. The practical and theological result of this division is to find a Jesus who is critical only of religious practices and not of social or economic ones. The message of the purely religious Jesus or the apolitical Paul has nothing to say to contemporary culture or to public policy. To isolate and spiritualize the person and message of either figure is to render them powerless as sources of vision or of transformation today. Such an apolitical model of biblical studies serves to maintain the benefits of the current economic and political system for those who work within it.

Horsley argues that the messianic movements of John the Baptist and of Jesus were popular movements of resistance to imperial leadership and policies.[6] The narrative arc of the Gospel according to Mark presents an interpretation of the followers of Jesus as joining in a renewal of Jewish civic life on the basis of the Mosaic covenant.[7] The Gospel according to Luke preserves traditions around the conception and infancy of Jesus that symbolically challenge the imperial representation of Caesar as savior, *sōtēr*, and agent of the good news, *euangelion*.[8] Paul imagined and organized the churches as alternative social spaces to the imperial structure of patronage and hierarchy.[9] All these arguments stress the fundamental point that rather than operating in a spiritual sphere beyond politics, the interpretations of Jesus on the part of Luke, Mark, and Paul are thoroughly political in that they speak to the power arrangements, the economic system, and the social order of their day.

Horsley contends for these political readings of the New Testament authors by describing the social, artistic, and economic structures of the Roman imperial world. Drawing on the work of classicists, ancient historians, sociologists, and other theorists and bringing that work to the attention of New Testament studies, he shows how the emperor cult, the system of patronage, and power relations were addressed and challenged either overtly or in a disguised and subtle fashion by the early Christian literature. The New Testament texts display and communicate a value system that counters the categories of honor and shame and of hierarchical patron and client relationships. By reading the New Testament authors in the context of Roman imperial ideology, Horsley encourages interpreters to see and hear protest and judgment on political systems that dominant interpretative models have obscured. The result of this shift in perspective has been a repoliticized Jesus and a repoliticized Paul.

One might summarize Horsley's strategy of interpretation and commentary in this way: Despite how we think, the past is not like the present. Religion and politics were indivisible. At the same time, the present is more like the past than we think in that religious language is still allied with economic and social systems in order to maintain and perpetuate them. A renewed appreciation of the interconnection of religion and politics implies that those who identify with Jesus and the movement that followed him do not do Jesus justice by assuming a completely individualized and spiritualized faith.

The historical Jesus whom Horsley reconstructs and describes is the model for political engagement in the present. Jesus criticizes the alliance of religious symbols with coercive power, as the Hebrew prophets did before him. Jesus reaffirms covenantal ethics over the values of the marketplace. Paul, too, in his use of the apocalyptic language of the conquest and subjection of the powers, does not escape the present concrete circumstances of his communities but launches a radical critique of them. Recognizing the close identification of political and religious symbols in the ancient world gives the contemporary interpreter the means to uncover and acknowledge the ways they are identified in political rhetoric in the present.

Both points depend on the use of historical analogies between the ancient world and the present. Horsley makes explicit parallels between the ancient Roman and the contemporary American empires in *Jesus and Empire*:

> Indeed many Americans cannot avoid the awkward feeling that they are more analogous to imperial Rome than they are to the ancient Middle Eastern people who celebrated their origins in God's liberation from harsh service to a foreign ruler and lived according the covenantal principles of social-economic justice.[10]

Movements of peasant resistance in the first century are structurally similar to resistance movements of today.[11] Global consumer capitalism is parallel to the imperial cultural domination of Rome in the first century. Using theoretical models from sociology and anthropology, particularly the work of James C. Scott and theorists of orality, Horsley reconstructs the ancient social world in which these texts were written and heard.[12] Convening groups of specialists, Horsley has encouraged historical reconstruction of Galilee and of the cities of Paul's letters which takes into account the lives of non-elite people.[13] Describing the social context of the Jesus movement and of communities around Paul results in a picture of the historical Jesus as a prophet who calls communities to resist imperial pressure and to renew covenantal values. Horsley uses historical analogies to relate scripture with the signs of the times and to cause a shift in reading Jesus and Paul from the confessional to the concrete.

Ways of Engagement

This method both offers historical reconstruction of the past and makes analogies with the present. Horsley's rhetorical strategy relies on his audience's acceptance of his reconstruction as accurate and agreeing with the comparisons he makes of past and present. He understands the work that he does to be correcting previous scholarship on Galilee and on the historical Jesus, and he appears reluctant to name explicitly the theological and ethical commitments that drive his work. The liberating message inheres in the biblical author or Jesus or Paul. In the decision to link interpretation closely to the claims of the historical text, Horsley differs from some of his colleagues who contribute to this volume.

Horsley presents Jesus, Paul, and the spirit-filled communities of the early church as those who imagined and expressed a vision of a world shaped by values of equality, inclusion, mutuality, and justice. Those who have power exercise it on behalf of those who do not, and those who have less share what they have with one another. Horsley describes and translates the phrase "kingdom of God" as a political idea with ancient roots in the imagination of Israel that Jesus enacted and his followers practiced. Horsley's description of Jesus' preaching and the impulses of the Pauline communities present an alternative vision to the structures of the Roman Empire. In this reconstruction, the historical figures of Jesus and Paul and the movements in which they took part are unambiguously positive examples to counter the Roman imperial values. Horsley's rhetorical strategy draws the sharpest contrast between the Roman Empire and the alternative vision of Jesus and Paul. In raising up this vision and articulating it in fresh ways, even in not primarily theological language, Horsley has proposed a shift in scholarship and offered to preachers and church people a compelling way of thinking and speaking of Jesus' ministry and mission.

The authors in this volume exemplify a diverse variety of ways that biblical scholars engage in contemporary political discussion. All of these authors, who are scholars and teachers of religion and some also pastors and preachers, employ different models for understanding what the biblical text offers to public life. They use distinctive rhetorical strategies and speak to specific audiences in particular contexts. They in their work, as Horsley does in his, use implicit and explicit historical analogies to link the past and the present. They demonstrate different levels of commitment to the historical-scientific paradigm and various degrees of self-awareness about their approach. The work of all these scholars shows commitment to an alternative vision of human community distinct from that of the surrounding empires. However, not all the essayists derive that vision from history, the world behind the text, in as straightforward a fashion as Horsley does.

Those who speak about the insights of the Bible in the present moment, in part one of this compilation, confront a world whose rhetorical landscape has changed dramatically since September 11, 2001. Warren Carter introduces the topic of empire for readers of the Bible in churches as he reports on his experience of teaching in parishes about how the New Testament texts negotiate the Roman Empire. Recognizing deep ambivalence about the idea of *empire*, and especially of America as an empire, Carter describes the Bible as a place of imperial negotiation that can provide a model for contemporary Christians who must do the same negotiation with the realities of empire. He understands his role as a biblical scholar to teach people new reading strategies.

Like Carter, each of the other voices in part one enters the discussion from the point where she or he feels the most urgency—Barbara Rossing with the reality and threat of global climate change, Cynthia Briggs Kittredge and Norman Gottwald around the issue of American foreign policy, Allen Callahan on the interconnection between slavery and empire, and Jonathan Draper on the role of biblical interpreters in the ongoing complex history of South Africa. Each scholar articulates a distinctive model for approaching and engaging with the Bible, an approach that is linked to their social context and to the audience whom they address in their teaching, writing, and preaching. Their approach, context, and audience all shape their rhetorical strategy.

Two essays describe models for the role of the biblical scholar in engaging with public life. Jonathan Draper describes an ideal process for reading the Bible in the public square in the postapartheid, now-secular state of South Africa. Noting the dearth of biblical and prophetic theology in recent years and neglect of the *Kairos Document* in current discussions of biblical studies in South Africa, Draper proposes a hermeneutical model of conversation with the text in which the self or community encounters difference, is provoked to self-criticism and transformation, and expresses the results as praxis. The process is constantly self-critical; central to it is the question of interest: Who benefits from this particular reading? Practiced within the now-secular state, such a model does not identify the church with the state nor does it privatize the Bible and its preaching.

Cynthia Briggs Kittredge sketches the model of rhetorical-critical biblical scholarship that explores and queries the rhetoric of both biblical texts and contemporary interpretation. She practices the model in an analysis of the rhetoric of the speeches of George W. Bush and their employment of the language of freedom and slavery parallel to that in Paul's Letter to the Romans. She addresses her analysis to an audience beyond that of the church, to a broader critical conversation among citizens and public intellectuals about public policy. Her exploration demonstrates one way that the expertise of a biblical scholar can generate critical questions to complicate and stimulate the discussion of politics.

The other essays in part one reveal their underlying models as they treat the biblical text. Barbara Rossing addresses those who preach and read the texts as the major part of the Christian tradition, who "seek biblical counsel" about the environment. The Bible is a resource for the work of environmental justice in its end-of-empire discourses in the book of Revelation. At the same time that she finds in one part of the Bible material for a healing vision of the world, she sees in 2 Peter's vision of the fiery end a "text of terror" to be strongly resisted. The role of the scholar is to highlight the strands of the biblical texts that offer joyful and compelling visions for abundant life. Allen Callahan treats Revelation as a text that possesses authority for those who read it. He affirms the analogy between America and the Babylon of the book of Revelation by using the modern terms "crimes on a global scale" and "murderous international regime" to paraphrase the biblical text. Callahan presents the speeches and sermons of intellectuals of African descent, including Maria Stewart, Theophilus Gould Steward, and Elijah Muhammad, and shows how they tie their contemporary America with Babylon from Revelation. The preachers and singers employ the vivid images and intense drama of Revelation to move and galvanize their hearers. The end-time fire, for example, is a hopeful, if violent, image. Callahan does not evaluate these rhetorical uses of the book of Revelation theologically but simply describes these readings and situates them in the particular social and historical location of the readers. Callahan's readers can hear, understand, appreciate, and, if they choose, judge their aptness.

Norman Gottwald's reflection uses the rhetorical form of a sermon in which he opposes the perspective of the Bible with that of the culture. Gottwald contrasts the exacerbation and manipulation of fear by the American administration since 9/11 with the images of fear and faith in the prophet Isaiah. Gottwald criticizes inaccurate historical analogies, such as equating Israel and Judah with America rather than America with the Assyrian empire. The moral directive of Isaiah and the prophets is for a nation to make its own internal integrity and justice its priority. All other choices lead to failure. Gottwald's final evocation of the fear of God stands as a force to relativize all other expressions of fear.

Placed side by side, the essays in part one can be read as a conversation. The essays of Allen Callahan and Barbara Rossing provoke reflection on the book of Revelation and the history of the effects of its interpretation for the environment, the incitement to violence, and resistance to empire. The rhetorical power of use of images from Revelation by African-American intellectuals invites comparison with the biblical language operating in the speeches of George W. Bush. All the essays that make up this conversation raise the question of the authority of the biblical text for its readers and the role of the scholar in speaking, translating, or proclaiming its themes.

The scholars in part two follow the example of scholars like Horsley in critically examining the presuppositions and interests of the field of New Testament studies in relationship to the churches and to the academic guild. Max Myers places the idea of American empire within a historical survey of empires and poses the challenge for people of faith to support or oppose empire. Speaking as a severe critic of U.S. presidential policies and assuming an audience with theological and ethical interests, Myers elaborates theologically on the implications of Richard Horsley's work on Jesus and the movement around him. Myers accepts and intensifies the historical analogies in Horsley's work and calls the New Testament an "oppositional document." He argues for the need for an anti-imperialist theology with a concept of God consistent with Jesus' religious ethics. He suggests that process theology provides such a concept.

All of them are self-conscious about the model of biblical scholarship that they employ; some of these scholars do not see the biblical text as a source for unambiguously positive anti-imperial material. Gerald West discusses the history of the Bible in the South African context as a "site of struggle," providing energy for both colonizing activity and anti-imperial movements. He cites the examples of the BaTlhaping people of southern Africa in the early 1800s, Isaiah Shembe of the early 1900s, and the contextual Bible study at the Ujamaa Centre. The role of the biblical scholar, as enacted here by West, is to investigate and clarify the dynamics of this public contestation, and also to assist readers in their liberative readings of the text.

For Abraham Smith a key role of the biblical scholar is to demystify myths of innocence in the field of biblical studies itself and in the biblical narratives. Smith shows how biblical scholarship in its history is implicated in colonialism. Despite the now-traditional view that Luke is inclusive in its emphasis on women and its concern for the poor, the book of Luke-Acts is thoroughly imperial in its orientation. For Smith, not to recognize the ambiguity of the text is to perpetuate a guise of innocence and to increase apathy.

Steven Friesen examines the biases in the discipline of New Testament studies against dealing with the topic of poverty in the early Christian communities. He surveys the genre of New Testament introductions, noting the selective attention of commentators to the poor in Paul's churches. He finds an explanation for this lack of interest in the social position and class interests of the professors in the field. Friesen urges ongoing self-criticism and renewed attention to economic inequality.

Robert Ekblad's Bible study of Matthew 27 with inmates and immigrants begins with a series of questions relating readers to Jesus in his passion and death. It concludes with a liturgical reenactment of the two final cries of Jesus, which release the Spirit and conquer the powers of death. Jesus in the biblical text of Matthew 27 is, for Ekblad and those with whom he reads, the embodiment of their suffering and sense of hopelessness. The pedagogy enacted in Ekblad's Bible study illustrates a powerful way that the Bible functions within a community of people on the margins.

The scholars in part three of the volume reflect on future prospects for engaging with the Bible in the public square. The essays by Elisabeth Schüssler Fiorenza and Antoinette Clark Wire frame the section, each sketching a process of reading the Bible in public to engender radical democratic thinking and provide vision for common life. Schüssler Fiorenza addresses realities that arise in many of the essays: the dual aspects of biblical rhetoric, which can act both to oppress and to empower, and the variety of ways the Bible is, and has been, read both to oppress and to free. She names these *imperial* and *democratic discourses*, and argues that the role of the scholar is to make visible both these strands of the text. Her proposal is harmonious with Gerald West's image of the Bible as a site of struggle and incorporates Abraham Smith's ideological criticism of the biblical text. She emphasizes the necessary choice involved in reading the Bible and the responsibility of the interpreter for her readings.

Sze-kar Wan deals with the notoriously imperial text of Rom 13:1-7. Using the categories of hidden and public transcript, Wan reconstructs the historical colonial context of the passage. He shows how the text, read from the top down, appears to support imperial values, while at the same time communicating, to those who read from the bottom up, Paul's proclamation of the supreme authority of God through Jesus Christ.

Neil Elliott focuses on the role of the churches in reading the Bible in the public square. Elliott describes vividly the multiple cultural forces that cause a contemporary "famine of the word," including the outlines of what he describes as a propaganda model in which the churches play an integral role. Elliott finds in the late William Stringfellow's critiques of church capitulation and complicity a precise anticipation of the current state of affairs and, in Stringfellow's understanding of the sovereignty of the Word, a powerful challenge for the churches today.

Antoinette Clark Wire's autobiographical reflections draw principles of interpretation from a lifetime of experience reading the Bible in community—in her childhood missionary home in China, in California among residents of a housing project in the Wider City Parish; among women in a parish group, the Lydia Circle; in an Oakland house church; and among rural Chinese singers and readers of the Bible. These principles—of open exchange, persuasive interpretation, and focus on the face of the other—emerge from the common struggle of people to understand their tradition. Public vision comes out of this common work.

It is fitting that the conversation set up among these essays should conclude with Wire's description of these particular communities of people reading the Bible. In its own way, this collection of essays constitutes a community of interpretation, academic in orientation but emphasizing engagement. All the authors try to read an ancient text in a changing world, a world that cares about this particular classic text both too little and too much. His role in the creation of such a scholarly community is one of Richard Horsley's most valuable achievements. His practice of collaborative scholarship has enacted the principles he most values and underscores most emphatically in the communities around Paul. He has generously encouraged other scholars, many at early points in their careers, and invited them to participate and to lead in the scholarly conversation. He has brought to the enterprise an infective spirit of optimism, even in the midst of the dire and discouraging realities of empire. Holding up an alternative vision of the Bible, he has inspired his readers to bring it into being. The contributors dedicate this volume to him.

PART I
Biblical Insight
into the Present Moment

1. Church Bible Studies, Ancient and Modern Empires, and the Gospel according to John

Warren Carter
Brite Divinity School,
Texas Christian University

FOR MANY YEARS, I have led Bible study sessions on Sunday mornings for adult Christian education groups in various mainline Protestant churches. I used to take a portable overhead projector with me; now I take a laptop and projector for the PowerPoint presentation. The churches to which I go tend to be large, suburban, educated congregations. The groups comprise lay folks who tend to take their theological education seriously. Some read prominent popular scholars and attend public talks. Sometimes the topics for the studies are given to me, sometimes they are my choice, and sometimes I am asked to do something that relates to my research or writing. Given my research and writing interests,[1] and hermeneutical proclivities, these sessions have in recent times often involved some discussion of how New Testament texts negotiate the Roman Empire. The topic seems to stimulate intellectual curiosity among group members as well as to strike a deep emotional chord. Inevitably, discussion turns to contemporary circumstances with group members readily employing the *e* word and acknowledging difficulty in negotiating the contemporary U.S. empire in which we are deeply embedded.

These types of Bible study group participants have been described as both "anxious about empire" and "eager for empire."[2] We are anxious (in part) because it has become apparent to us as world citizens that our nation's quest for security through economic and military control has wrought more chaos, death, repression, and resentment than it has order, life, human rights, and gratitude. We are anxious about our nation's role in the world, fearing that we will reap a whirlwind from what has been sown. Yet we are eager for empire because we know ourselves to be (in part) a community that is shaped by *another* empire, the reign/empire (*basileia*) of God present among us. It is a community that anticipates the yet-future establishment of God's life-giving, inclusive, and just purposes for all creation.

This binary of "anxious about/eager for empire" cannot of course embrace all of the complexities of our contemporary experiences. It does not identify, for instance, religion's capacity to be both an agent, supporter, or ally of imperial power and the inspirer of resistance. Richard Horsley has observed:

> Once aware of how religion can inspire resistance to imperial domination on the one hand and become the expression of imperial power on the other, American Jews and Christians may want to challenge the ambiguity of their own religious traditions. . . . The Bible "speaks out of both sides of its mouth," sometimes providing scriptural authorization for imperial domination, and at other times inspiring further struggles against empire.[3]

Yet, despite its limitations, the binary of being "anxious about/eager for empire" usefully names important aspects of the difficult task of negotiating empire.

Rarely do group discussions stop to define carefully the term *empire* as it might apply to contemporary situations. My role often includes naming the need to do so, highlighting differences between empires now and then, and reporting on discussions of the term's contemporary use.[4] Michael Walzer, for instance, complains that in current parlance the word *empire* is more a "term of denunciation" than of "enlightenment," so he prefers to speak of "hegemony."[5] Of course, for some on the religious right the term is a welcome euphemism for Republican politics and for claims of divine sanction for U.S. self-interested action. Jean Bethke Elshtain contrasts "past imperialisms" like those of Rome, with contemporary U.S. "robust powers of intervention" intended to accomplish international justice.[6] Michael Ignatieff also contrasts contemporary "empire lite," comprising free markets, human rights, and democracy (ironically reinforced by military power!) with past empires that employed colonies and conquests to civilize natives.[7] Whatever the language, definitions, and nuanced differences between ancient and modern empires, participants in the Bible study groups sense some significant similarities: unaccountable power exerted internationally and domestically, elite control, rewards for a few, and damage to many. They view such dynamics as integral but regrettable parts of our present society and political enterprise.

They are, however, often surprised that New Testament writings engage the task of negotiating empire and that these writings might offer resources to assist their own negotiation. Various oft-identified factors no doubt account for some of this surprise. American civil religion has taught mainline churchgoers to see themselves as integrated and supportive parts of the civic fabric, without any sniff of being dissenters from, critics of, or an alternative to it. Coupled with this is a ready acceptance of and submission to civic authority and officeholders, Rom 13:1-7—or at least a sentiment possibly akin to one reading of it—is regularly quoted as though it were the Bible's sole and obvious word on the matter. The confusing relationship between faith and politics is also in play. Social forces encourage alignment of the two, yet the separation of church and state is received doctrine. Participants are also suspicious of the so-called *religious right*, uncomfortable with the aggressive promotion of a conservative Christian agenda, increasingly resentful of its presentation as normative Christianity by uninformed media reporting, yet often sensing they themselves cannot articulate a biblically or theologically informed alternative. These factors, among others, contribute to the surprise that New Testament writings might assist in the contemporary task of imperial negotiation.

But another factor, frequently to the fore in group discussions, needs to be added. Often Bible study groups from mainline denominations lack reading strategies by which to access the New Testament texts in ways that could usefully inform their struggles with imperial negotiation. When groups engage scripture, the dominant reading strategy comprises "spiritual" readings that value the inner or individual life in relation to God. Such strategies I suspect are shaped, among other things, by preaching practices. Rarely do the strategies include communal dimensions even though New Testament texts address communities of believers much more than individuals. Such spiritualized, interiorized, individualized reading strategies rarely embrace the somatic, material, societal, and political as spheres for encountering God. I recall vividly the incredulity with which one group member reacted to my observation that the gospel narrative of feeding the five thousand concerned feeding hungry people with real bread. Hunger and bread were irrelevant, this participant asserted. Jesus was meeting their spiritual needs. My observation is that such "spiritualized" approaches might provide individuals with strength for daily living, but the limited focus of this approach cannot help communities of faith with the systemic and societal challenges of negotiating empire.

Some New Testament scholars are engaging the task of recovering and reappropriating New Testament texts as works of imperial negotiation. This work is fed by various streams: an extension of historical interests beyond communities of believers or beyond first-century Judaisms, interest in social-science models of empire,[8] emergence of postcolonial approaches in various disciplines, a renewed interest in classical studies, graduate students looking for unexplored areas to engage, and the impact of current world circumstances on scholars and the communities (such as churches) in which they participate. To date, studies of imperial negotiation have involved, for example, the historical Jesus, Paul, Mark, Matthew, Colossians, and Revelation to name but some.[9]

The Gospel according to John has not received much attention in this work. Undoubtedly, throughout the last two millennia, the "spiritual" gospel has exercised considerable influence on ecclesial doctrine and personal piety by means of individualized readings. It is without a doubt a central text in many personal canons as well as the ecclesial canon. Inevitably in Bible study sessions, as commonly as appeals are made to Romans 13, someone will cite John 18:36a ("My kingdom is not from this world") to refute any suggestion that Jesus had any interest in anything political or imperial, or that the Gospel according to John might be involved in political or imperial negotiation. When I press for elaboration of how the verse disqualifies imperial interest, commonly the explanation indicates a reading divorced from any societal realities. The verse is spiritualized; Jesus' kingdom has nothing to do with everyday (political or material) life. Jesus is not interested in such life. He only cares about spiritual matters.

But five quick observations indicate that citing John 18:36a does not refute the suggestion that the gospel might be interested in imperial negotiation. First, the gospel's plot narrates the death of its main character Jesus on a Roman cross. One did not get crucified for being spiritual, nor did Rome happily cooperate with the Christian God to take away the sins of the world. One got crucified for threatening Roman interests.[10] Second, the claim that 18:36a disqualifies any imperial or political interest misses the point that the verse concerns the origin of Jesus' mission and not its sphere. In the Gospel according to John, the Greek word often translated as *of* commonly denotes origin (see, by way of comparison, 1:12-13) as the NRSV translation of 18:36a indicates with its wording "*from* this world."[11] The Greek word translated as *world* is used in John's Gospel with a particular spin. It signifies not just the physical world created by God, but also the "world" of human beings that rejects God's purposes (1:10). John's Jesus claims that his rule or empire does not originate in the "world" created by God that rejects its creator as do empires like Rome's. Yet it is precisely in and for that world that he reveals God's life-giving purposes through, for example, healings and feedings (see John 6:2-14). Jesus' claim is that his empire derives from God and expresses God's purposes for life among humans (1:1-5; 20:30-31). Far from being disinterested in or uncaring about the political or imperial, Jesus' mission comprises a significant challenge to it through enacting an alternative way of being human.

Third, there is an important translation issue in John 18:36a. The common translations use the term "kingdom" which gives the verse an antiquated and non-political sense because "kingdom" is not a word we use much in contemporary political speech. The Greek word *basileia*, though, is a word commonly used to refer to empires such as Rome's. A different translation, "My empire is not from this world," immediately evokes political structures countering tendencies to read the verse apolitically. Fourth, when group members cite John 18:36a, they usually omit 18:36b: "If my kingdom/empire were from this world, my followers would be fighting to keep me from being handed over. . . ." Jesus' comment puts his empire into explicit conversation with conventional empires, contrasting his "empire" explicitly and sharply with them. Violence is the defining mark of empires "from this world" that reject God's purposes. Jesus' comment forbids violence to his followers. It is not a legitimate means of expressing God's life-giving purposes. He draws a sharp contrast with conventional imperial ways of being. And fifth, while we do not know for certain where John's Gospel was written, ecclesial traditions link the gospel with the city of Ephesus. Ephesus was the capital city of the Roman province of Asia, the center of Roman control in the province and a city in which a temple dedicated to the Roman emperors was dedicated in 89/90 C.E., about the time John's Gospel was written. That is, Roman power was a daily reality for John's audience who as followers of Jesus lived their discipleship in its midst.

Because of these factors, the repeated quotation of John 18:36a ("My kingdom/empire is not from this world") to indicate that John's Gospel has no interest in political matters indicates an inadequate reading strategy. The Gospel according to John is not concerned only with individualized religious matters and oblivious to all other areas of life. Such a reading strategy prevents access to the Gospel according to John as a work of imperial negotiation and as a resource for contemporary mainline congregations. It suggests that a task of recovery and reappropriation needs to be undertaken to render this text available to contemporary congregations struggling with imperial negotiation.

Also preventing access to the gospel as a work of imperial negotiation is the pervasive focus of contemporary Johannine studies. Since the initial publication of the Dead Seas Scrolls in the 1950s and the pioneering work of J. Louis Martyn and Wayne Meeks in the 1960s and 1970s, much Johannine scholarship has read John in relation to first-century Judaism and the expulsion of Jesus-believers from a synagogue to form a sectarian community.[12] There is little doubt that this approach has offered vast insight into the Gospel according to John. It also has, since the Holocaust, provided a much-needed focal point for the discussion of anti-Semitism and the contribution of the canonical gospels and critical scholarship to that serious problem.

But numerous aspects of this historical reconstruction have increasingly been questioned. Daniel Boyarin concludes a recent survey of the debate with the assertion that "Martyn's reconstruction simply cannot stand because the historical foundations upon which it rests are so shaky that the edifice falls down. . . . There are, therefore, it seems hardly the slightest historical grounds for accepting Martyn's elegant hypothesis."[13] Further, this dominant approach has ironically produced a decidedly ahistorical "historical context" in which Jesus-believers are concerned only with ideas, religion, and a synagogue community, but not with bodies, politics, or empires. Moreover, the discussion has generally ignored the emerging scholarship on first-century Jewish communities that shows synagogues were not isolated and culturally withdrawn enclaves of *pure* Jewish identity.[14] Rather, synagogues were places of imperial negotiation carried out in various tensive and complex combinations of accommodation to imperial society and observance of distinctive cultural practices. To locate John only in relation to a synagogue as a religious community is to miss the synagogue's embedment in the empire and to exclude the question of how Jesus-believers engaged the empire that pervaded a Roman provincial capital like late-first-century Ephesus, a traditional location for the gospel's final form (though by no means a location universally accepted by scholars).

When a few brave Johannine scholars have wondered about how the Gospel according to John might have interacted with Rome's imperial world, they have suggested three scenarios. All involve persecution, all center on failure to honor the emperor by not participating in the imperial cult, and all are quite unsustainable. Persecution cannot be established as the central dynamic of John's imperial negotiation.

The first scenario erroneously claims that Judaism enjoyed a protected status of *religio licita,* whereby Rome guaranteed its religious liberty with charters of rights.[15] The separation of John's Jesus-group from a synagogue community (9:22; 12:42; 16:2), so the argument runs, left the group without the protection of these charters. Unprotected, Jesus-believers were persecuted for their failure to participate in the imperial cult.[16]

There is, however, no evidence for an official category of *religio licita* before Tertullian refers to it around 200 C.E., some hundred years or so after John's Gospel was written. No evidence attests that Rome approved religions and protected them with a universal charter of rights.[17] As other scholars have shown,[18] the decrees that Josephus records in *Antiquities* 14 and 16 point to specific and atypical situations of tension when traditional rights were challenged or denied, and Jewish groups appealed to Rome for protection of traditional practices. These decrees were situation-specific, necessary to protect Jewish groups in situations of unusual tension. They were not universal charters. Rather, synagogue communities seem to have negotiated their local civic and imperial contexts with a mixture of participation and observance of traditional practices. To leave a synagogue community—even if that scenario could be established for John's Jesus-believers—would not leave a group unprotected by a legal charter (since one did not exit) nor open to persecution (there is no evidence). Rather the group would have to negotiate its own place in the civic and imperial context. Nor is there any evidence for Roman persecution of Jesus-believers in Ephesus in the late first century. John 16:2 suggests a future scenario with its future tenses and framing of "killing" as "offering worship/ service." Persecution is envisaged in the future and not experienced now.

A second scenario asserts that the emperor Domitian (81–96 C.E.) persecuted John's Jesus-believers.[19] Space prohibits a discussion of the nature of Domitian's reign except to observe that it was probably no worse than any other emperor's.[20] Problematic for claims that Domitian persecuted Jesus-believers is the lack of compelling evidence. The supposed "evidence" comes from Eusebius in the fourth century, over two centuries after Domitian's reign. Eusebius appeals to Irenaeus as a source for information about Domitian persecuting believers. But Irenaeus, writing a century after Domitian, refers to Domitian only in relation to the date of the book of Revelation, written "almost in my own lifetime, at the end of Domitian's reign,"[21] but says nothing about persecution.[22]

The situation for this supposed persecution is usually identified as Domitian's aggressive promotion of the imperial cult. But this claim also lacks evidence. Imperial cult observance was well established in Ephesus throughout the first century.[23] Local Ephesian elites had actively participated in its promotion. Jesus-believers had, in various ways, negotiated it for decades without persecution. Participation was voluntary and not mandatory, though some social pressure was doubtless exerted in associations and civic observances, especially when the temple to the *Sebastoi* was dedicated in Ephesus in 89/90 C.E. The claim of heightened demands by Domitian to be worshiped is undercut by Ephesus's dedication of the temple not to the one emperor Domitian alone, but to a collective imperial entity, the *Sebastoi*. The temple dedications do not address Domitian as "Lord and God" but as emperor, *autokratōr*.[24] This form of address would be crassly insulting, and quickly remedied, if the claims about Domitian's demand to be addressed as "Lord and God" were reliable. Likewise when the Greek writers Dio Chrysostom (*Discourse* 45.1) and Dio Cassius (67.4.7; 67.13.4) do refer to Domitian as "Lord and God," they employ the Greek terms *despotēs kai theos*, which are not the same terms used in John 20:28, *ho kyrios mou kai ho theos mou* ("My Lord and my God").[25] That is, if John's Gospel was specifically rejecting Domitian's supposed heightened demands to be worshiped as "Lord and God," we would expect these references to share standard language.

A third scenario posits persecutory situations akin to that attested by the correspondence between Pliny, governor of the province of Pontus-Bithynia, and the emperor Trajan around 112 C.E. (*Epistulae* 10.96–97).[26] Governor Pliny writes to the emperor because of negative reports from locals about Christians. The exact nature of the complaints is not clear, and the reports do not concern Pliny enough to search out believers.

The localized nature of this activity warns against universalizing it to the rest of Pliny's administrative area of the province of Bithynia-Pontus, let alone to Ephesus, over which Pliny had no jurisdiction. No evidence links John and Pliny. No evidence suggests that Christians in Ephesus encountered situations of persecution in the 90s akin to that described by Pliny several decades later when he as governor requires reported believers to offer worship to images or die. Pliny makes clear that part of his uncertainty in knowing how to respond is that there are no precedents for his response.

Though persecution has often figured prominently in the limited discussions of interactions between John's believers and the empire, no evidence sustains these three scenarios. Persecution does not comprise the central dynamic for the gospel's complex interaction with the empire.

More helpful would be to employ an interdisciplinary approach that frames the question in terms of intertextual interactions between imperial structures, personnel, and claims on one hand, and on the other the Gospel according to John's story of Jesus crucified by Rome, whose power is shown to be death-bringing and not ultimate by God's act of raising Jesus.[27] Julia Kristeva describes such cultural intertextuality as locating a text "within [the text of] society and history," placing this specific gospel text "within the general text [culture] of which [it is] a part and which is in turn part of [it]."[28] This approach requires historical analysis of late-first-century Ephesus with particular attention to the experiences of empire. Postcolonial studies, along with studies of disparities of societal power, provide important means of elucidating these experiences, as do classical studies and archaeological studies from Ephesus.[29] Literary attention to the telling of the gospel story and theological analysis of leading themes are necessary for intertextual attention to the interplay between the gospel and practices and understandings of the Roman Empire in a provincial center such as Ephesus.[30] Such a discussion that foregrounds the Gospel according to John as imperial negotiation offers a reading strategy for contemporary Jesus-believers in mainline churches struggling to negotiate contemporary empire.

Numerous aspects of the Gospel according to John can be explored through this approach of cultural intertextuality.[31] For instance, what happens in the intertextuality involving titles used for both Jesus and the Roman emperor (Son of God, Savior of the World, Lord, and God)? What comprises the intertextuality between a gospel that offers "eternal life" (John 3:16; 10:10; 20:31) in the midst of an empire centered in Rome, the eternal city (Livy, 4.4.4; 28.28.11; Tibullus, 2.5.23; Ovid, *Fasti* 3.72), that claimed an eternal empire (Virgil, *Aeneid* 1.279)? What happens in the intertextuality between the gospel's repeated description of God as Father and the emperor's title "Father of the Fatherland"? Of what significance is it that the empire proclaims its active good faith (*fides; pistis*) while the gospel insists on "faithing" (*pisteuō;* 1:12; 3:16) as the central means by which Jesus-followers encounter God's life-giving possibilities? How does a community whose dominant practices comprise service and love (13:13-17, 34-35) engage Roman imperial society where domination and patron-client relations are normative?[32] I am suggesting that investigation of John's Gospel as a work of imperial negotiation will involve at least its context, plot and genre, theology (understanding of God), Christology, soteriology (salvation), eschatology (end things), and ecclesiology (church).

How might an adult Sunday school class learn such a reading strategy? In classes I have taught, I have employed several points of entry involving realities of Roman power. One entry point comprises talking about a model of empire formulated by Gerhard Lenski that highlights the use of power (including alliances with local elites) and distribution of resources.[33] Another involves archaeological material: The statues and panels that were part of the approach to the *Sebasteion* in Aphrodisias are effective testimonies to Roman power and provincial honoring.[34] So, too, are images of various coins, especially those that depict emperors with images of various gods and goddesses on the reverse (Jupiter, Victoria/Nike, Ceres, and so on). Such images depict the imperial theology comprising claims of divine sanction for Rome and presentation of Rome as the agent of the gods' sovereignty, blessing, and will.[35] By engagement with such material, something of the imperial societal vision and structures can be glimpsed as a context for engaging Johannine texts and the vision of human well-being that they offer. Pursuing the question of why Jesus was crucified (a Roman form of execution) highlights the clash of visions.

Another approach is to begin with a Johannine scene and elaborate its cultural intertextuality. The entry to Jerusalem (12:12-19) evokes protocol concerning the welcome of imperial figures to a provincial city. Jesus' entry at points imitates yet mocks, copies yet resists, aspects of such scenes while it celebrates and redefines greatness.[36] The turning of water into wine scene (2:1-11) invites exploration of several Hebrew Bible images (wine, weddings) that point to the establishment of God's purposes marked by (material) abundance, fertility, and justice.[37] The temple scene (2:13-22) requires exploration of the functions of temples in the imperial world and in Judea, collapsing the contemporary secular-religious divide,[38] and investigation of the eschatological intertext of Zechariah 14 (John 2:16 NRSV) in which God's rule over the nations is established, and of the lament of Psalm 69 (John 2:17). That is, guided and informed elaboration of the cultural and biblical intertextuality of the scenes will lead groups into recognitions of various ways in which this gospel negotiates Roman power and will provoke consideration of how contemporary communities of faith negotiate empire.

Our age is, of course, not the first occasion in the history of Christianity in which the task of imperial negotiation has loomed large. Our traditions, including our foundational biblical texts, have frequently negotiated empire, sometimes from positions of ascendancy and sometimes from below. Recovery of our traditions' wisdom and mistakes, along with apposite reappropriation, can assist us in our contemporary challenges to discern faithful living in the midst of empire. The possible contribution to this task of the Gospel according to John, a central ecclesial text, has been neglected. Recovery work requires a reading strategy that engages the imperial dimension of the gospel's context and text, thereby enabling congregations to use this gospel as an informing voice in their struggles with contemporary imperial negotiation and with formulating faithful practices of discipleship to be lived in the public square.

2. Hastening the Day when the Earth Will Burn: Global Warming, 2 Peter, and the Book of Revelation

Barbara Rossing
Lutheran School of Theology at Chicago

FORMER VICE PRESIDENT AL GORE has likened the catastrophic effects of global warming on the world to "taking a nature hike through the book of Revelation."[1] Better still, his nature hike could also include 2 Peter 3, a terrifying chapter that raises troubling questions for those seeking biblical counsel on the environment because it consigns the earth to burning up by fire.

We are well on our way to that burning.[2] Three recent reports from the Intergovernmental Panel on Climate Change (IPCC), released in 2007, read more like the plague sequences of Revelation than like typical scientific reports, with predictions of higher sea levels, more acidic oceans, fiercer storms and weather events, deadlier forest fires, more heat-related deaths, longer dry seasons, declining water supplies, catastrophic floods, and increasing infectious disease. In an ironic coincidence, one of the reports, "Climate Change Impacts, Adaptation and Vulnerability," was released on Good Friday, April 6, 2007.[3] Even after the U.S. and other governments watered down the text, the report still predicts the future passion and suffering of at least 200 million of the poorest and most vulnerable people of the earth who will be displaced or otherwise affected by climate change if temperatures rise only as much as 3.6 degrees Fahrenheit (2 degrees Celsius). This is on top of the suffering of rivers, oceans, coral reefs, and ice sheets, and the consequent extinction of 20–30 percent of the world's living species. News reports that whole islands and even island nations have already disappeared in the Pacific bear eerie resemblance to the prophetic voice of Rev 16:20 that "every island fled away."[4]

A few fundamentalist Christians may welcome the prospect of calamitous events as if they were signs of the end-times and Jesus' return. For most Christians, however, the urgent question is whether and how the Bible might provide resources for addressing our new situation of living at the *end*.

It is becoming clear that we do face the prospect of some kind of an end. At the present rate of emissions growth, atmospheric concentrations of carbon dioxide will rise above 500 parts per million—almost double the preindustrial levels—by the middle of this century. America's premier climatologist, James Hansen of NASA's Goddard Space Institute, says that we can probably survive those levels but that it would be on a "different planet."[5] If the concentration of carbon dioxide ever were to rise to 666 parts per million—Revelation's number of the beast—we would be toast. Unfortunately, even this number is below the top of the range in the scenarios that may well happen within the lifetime of our children and grandchildren.[6]

Moreover, scientists now think the IPCC projections are too conservative, since they do not take into consideration new data regarding the faster-than-expected melting of both the Greenland and Antarctic ice sheets and mounting evidence, since March 2006, of climate changes much more serious than previous models predicted.[7] The reports also do not consider the scenarios of irreversible feedback loops or what scientists call "tipping points." To be sure, the world has so far dodged other planetary perils in the past—most notably the threat of nuclear annihilation. In the past, the *Bulletin of Atomic Scientists* has moved the hands on its "Doomsday Clock" even closer to midnight than at present.[8] But previous crises did not portend tipping points that would be irreversible, such as the "albedo effect" by which melting Arctic sea ice itself accelerates further warming (since ice is white and reflects heat back to the sun, whereas sea water is dark in color and absorbs more heat).

NASA climatologist James Hansen believes that we still have time to avert dangerous sea level rise—but we must reduce carbon emissions significantly in the next ten years, and by 90 percent by the year 2050. Otherwise it will be too late to save the Greenland ice sheet and avoid other catastrophic tipping points. Even the IPCC report itself states that global carbon emissions must peak and begin declining within eight years, by 2015, if the world wants to have any chance of limiting the expected temperature rise to 2 degrees Celsius (3.6 degrees Fahrenheit) above pre-industrial levels.[9] Scientists, religious leaders, and world political leaders underscore the urgency of acting now to reduce carbon emissions. If not, we risk losing the ten-year window past which we would be unable to avert irreversible, catastrophic, climate change.[10]

So how can we draw on the Bible publicly to address this crisis, underscoring especially the urgency of that ten-year window?

Since early Christian apocalyptic texts address the sense of an *end*, it might seem logical to turn to these texts to speak to our current situation. We must carefully distinguish among various strands of early Christian apocalyptic, however. The New Testament presents a range of perspectives on the end of the world. This chapter will first contrast two apocalyptic texts, Revelation and 2 Peter, in terms of how they might help us address global warming. I will argue that whereas the end-of-empire perspective of Revelation can be helpful ecologically, 2 Peter's claim that the world is destined to be burned up with fire must be viewed as highly problematic. Building on previous ecologically oriented work on Revelation, this chapter will then explore two elements— Revelation's anti-imperial perspective, including the millennium vision for life beyond empire, and its sense of the urgency of the present moment—that may prove helpful in addressing the crisis of global warming.[11]

The Sense of an End: Revelation versus 2 Peter

A strong sense of an impending end pervades much of the apocalyptic discourse of the New Testament. Early Christians definitely believed they were living at the end of the age, the end of the world. But the question is: The end of *what* world? What was it that early Christian texts view as coming to an end? With the exception of 2 Peter, the *end* that New Testament texts envision is not primarily the destruction of the earth or the created world. Rather, in proclaiming the dawning of a new age in Christ, they envision an end to the Roman imperial world of oppression and injustice, an end to the *oikoumenē*.[12]

I draw a distinction between several different Greek words for "world." Revelation unveils the end, not of the physical world or earth (the Greek words *kosmos* and *gē*), nor creation (the Greek word *ktisis*), but of the imperial world, the *oikoumenē*. In my view this distinction can help us navigate the sense of an end today as well.

In Revelation, the earth (*gē*), the world (*kosmos*), and the entire created world (*ktisis*) belong to God. For all its imagery of destruction, Revelation continues the biblical tradition of affirming the fundamental goodness of creation as declared by God in Genesis 1. Commands to "worship the one who made the heaven and the earth, the sea and springs of water" (Rev 14:7)[13] make clear that God created heaven, earth, springs of water, and the sea; they are considered God's creations throughout the entire book. The use of creation-oriented terminology (the Greek root *ktiz-*) in Revelation is overwhelmingly positive: Rev 3:14; 5:14; and especially the emphatic declaration of Rev 10:6 (see also 4:11) that God "created the heaven and what is in it and the earth and what is in it, and the sea." God does not consign the creation to destruction in Revelation.[14] A key text is Rev 11:18, in which Revelation proclaims not that "the time has come to destroy the earth" but that "the time has come . . . to destroy the *destroyers* of the earth," that is, the Roman Empire.

This is quite different from the perspective of 2 Peter 3, a chapter that I have come to view as the most ecologically problematic chapter in the entire New Testament. I regularly receive e-mails from Christians asking for help in dealing with 2 Peter's images of planetary conflagration. Second Peter makes extensive references to God's plan for a fiery end to the planet, warning that "the present heavens and earth have been reserved for fire" (3:7) and that when the day of the Lord comes, the "heavens will be set ablaze and dissolved, and the elements will melt with fire" (3:12). This epistle draws an analogy between the Genesis flood and end-times fire: Just as the world (*kosmos*) that existed at the time of Noah and the flood was deluged by water and destroyed, so too the present heavens and earth (*gē*) are destined for fire and destruction (3:6-7). The King James and Revised Standard Versions include an additional reference to fire at the end of verse 10 that has been modified in the New Revised Standard Version on the basis of manuscript evidence. The text-critical question is whether the earth and the works that are in it "shall be burned up" (*katakaēsetai*, KJV, RSV) or "shall be disclosed" (*heurethēsetai*, NRSV).[15] Even without this additional reference to fire in verse 10, there is more than enough burning in 2 Peter 3 to fuel end-times speculations!

Most problematic from an ecological viewpoint is that 2 Peter not only describes the fiery destruction, it actually calls on believers to "hasten" (*speudontas*) the day when the creation will be set ablaze:

> Since all these things are to be dissolved in this way, what sort of persons ought you to be in leading lives of holiness and godliness, waiting for and hastening the coming of the day of God, because of which the heavens will be set ablaze and dissolved, and the elements will melt with fire? (2 Pet 3: 11-12)

This call to readers to "hasten" the day makes the burning of the planet not just a far-off future scenario. Rhetorically, it functions to bring the future burning into the present, giving an active role to readers. Today, in the face of nuclear proliferation and global warming, 2 Pet 3:11-12 risks becoming a terrifying, self-fulfilling prophecy.

Throughout Christian history, 2 Peter's scenario of end-times burning has spawned a potent legacy that continues today. [16] When parents in the Seattle suburb of Federal Way succeeded in blocking the showing of Al Gore's film *An Inconvenient Truth* in public school on the grounds that "The Bible says that in the end times everything will burn up," they were referencing 2 Peter.[17] Televangelist Jerry Falwell likewise appealed to fiery imagery to debunk global warming in a February 25, 2007, sermon: "The earth will go up in dissolution from severe heat. The environmentalists will be really shook up, then, because God is going to blow it all away, and bring down new heavens and new earth."[18] While Falwell himself did not equate global warming with the end-times fire of 2 Peter, other Christians draw that equation. A forum on the WorldNetDaily website called "The Great Global Warming Debate," which discusses whether or not global warming is human-caused, contains this post:

> God planned for global warming even before He created this planet. . . . Please consider with me God's words recorded in the third chapter of Second Peter in verses 10 and 12. Verse 10: "But the day of the Lord will come as a thief in the night; in which the heavens shall pass away with a great noise, and the elements shall melt with fervent heat, the earth also and the works that are therein shall be burnt up."[19]

Similarly, on a website titled GotQuestions.org, an answer to the question "How should a Christian view global warming?" cites 2 Peter's fiery vision to claim that "The Bible does in fact mention a form of 'global warming.' 2 Peter 3:7-13, 'By the same word the present heavens and earth are reserved for fire, being kept for the day of judgment and destruction of ungodly men. . . . The heavens will disappear with a roar; the elements will be destroyed by fire.'"[20]

It is not just fundamentalists who have speculated on the fiery destruction of creation described in 2 Peter 3. A trajectory of interpretation, beginning in the second century, developed from this text and has continued to influence Christian understandings of the end.[21] One Lutheran professor describes the prevalence of 2 Peter 3 in the church of her childhood: "I often heard missionaries speak of the end times. It was still their urgent mission to hasten the day of the Lord, when, as 2 Peter says, the heavens will be set ablaze and the elements will melt with fire. They looked for it, prayed for it, and worked for it with all their hearts, even on the prairies of North Dakota."[22]

I have pondered the e-mails and questions from ecologically concerned Christians asking what to do with 2 Peter 3. Many churches' lectionaries assign this text to be read during the season of Advent.[23] We cannot simply ignore 2 Peter 3 and its apocalyptic imagery of a divinely ignited burning planet. But we must also insist that 2 Peter not become the lens through which the rest of New Testament apocalypticism is read.

For preachers and others who grapple with this text, I offer these suggestions: First, we should not attempt to harmonize the New Testament's various apocalyptic cosmologies. The idea of a fiery eschatological conflagration that consumes the entire planet at the end of the world is found only in 2 Peter, an epistle written in the early second century or possibly the end of the first century by a pseudonymous author.[24] Other biblical texts use the image of a refiner's fire or the fire of purification. But no other New Testament text speaks of a total world-destroying fire, and certainly no other text exhorts believers to hasten the day of burning.[25]

Some scholars claim that 2 Peter 3 draws on a Jewish apocalyptic strand that envisions two destructions—one destruction by water in the past, the Noachic flood, and a future destruction by fire—but this tradition is late.[26] A more probable source of influence is the Greco-Roman philosophical notion of *ekpyrōsis* or world-destroying fire, a much-discussed topic in pagan philosophical debates dating back to Plato's *Timaeus*.[27] The author of 2 Peter may have transposed the Jewish notion of the burning of the *wicked* into the more Greek notion of the burning of the *whole created order* as part of his effort to convince a Gentile audience that God is indeed involved in history. The second-century theologian Justin Martyr, for example, makes reference to the well-known Stoic version of conflagration in delineating his own Christian version of end-times fire.[28]

Later in the second century, however, when the idea of an end-times cosmic conflagration became a favorite notion of the Valentinians and other Gnostics who thought of the created world as evil, theologians such as Irenaeus and Origen distanced themselves from this tradition.[29] The important point to note is that already in the second century, Christians realized that there are different trajectories of apocalyptic speculation, and the trajectory of a world-destroying fire ran the risk of being used in a Gnostic, world-denying way. Cosmic conflagration traditions are not shared by Revelation or any other New Testament texts.[30]

Second, we should note that even within the polemic of 2 Peter, cosmic speculation about the burning of creation is secondary to the main point of the letter.[31] While many fundamentalists today fixate on the chronology of end-times burning, that is not at all the intended focus of 2 Peter. Rather, the letter uses such end-times threats as a tool to exhort individual sinners to repentance. The epistle's references to the coming burning of creation address a situation where "scoffers" (2 Pet 3:3-4) have apparently latched onto the continuity of God's care for creation to mean that they can do whatever they want because there is never going to be a judgment day.[32] It is in response to these scoffers that 2 Peter unleashes threats of burning, not out of a desire to see the planet burn per se, but rather in order to assure scoffers that there will be a "day of judgment and destruction of the godless" in the future, just as God sent a destructive flood in the past (2 Pet 3:5-7). God's patience in delaying the day of the Lord should not be used as justification for complacency, but rather as evidence for God's graciousness (2 Pet 3:9).

Most problematic is the exhortation to "hasten" the day of the Lord and the burning of the planet—a verse that must be regarded as a text of terror in our age of nuclear weapons as well as global warming (2 Pet 3:12). This verse should probably not be read in churches' lectionaries as the word of the Lord. To be sure, the notion of hastening the day of the Lord does not counsel a cavalier "bring it on" attitude toward the fiery destruction, even if, in light of our acceleration of global warming today, it could be tempting to take it that way. Hastening the day of the Lord has rather the sense of "active waiting," as one Latin American liberation scholar has suggested; it is part of the letter's overall strategy of "resistance."[33] Other scholars emphasize that "hastening" is the "corollary" to the assertion in 2 Pet 3:9 that God defers the *parousia* out of a desire for Christians to repent, the idea being that believers' repentance and good works could hasten the Lord's return.[34] Nevertheless, in order for this to become a liberating text, sinners who repent would have to be provided with something analogous to the ark that saved Noah and his family from drowning in the flood. But neither Noah nor the ark is mentioned in this chapter of 2 Peter, only a total end-times burning of the earth, the heavens, and all the elements. As we face the prospect of global warming that will irreversibly endanger the entire planet, perhaps we need to shift our interpretation of the Genesis flood story away from 2 Peter, so that we begin to view the renewed earth itself as our ark.

All the fiery rhetoric of 2 Peter leads up to the final promise of the new heavens and new earth: "In accordance with his promise, we wait for new heavens and a new earth, where righteousness is at home" (2 Pet 3:13, NRSV). The "new heavens and new earth" reference has led some scholars to argue that 2 Peter shares with Revelation a notion of the transformation of the planet rather than its total annihilation.[35] In their view, the analogy of the fiery end-times conflagration to the Genesis flood means that 2 Peter does not have in mind the total obliteration of the creation, but only its purification, since the Noachic flood did not completely destroy the plants, sea creatures, and the earth. But this letter does not develop the theme of new heavens and earth in any positive way, except as a reward for the righteous after the wicked have been destroyed. As Ernst Käsemann points out in his critique of the theology of 2 Peter, "This eschatology only presents us with a straightforward doctrine of retribution."[36]

Aside from the reference to "new heavens and a new earth," chapter 3 of 2 Peter has little in common with Revelation, despite apparent similarities. Even the exhortations to repentance function quite differently—perhaps not surprisingly, since 2 Peter was probably written later.[37] While 2 Peter shares with Revelation, and most other apocalyptic texts, the element of exhortation, 2 Peter focuses much more on an individualistic moralism than on the anti-imperial exhortation of Revelation. Only individuals are addressed in 2 Peter's exhortations and references to the Genesis flood. As Elisabeth Schüssler Fiorenza has pointed out, apocalyptic language can function in two ways, either to control the behavior of individuals or to provide an alternative vision and encouragement of new community structures in the face of oppression. [38] These observations allow us to recognize that 2 Peter definitely represents the moralistic use of apocalyptic threats to control individual behavior. By contrast, Revelation targets its primary threats of judgment against the system and structures of empire, especially the economic system (Revelation 18). The New Jerusalem vision (Revelation 21–22) serves to encourage people toward citizenship in God's counterimperial polis. The book exhorts God's people to "come out" of empire (Rev 18:4) so that they can enter into God's city of blessing and promise.

To summarize: Within the spectrum of early Christian apocalyptic literature, Revelation and 2 Peter represent two very different eschatological perspectives on the *end*. Whereas 2 Peter envisions an end to the earth and the whole created world, Revelation envisions an imminent end to the Roman imperial world.

End of Empire, Not the End of the Created World

This crucial distinction between the *end of empire* and the *end of the created world* is one that I believe can serve us in these next years. Public theologians and biblical scholars will need to articulate this distinction much more forcefully in order to equip people of faith to address the crises of empire today, manifested in global climate change as well as attendant crises such as "peak oil" (the projected decline of world oil production as supplies become depleted), deforestation, water shortages, and the environmental justice crises being experienced by vulnerable communities throughout the world. What must come to an end today may well be the unsustainable way of life in U.S. culture—a carbon-addicted way of life that could be defined as the most dangerous manifestation of empire today—but not the earth itself. Our task as public scholars will be to lift up New Testament end-of-empire discourses to help people envision life beyond this empire, articulating the Bible's joyful and compelling visions for abundant life in local communities as counter-visions to imperial violence and exploitation.

The New Testament is full of end-of-empire discourses, as Richard Horsley has helped us to see. Horsley is a "pioneer among biblical scholars who have emphasized the anti-imperial, political strategies of the Jesus movement."[39] Through their work on the first-century Roman imperial context of Galilee, Judea, and Asia Minor, Horsley and others have demonstrated that the terminology of empire is everywhere in the New Testament. New Testament authors redefine and subvert political terms such as "gospel" (*euangelion*), "savior" (*sōtēr*), and "kingdom" (*basileia*) in deliberately counterimperial ways.

Another imperial term employed by the New Testament is *oikoumenē*. Standard English translations of this term simply as "world" or "inhabited world" mask the aggressively imperial cast this term had taken on by the time of Augustus, as evidenced in imperial propaganda asserting Rome's dominance over the whole *oikoumenē* through military, political, and economic means.[40] We should translate *oikoumenē* as "empire."

Luke Johnson argued already in 1991 that *oikoumenē* should be translated as "empire" rather than "world" in birth and temptation narratives in the Gospel of Luke (2:1, the imperial census; 4:5, the "kingdoms of the empire"), as well as in some of the conflict scenes of Acts (11:28; 17:6; 24:5). But Johnson did not extend the translation of *oikoumenē* as "empire" into passages about the *oikoumenē* falling under judgment or coming to an end.[41] In my view, the translation of *oikoumenē* as "empire" should be applied also to the New Testament's end-times discourses. When the Gospel of Luke uses the word *oikoumenē* in the context of end-times tribulations that will come upon the nations ("There will be distress of nations . . . people fainting with fear and foreboding of what is coming upon the *oikoumenē*," Luke 21:25-26), this text signals the end of *empire*, not the end of the physical, created world. Similarly, in Revelation, the "hour of trial that is coming upon the whole *oikoumenē*" (Rev 3:10) should be read not so much as a general end-times tribulation that God will inflict upon the planet earth to destroy it, as many of today's fundamentalists like to claim, but more pointedly as the time of trial or judgment that God will bring upon the entire Roman Empire and on all those who benefit from Rome's injustice. Two other uses of *oikoumenē* in Revelation (Rev 12:9; 16:14) are also anti-imperial, drawing on highly mythological language of beasts and dragons to counter Rome's own mythological claims of omnipotence.[42]

As we face the global warming crisis, this distinction between the end of empire (*oikoumenē*) and end of the created world (*kosmos* and *gē*) will become crucial. Our unsustainable way of life—the empire of a carbon-consuming system that is destroying the earth and endangering its most vulnerable people—must come to an end. But from a biblical perspective, end of empire does not have to mean the end of the physical, created world.

Indeed, Revelation, perhaps more than any other New Testament text, helps us envision this distinction between empire and the created world, with its picture of the millennium in chapter 20, after the destruction of Babylon/Rome in Revelation 17–18. Revelation introduces the millennium as a symbolic thousand-year period of time after Satan has been tied up, that is, after the fall of the empire (Rev 20:4). Such an image is not meant to furnish a literal chronology of linear time. The entire book presents us with "vision time," as Steven Friesen describes it, the journey-like experience in which Revelation moves between "different phases of historical time and records them in a disorienting fashion."[43] The millennium of Revelation represents what Friesen calls "vindication time" for the victims of Roman imperial rule, a concrete period of time after the fall of the Roman Empire.[44] Pablo Richard's interpretation of the millennium of Revelation 20 as "not a chronology but a logic" can be helpful.[45] The important point is that Revelation teaches a logic that embraces life on earth beyond empire, that is, after the satanic power of empire has been dethroned.

Other New Testament texts share the conviction of Revelation that the old imperial order was passing away, and the realm of God was already dawning on earth in Jesus Christ. Apocalyptic language of the *end* seems deliberately chosen to counter Rome's imperial and eschatological claims to eternal hegemony, and to underscore the urgent advent of a new age.[46]

The Urgency of the Present Moment: Time for Repentance and Public Testimony

Time is of the essence in Revelation. But interestingly, the book's perspective is not simply of time hurtling towards an inevitable end. Rather, Revelation puts great emphasis on the present moment as a moment for decision and repentance. Shifts from past tense to present and future tenses, along with calls for repentance and use of deliberative rhetoric, all serve to draw the audience into what Harry Maier calls "an abiding sense of the imminent," extending the urgency of the present moment.[47] The entire book of Revelation calls on the audience to "come out" of empire before it is too late (Rev 18:4), in order not to fall prey to the catastrophic judgment and plagues, in order not to share in the collapse of the empire.

Revelation's focus on the urgency of the present moment as a time for repentance and testimony is an aspect of the book that can help us face the crisis of global warming. Scientists tell us that halting carbon emissions at 440 parts per million is possible with existing technology.[48] What is needed is massive public, political commitment that would undertake the actions necessary to reduce carbon emissions by 80–90 percent by the year 2050, with a 50 percent reduction by 2020. How do we mobilize that massive public, political commitment?

Repentance is the first action for which Revelation calls. The writer of Revelation believes that people can still make the changes necessary to "come out" of empire. It is not too late for repentance. To be sure, the book's positive calls for repentance (the imperative of *metanoēson* ["repent"]) are concentrated in the seven opening letters (for example, Rev 2:5, 16; 3:3, 19), whereas later references to repentance are phrased negatively ("they did not repent from . . . " Rev 9:20-21; 16:9, 11). Yet Schüssler Fiorenza has made a persuasive case that even these negative references to repentance in chapter 9 serve as part of the book's rhetorical appeal to the audience to repent.[49] Moreover, in a departure from the book's extensive use of the Exodus story, hearts are never hardened in Revelation. Rather, Revelation 11 lifts up a concrete model of successful repentance, with the "rest" of the people who heeded the testimony of the two witnesses and "gave glory to God" (Rev 11:13).

The book describes plagues that contribute to the call for repentance. They project out into the future the logical consequences of the trajectory that Rome is on, so people can see in advance where the dangerous imperial path is taking them. The terrible calamities of ecological disaster that are described as befalling the earth, rivers, and oceans are not intended as *predictions* of future events that God has preordained *must* happen to the world. The plagues serve rather as warnings, as wake-up calls, like Ebenezer Scrooge's visionary journeys in Charles Dickens's *A Christmas Carol*, where Scrooge is shown horrifying future scenarios not because they must happen, but so that he can alter the course of his life.[50]

We, too, need to alter the course of our life before it is too late.

Even nature itself participates in the warning of the plagues, crying out about the consequences of the deadly actions of imperial oppressors. When waters and springs turn to blood in the third bowl plague, the angel ("messenger") of the waters interprets this through the logic of natural consequences, as a boomerang-like effect: "You are just, O Holy One . . . for you have judged these things. Because they shed the blood of saints and prophets, you have given them blood to drink. It is axiomatic (*axios estin*)" (Rev 16:6). Today, what is axiomatic is that if we continue on our perilous path we will bring about our own demise.

Although the end of the empire is inevitable and axiomatic, the destruction seems to be deliberately delayed in Revelation so that the audience can come out of empire, and so it can have the opportunity to give public testimony. Analyzing what he calls Revelation's "games with time," Maier argues that Revelation makes ingenious use of delay in order to open up the present moment as a time for decision on the part of readers: "Like advertising with its urgent appeal to buy 'while quantities last,'" the Apocalypse "uses the threat of an imminent end to break open an urgent reconfiguration of the present." Revelation offers a kind of never-ending "not yet," a "'not yet' that insists on present action."[51]

Testimony or witness (*martyria*) is the second action to which Revelation calls the community, following the model of the testimony of Jesus the Lamb. "Testimony is not just any word, but a public word," Pablo Richard explains, drawing on his experience of resistance in Latin America. "In Revelation, testimony always has a power to change history, both in heaven and on earth."[52] Revelation places the Christian community in the role of the two witnesses of chapter 11, "calling for a witness of active, nonviolent resistance to Rome's claim of lordship over human history," as Brian Blount argues in *Can I Get a Witness?*[53] Perhaps the analogy today would be the call for a massive witness of active nonviolent resistance to the dominating claim of carbon consumption over human history.

"Can I get a witness?" The question that Brian Blount hears at the heart of Revelation is a question we must ask today. We are called to give witness or testimony to the stories of those most affected by climate change—people in the island nations of Kirabati or Tuvalu who have done nothing to cause this crisis, but who will lose their island homes because of our carbon emissions; people in Bhutan in the Himalayas who risk being killed by "glacial lake outburst floods" because of glaciers melting that have never melted before;[54] people in Chicago and other major U.S. urban areas where asthma deaths will rise, aggravated by higher summer temperatures; people in Africa and Central America who will become climate refugees because of severe drought and drinking water shortages. We are called to witness to Revelation's urgent wake-up call, as well as its vision for justice and the healing of the world.

Public testimony must call upon the world, and especially its richest nations, to change our addiction to a carbon-consuming way of life, so that hundreds of millions of people, and creation, itself, can live.

It is not yet too late for us to "come out" of this empire. But scientists tell us—and I believe them—that we probably have less than ten years to do so.

3. Biblical Hermeneutics in a Secular Age: Reflections from South Africa Twenty Years after the *Kairos Document*

Jonathan A. Draper
University of KwaZulu-Natal

Biblical Theology Twenty Years after the *Kairos Document*

MANY HAVE SEEN, AND PERHAPS CONTINUE TO SEE, the end of apartheid and the social and political transformation in South Africa as one of the beacons of hope in an otherwise rather bleak history of the twentieth century. Without wishing to overemphasize the role of the church and Bible in this process, there is no doubt that both were integrally involved in the struggle for transformation on both sides. One of the decisive moments for the involvement of the church—a term that is used here generically to include the full variety of denominations and movements—was the publication in 1985 of the *Kairos Document: Challenge to the Church: A Theological Comment on the Political Crisis in South Africa*.[1] The document was signed by a number of eminent theologians and provoked a flurry of debate in both church and society—occasioning a full-scale attack by the apartheid government and conservative churches on theologians and church leaders who supported it. However its challenge also inspired a new generation of conscientized and radicalized Christians to participate alongside secular liberation movements in the struggle to remove apartheid. In the great demonstrations that accompanied and hastened its demise, bishops, moderators, clergy, and Christian activists inspired by the message of the *Kairos Document* marched alongside other religious and secular movements, often at the front.

Yet it is one of the ironies of recent South African history that the *Kairos Document*, which made such an impact not only in South Africa but around the world when it was published in 1985, scarcely received a mention on its twentieth anniversary. A web search came up with only twenty-two hits, of which half related to the *Kairos Europe* initiative, and most were quite old.[2] The institution responsible for the drafting of the document, the late Institute for Contextual Theology, fared even less well in an Internet search.

The *Kairos Document* shaped the academic and popular theological debate in South Africa—and indeed in many places around the world—for a decade. It no longer saw the church intervening against injustice in society, but rather saw the church itself as a "site of struggle," using the Gramscian terminology that became popular among Kairos theologians.[3] It also posed a direct challenge to biblical interpretation, with its blunt denial that there are *neutral* zones where biblical research and teaching can be done without regard for their social consequences. For the *Kairos Document* called itself a "biblical and theological comment on the political crisis in South Africa today" and campaigned for an "alternative biblical and theological model" to produce a Christian response that "is biblical, spiritual, pastoral and, above all, prophetic."[4] A biblical prophetic theology is opposed to "Church Theology" and "State Theology."[5] That this statement gave academic biblical interpretation a new urgency and relevance did not escape the interest of socially engaged biblical scholars in Europe and America, such as Richard Horsley, Norman Gottwald, Walter Wink, and many others, who lent what support they could to the anti-apartheid movement. Yet today there is little sign of biblical and prophetic theology at the center of either the church or the state in South Africa, nor, for that matter, in the academy. In fact, at a meeting of the New Testament Society of South Africa in 2005, which was devoted to ethics in Paul, the keynote speaker, ethicist Professor Piet Naudé, asked what had happened to the role of biblical interpreters on the public *agora*, the marketplace of ideas and the seedbed of public action.[6] The signs appear no more favorable elsewhere in the world.

Does this mean that the *Kairos Document* was wrong or that biblical scholars no longer have anything to say in the public square? Part of the change that has taken place since the publication of the *Kairos Document* is that South Africa has moved from being a state in which Christianity was the established religion enshrined in its constitution to being a secular state in which Christianity has no exclusive or privileged role. This coincided with the collapse of the Soviet Union and the end of the Cold War, which brought to an end the myth of a Christian West confronting Marxist atheism and ushered in a new age of secularism dominated by global economic interests. So the question of the role of the Bible and its interpretation in a secular age, or if indeed it does have a role, is an important one, not only in South Africa and the global South, but also in Europe and North America. What kind of hermeneutics would be appropriate for New Testament scholars and Christian leaders concerned to make a significant public contribution in a secular state in a globalized age? And is anyone listening out there?

Essentially the hermeneutic offered by the *Kairos Document* based itself on the suggestion of Luke 19:44 that, in a time of crisis, God confronts his people with an opportunity to respond before it is too late. This is a special decisive moment in time, a *kairos*, that is also a moment of judgment when "the Church is . . . shown up for what it really is and no cover up will be possible."[7] The *Kairos Document* argues that to discern the present crisis, the church needs to undertake social analysis. In order to understand what God calls the church to do, the Bible, rightly understood, provides an insight into the nature of God as a God of justice and compassion, working out God's redemptive will to liberate the whole creation from oppression. This is seen as the "central theme that runs right through the Old and New Testaments."[8] Once the Bible reader has analyzed the social context that confronts her or him with a crisis, the text provides a spotlight of God's purpose in history, a purpose that enables the reader to speak prophetically, to call for justice, and to engage in transformative praxis. This prophetic message is not only a pronouncement of judgment on injustice, but a message of hope, since God's purpose does not fail. God's oppressed people, and indeed the whole created order, will be set free.

Discernment in a Secular Society

As has already been noted, part of the potency of the *Kairos Document* was that it spoke what it presented as a biblical prophetic message into a society that declared itself a Christian state and appealed to the Bible for its legitimization. It is neither realistic nor proper to speak in the same way today, when the Constitution promulgated in 1996 guarantees the freedom and equality of religious expression in an entrenched Bill of Rights.[9] This means that Christianity is allowed—at least in theory—no privileged position in the new secular South Africa.

Indeed, when church leaders raised questions about the behavior of ruling African National Congress party leader, Jacob Zuma, who was acquitted of rape but reprimanded by the judge for irresponsible sexual behavior, this point was forcibly made by a senior leader of the Congress of South African Trade Unions in Zuma's defense. National Union of Mineworkers President Senzeni Zokwana declared at the twelfth annual conference of COSATU, "We are not Christians. We don't listen to the Ten Commandments, and we don't have to listen when Christians tell us adultery is wrong. We also don't need Christians to tell us who our leaders should be. We can't have people telling us that our president must be a woman."[10] Likewise the supporters of Jacob Zuma turned savagely on eminent liberation theologian Archbishop Desmond Tutu when he raised issues relating to the same episode, questioning his right to speak publicly as a religious leader on political issues.[11]

In this new political and social climate, many, if not most, South African Christian leaders have retreated into the private spiritual sphere of the church and, despite some pious statements here and there, are leaving the politicians to get on with the show. Church leaders appear at public functions to bless and to pray at the bidding of the politicians, thereby legitimating processes over which they have rarely had any influence.

Denominationalism has reasserted itself strongly, where before there was a real attempt to get the churches to speak into urgent social questions with a united voice. (This might not have ever really happened in a sustained way, but it was at least a sought-after ideal.) This new denominationalism, besides splitting the voice and influence of the church in South Africa, has had the result that interest blocks within the church simply raise issues relating to sexual morality or their own ecclesiastical and doctrinal concerns—abortion, birth control, homosexuality, AIDS, pornography, the environment—without engaging with one another. This is a familiar scenario in the modern secularized world.

The danger of such privatization and compartmentalization of religion is that it either retreats into pietism, or else it becomes a breeding ground for new fundamentalisms in religious communities that seek to control the political process. Both of these trends are unfortunate. In the new secular South Africa, as generally in the West, the kind of emphasis that the *Kairos Document* advocated is not irrelevant; rather, it points the way forward to a hermeneutics for the church in a secular society. There is the same need for social analysis of the context; for exploration of the biblical text as the primary channel for the expression of the will of the God of justice and compassion; for identifying God's key moment of judgment and opportunity, or *kairos*, when it comes; for speaking prophetically into the social context out of that exploration of the God of the Bible; and, finally, for engaging in appropriate praxis. Christian theologians and biblical scholars need, of course, to operate differently within a secular state, but they still have important insights to contribute in the public arena.

The Self and the Other

The *Kairos Document* recognized three kinds of theology: state theology, church theology, and prophetic theology. "State Theology" is "simply the theological justification of the status quo with its racism, capitalism and totalitarianism," using texts like Rom 13:1-7 to silence criticism and demand total obedience on the grounds of its duty to uphold "law and order" in the face of a supposed "community threat." The "idolatrous god" of the state oppresses and kills the poor and protects the rich and powerful, legitimated by a "heretical" and "blasphemous" theology.[12] "Church Theology" criticizes injustice but uses "superficial . . . stock ideas" of "reconciliation (or peace), justice and non-violence." It fails to see that reconciliation cannot be achieved without justice, and hence that it requires repentance and restitution. It seeks the "justice of reform" determined by the ruling whites and rejects the kind of "more radical justice" which comes from below and is determined by the oppressed majority. It envisages justice coming about by reforms driven by "individual conversions," an approach which "has not worked and . . . never will work" because the problem is one of structural injustice and not simply of personal guilt. Such Church Theology calls for peace and an end to all forms of violence, "but this *excludes* the structural, institutional and unrepentant violence of the State and especially the oppressive and naked violence of the police and the army."[13] By way of contrast, "Prophetic Theology," which begins with social analysis of the structural problems, moves to an understanding of the biblical trajectory of liberation through structural transformation and finds a message of hope for the future in the coming of God's kingdom and the doing of God's will "on earth as it is in heaven." This involves understanding that God takes sides with the oppressed and calls the church to do the same. It calls Christians to participate in the struggle against injustice. It requires the church to name the evil forces, to share solidarity with the masses of the people in their struggle for liberation through civil disobedience to unjust laws and policies of a morally illegitimate regime. The *Kairos Document* appealed to the Bible in support of a prophetic theology for the time of crisis it perceived in South Africa after the conflagration that began in Soweto in 1974, after a series of marches against the racist policy of apartheid had been met with major violence by police and army. This culminated in a State of Emergency being declared in 1986, which lasted until the lifting of the ban on the liberation movements and the freeing of Nelson Mandela on February 12, 1990, after twenty-seven years in prison. It called for social analysis of the reader's context as the basis for a truly biblical prophetic theology, and it referred to the importance of understanding the biblical text's historical context in order to avoid a false reading of the text. Its goal was praxis, living out the biblical text. I affirm these three aspects of the hermeneutical task, but wish to reformulate them to take account of the reality of a post-apartheid South Africa and, indeed, of secular society elsewhere. The *Kairos Document* was rather narrowly focused on the role of the church in the political struggle, and the church and the Bible have, quite frankly, become largely marginalized in this sphere. South Africa's option for a secular state in its constitution required a new hermeneutics and a new praxis.[14]

A key aspect of a hermeneutics for a secular age is recognizing our own particularity as readers and the otherness of the text over against us. Until we are able to reach this moment of recognition, we cannot meet the Other in the text, the one who meets us in the Word and calls us to embrace the other in ourselves[15] and in our society. Without this openness to the other/Other, we hear in the Word only what confirms and comforts us in our own closed world. The exclusion of the other in ourselves and in our world supports an uncritical validation of our group and a demonization of other groups. This, I believe, lies at the heart of fundamentalisms of all kinds, or, to use a more neutral term, what Edward Said called "essentialisms."[16] We construct "essentialisms" of the other that then essentialize us in turn. Fundamentalisms play a largely destructive role in our modern secular world by leading to extreme and violent behavior, since they are easily manipulated by politicians, religious leaders, and demagogues. We consequently beat up on the stranger and the deviant. But God is present in the stranger and the deviant, inasmuch as God is always a stranger to us and a deviant to our ways ("For my thoughts are not your thoughts, nor are your ways my ways, says the LORD," Isa 55:8).

The starting point of our hermeneutics must, therefore, be the recognition that the Bible was not written for us but for others long dead, for a society very different than our own. It has been two thousand years since the New Testament was written, centuries more beyond that since some of the books of the Hebrew Bible were written. To some extent, the ordinary reader depends on the trained reader to supply information that makes clear that difference. So the *Kairos Document,* which continually emphasized the ownership and agency of the masses of ordinary Christians, nevertheless had to turn to expert knowledge to reject the contention of state theology that Romans 13 called ordinary Christians to obey the government of the day as put there by God, something a surface reading of the text would seem to require. Recognition of this need for the guidance of trained readers can provide a safeguard against abuse of the text by the status quo. But not everything can be resolved in this way. So, for example, there are passages where women are simply told to submit, to find their identity in their husbands and their children, or to stay in the closed world of the home. Slaves are told to submit to their masters as types of God. Gay and lesbian (if we may be permitted to use anachronistic language) people are told that their behavior is unnatural. The discovery of difference between the culture(s) of the Bible and the culture of our own time is not an end in itself, but only the starting point of a dialectical process.

The modern reader in a secular society should begin by posing questions to the text, expressing difficulties with what it says, and asking why it says those things. At the same time, the modern reader also needs to listen patiently and openly to the text, even when having profound difficulties with what it says on first reading. What is the text really saying: Is it what we thought when we first approached the text? Is it unexpected? Is it offensive? How do its solutions to problems differ from ours today? Do we have to challenge those answers on the basis of the deepest principles within the Bible itself?

Do we have to challenge our own presuppositions on the basis of what the text says?

Hearing the voice of the text can be achieved only by this process of letting it be different and creating space for it to speak, in a process of "differentiation."[17] To achieve this, we need to undertake a careful and close reading of the text, using tools that foster differentiation. Obviously, historical-critical tools are very effective in this process, but they can be very challenging and alienating to ordinary readers. They require expert knowledge and advice. This does not excuse ordinary readers of today from undertaking historical-critical study to a greater or lesser extent, particularly given the enormous diffusion and availability of such study tools today through books, films, study guides, and so on. The goal of hearing the voice of the text also challenges Christian leaders to take their task of providing such information very seriously. It is all too easy for Christian leaders to simply ignore what challenges and disquiets their people, but it is shortsighted. In the new secular age, films, TV, radio, and newspapers are constantly picking up on the unfinished debates of academic study and packaging them deftly for mass consumption (for example, *The Da Vinci Code*, the Gospel of Judas, the Gospel of Mary, various sarcophagi with inscriptions from archaeological digs in Palestine, Dead Sea Scrolls, Nag Hammadi texts, all mixed up in an undifferentiated mix of conspiracy theory). The half-remembered bits and pieces of such debates continue to operate in the background of the minds of many ordinary Christians, with an uneasy suspicion that they are not being told the whole truth. These suspicions have a basis in reality, in that the church is often evasive in facing up to uncomfortable critical questions about historical data in the Bible.

On the other hand, literary tools and cultural information can also help readers to hear the otherness of the text, to challenge their own assumptions. The connection between text and context is usually reflected in the structure of the text and can provide an insight into the different world of its community. Narrative and structural analysis can be as important in the process of differentiation as historical-critical analysis. Indeed, in a good exegesis they should go hand in hand. This process of differentiation is not the same as the attempt at scientific objectivity in the old Enlightenment sense, though obviously it relates to that enterprise. The biblical text is not, in this approach, so much an *object* of our inquiry, but a *subject*, an "other" in a conversation about a matter of mutual interest.

The Other and the Self

However, the biblical text is in many respects not just the "other" for Christians, but an aspect of their own identity, their "shadow." Christians do not approach the text as strangers but as those for whom it is normative, those for whom it is the "bread of life," to paraphrase the language of the Gospel of John (6:63). We are heirs of two thousand and more years of interpretation and praxis. The thousands, or perhaps we should say, millions of readers over the millennia have each contributed to the meaning of the text. Its meaning for us is not only determined by what it meant, but by what it means and continues to mean for our community of faith. The text has what J. Severino Croatto called a "reservoir of meaning" that is deep and broad.[18] We are not objective first-time readers of the text. We stand in a tradition and a community of readers. We cannot approach the text as neutral and objective readers, since we read as those whose history and identity are rooted in the text and its continuing community. This is true even for readers who approach the text as those who have lost or rejected their Christian faith or those who belong to different faith communities. Muslims, Hindus, or even people of no faith in the new globalized world, inherit a historical (often conflictual) interaction with the Bible and the Christian faith, just as Christians inherit a set of historical interactions with them and their texts. Even where we stand outside a faith community that produced a text, we read as those caught up in human history, as ourselves subjects in relation to other subjects. Our approach to the text is already marked by a "long conversation."[19] Whatever our own faith tradition and position, it will contribute substantially to our reading of texts that make faith claims on us.

What this means is that, as Wilhelm Dilthey and Hans-Georg Gadamer have argued, when we interpret history we are actually interpreting ourselves.[20] Or to put it more generally, our interpretation of the other is an interpretation of ourselves. To understand the historical context of the biblical text we need to understand our own context, our own questions, our own insights and fears and problems, our own dark side. This "paradox of otherness" opens us to the possibility of hearing the "word addressed to me."[21] Thus a hermeneutics for a secular society requires not simply openness to learning about the other, but openness to learning about ourselves. The text poses questions to us and challenges us as those who are other to itself. This creates a dialectical relationship between the text and the reader, an existential tug-of-war, which is so well described by Karl Barth in the preface to his famous *Commentary on Romans*.[22] Honest reading impels us back to further study of our own social, political, and economic context and to critical analysis of ourselves and our interests.

The Othered Self

I have chosen this title provocatively. I thought to speak of "the new self" in order to stress that something new comes out of the wrestling between the context of the text and the context of the reader: The text projects a world that we can enter momentarily by suspending self and living in that world, experiencing it, and potentially being transformed by the experience, in the terminology of Paul Ricoeur.[23] But speaking of "the othered self" keeps a focus on the self and the other considered above. It also suggests that the interpretive process leads to recognition of the other in ourselves: that the moment of openness to the other helps us to recognize that the stranger is not really a stranger, but an aspect of our own deepest self. In other words, we recognize our common humanity in the other. For those of us who are people of faith, whatever that faith may be, the recognition of our common humanity is recognition of the *imago dei* (image of God) in the other (however that may be understood). God meets us as Other in the otherness of the human other, which is a rejected or neglected aspect of the self.

So the final aspect of our biblical hermeneutics for a secular age lies in the recognition that reading is and should be transformative. When Christians read the Bible honestly and openly, they need to be changed by a new understanding of how different communities live and work and by a recognition of the challenge and call this presents to them, whether they understand themselves as people for whom this book is significant and normative as an expression of the faith of others with whom we stand in continuity as people of faith, or simply as people in solidarity with others as human beings caught up in history. An acceptance of this transformative potential of the text is the moment of our appropriation of the text. We make it our text, our story in some significant way.

Finally, a new understanding is related to a new praxis. Even if it means only a recognition that other people are different from us and do things differently, and an acceptance of the legitimacy of that difference, our appropriation of the text should lead us to live differently, to hear and respond to the call to be different. Otherwise we are like those who see our faces in a mirror and go away and forget what we look like to others, as the book of James (1:22-24) says perceptively. Transformative engagement with the text leads to transformative engagement with our social, political, and economic contexts and to the insertion of the prophetic word into the public sphere—not as an attempt at a new Christian hegemony, but as a contribution to the public discourse on the part of a faith tradition that is normative for a particular faith community.

The Othered Self and the Secular Society

One of the key problems in the new globalized secular society which is increasingly becoming the norm is the formation and maintenance of a common life and of an identity that moves beyond the racial or cultural homogeneity of the European nation state: one people, one race, one nation, to which one might add, one religion. This is obviously a key issue in the new South Africa, which is trying to move beyond the devastating effects of colonialism and racism. But the lingering concept of the nation state remains a problem for Europe as well, as the unease about the admission of Turkey to the European Union has shown. Humanist, post-Christian Europe has been able to rely on an unspoken and undefined commonality based on its common Christian heritage, whatever wars it has fought over the definition and control of that heritage. The question of a cohesive national identity is a critical issue in the United States of America as well, where the last two national elections have shown that similar deep and fundamental issues divide it. The opening up of this divide was analyzed and predicted by the American sociologist Robert Bellah and his research team decades ago in *Habits of the Heart* as they tried to chart a way forward through this looming nightmare.[24]

The problem is rooted in the need for a shared identity.[25] Society holds together by means of an agreed set of understandings and values that are not always explicitly stated, but may be projected by means of "master myths" (the common assumptions under which cultures operate when they are not challenged)[26] and metonymic referencing (the word, concepts, and phrases which stand for much wider common cultural systems, *pars pro toto*, even when they are not fully understood by the users).[27] In other words, society depends on a world of meaning that has hegemonic force precisely because it is not stated but assumed. If it were stated and brought out into the open, it would become ideology, something that might be contested and therefore could no longer command universal assent. The moment when hegemony becomes ideology is also the moment of "play" or *bricolage* (in which new and productive fusions can be made out of disconnected fragments of competing cultures).[28]

If, for instance, someone in a Western society says, "It's my right," others might discuss whether the person's claim to a specific right is acceptable, but would not challenge the idea that he or she actually has rights: *Rights* are therefore a master myth of Western culture. Such a statement would lose its hegemonic role in a society that denies the existence of human rights, however, and there would have to be introduced and defended as ideology. It was quite common for white children growing up in South Africa in the apartheid era to be told, "You have no rights, only duties." The fact that such a thing could be said to children is significant. Such a statement would probably be classed as deviant in Europe and North America today, but was rooted in a particular kind of Christian worldview. This statement carried specific social consequences in South Africa because it operated with hegemonic force and underpinned the totalitarianism of the apartheid state. It assisted in the militarization of white society. Reading with the other in the biblical text brought, and brings, this kind of hegemony into question, and opens up possibilities for new kinds of agency in situations of legitimized oppression.

The emergence of a secular state in a society marked by racial, religious, and social diversity is a feature of the new South Africa in particular, but it is also an aspect of globalization. It has become impossible for states or even groups of states to go it alone. We define one another. Our proximity to one another in terms of global communication, trade, and transportation means that more and more of what was once assumed can now only be asserted: What was once hegemonic now becomes ideological. While the sociology of knowledge, as formulated by Peter Berger and Thomas Luckmann, might suggest that religion and culture are simply *projections* of the human reality, it is clear that their role is more complex than this.[29] The landmark study of Clifford Geertz on changing rituals in Javanese society indicates that there is a dynamic and creative interaction between a given society and its "universe of meaning."[30] Precisely because this projection (whether it refers to a real entity, that is, God or gods, or not) opposes what *should be* to what *is*, it provides the kind of tension that allows new social arrangements to come into being. For the major world religions, sacred texts represent the most potent objectification of the projected "universe of meaning," so that interaction with these texts at a deep level in the interface between what is and what should be, in the interface between the self and the other, can be productive of new and potentially life-giving transformation. It also provides the engaged biblical scholar and Christian leader with the space and the responsibility to contribute to the debate and formation of public policy in the secular state in a constructive way.

This is where I find a conversational model of hermeneutics helpful, because it focuses on the *other* as an opportunity and not a threat. The recognition of the nature of the historical text (or any text for that matter) as "other" challenges us to explore difference and identity without alienation. At the heart of the Christian faith is a text that is both other to us and an aspect of ourselves. A two-thousand-year-old collection of diverse texts, mostly from the region of the Mediterranean, coming from communities so different from our own in their languages and cultures, and reflecting a history of continuing challenges to their own identity and survival, the Bible is foundational and, in some sense, normative to our own identity. Until we engage with the otherness of the text, it is silent. If we hear anything, it is only the echo of our own voice. We do not convince ourselves or others when we thump the Bible and assert its inerrant truth, no matter how loudly we shout—and we shout because we are trying to drown out our own doubts. When we do engage with the otherness of the text, its fundamental difference challenges our master myths and speaks strange and, at first, alarming words in a foreign accent. Our own otherness questions the Bible's assertions and is sometimes rightly horrified by its master myths.

Who could read the profoundly evocative lament of Psalm 137, verse 1 (REB), "By the rivers of Babylon we sat down and wept as we remembered Zion," without being moved, and who could read its concluding savagery in verse 9, "Happy is he who seizes your babies and dashes them against a rock," without being shocked? But it is in listening to these texts and talking back to them that we move beyond what is comfortable to what is transformative. In the Anglican liturgy and prayer books, those last words of the Psalm are always bracketed out. Indeed, it is hard to recite such words in church today, but I believe that even if we don't recite them liturgically, it has become, more than ever, important to read them and engage with them in our era of localized and international savagery. Only then will we hear the depth of pain and loss of the oppressed and understand their responses, and only when we have entered into that experience, and our own responsibility for it, can we talk to others about the sanctity of human life. As Ricoeur phrased it, when we read texts in this way, we enter into and experience another possible world, "a proposed world, a world I may inhabit and wherein I can project my ownmost possibilities," and this process has the potential to transform us and our own world.[31]

What I say here about the Christian tradition is not really different for Islam, Hinduism, Buddhism, and African Traditional Religion(s) in the new globalized secular context, although perhaps some of these religious systems can still point to more homogenous societies than post-Christian Europe and North America. It is unlikely that they can escape the impact of globalization for very long even if that were true. For instance, immigration into Europe and North America, settlement forced by slavery or economic pressure in former colonial settlements like South Africa, and mass media and modernization have all driven an increasing wedge between traditional Islam and the experience of Muslims today. The emergence of new Islamic fundamentalisms is not dissimilar to the emergence of Christian fundamentalisms: It is an attempt to drown out the doubt and dissonance by shouting louder, but it cannot restore the old feudal Islamic states or even preserve them. Whatever emerges from the current world conflicts will be new, not a restoration of something lost. Thus, once Iran installs nuclear energy and builds nuclear warheads, it enters the terrain of modern science with all its attendant presuppositions. In the end, utilizing Western technology and adopting Western weapons to undergird Islamic separatism will only increase cognitive dissonance, not diminish it.

The way forward lies in a hermeneutics of conversation, meaning conversation with the otherness of our own faith traditions and universe of meaning, and conversation with the otherness of different faith traditions and social universes as well, rooted in the analysis of our own social, political, and economic context(s).

On the other hand, talking is dangerous if it is seen as an end in itself. For instance, international negotiations may do more harm than good if they are perceived by oppressed people as a talk shop designed to silence their legitimate aspirations and to bind them, in a position of weakness, to an agreement that will damage their long-term interests. What that kind of talking does—and there is a lot of it about—is to undermine the credibility of the leaders of oppressed people who are suckered into taking part in the negotiations, and to lead to the emergence of more radical leaders who understand the futility of talking from a position of weakness. If negotiations do not lead to real and perceived benefits in practice, then they are, at best, useless and, at worst, harmful. For example, at a time when there is real evidence for the emergence in England of a radicalized Islamic youth, news broadcasts there produce frequent statements from moderate Islamic leaders to the effect that they have been talking for years and have reached numerous agreements without producing any real change in government or society to transform the social conditions that breed radicalism.

In terms of the sort of conversational hermeneutic that I propose, this means that the whole hermeneutical cycle must issue in transformed praxis.

The Othered Self and Transformative Praxis

To return to the *Kairos Document*, perhaps its most insistent declaration was that there can be no compromise with injustice. There cannot be a middle path that allows entrenched and institutionalized injustice to continue. There may be moments that are *kairos* moments that call for a decision that cannot be evaded because failing to make a decision is already a decision for injustice. The *Kairos Document* sets out the goal of its hermeneutics as the identification of a *kairos* and the unequivocal commitment to God's call for transformation. To quote the line of a famous hymn by James R. Lovell, written in 1845 to protest America's war against Mexico and much sung in the struggle against apartheid in South Africa:

> Once to every man and nation comes the moment to decide,
> In the strife of truth with falsehood, for the good or evil side;
> Some great cause, some great decision, offering each the bloom
>   or blight,
> And the choice goes by forever, 'twixt that darkness and that
>   light.

This is not to call for the adoption of new fundamentalisms or essentialisms, but a recognition that hearing the voice of the Other in our conversations with the other confronts us with real choices, sometimes stark choices. It transforms our understanding of what is normative in our faith tradition and of how this should be lived out individually and corporately, not just in church but in society. This is the prophetic voice that leads to prophetic action.

How can we distinguish the prophetic voice from new fundamentalisms? Of course we could take our way from Deuteronomy 18:15-22—does the prophecy come to pass? But that is not very helpful, since it is easy to speak from hindsight when the battle is over! We are also likely to be swayed in our judgment by whether what came to pass benefits us personally or communally. Perhaps instead we can adopt the cryptic rule of thumb provided by the early Christian rule of life, the *Didache*, which struggled with the very practical issue of how to discern whether someone claiming to be "speaking in the Spirit" should be obeyed or not:

> And every prophet ordering a table in the Spirit
> Shall not eat from it[32] (11:5).

The prophet may demand that food be provided for those in need, but she or he may not benefit personally from the prophecy or else it is a false prophecy. We have constantly to ask ourselves: *Cui bonus*, to whose benefit? Most of the voices on the public stage are the voices of self-interest. Christians in general and academic theologians in particular, who intervene in the public arena without going through the process of the othered self, are liable to be co-opted in a way that identifies and confirms their own interests in the service of some other political, social, and economic interest. What emerges from real engagement with the other in our own sacred texts and traditions, however, is always searching and painful because what remains at the end of the conversation is neither the self nor the other as they were, but the creative and transformative othered self where self-interest has been surrendered to a new common good. The prophet does not get a free lunch. The Word that speaks into and through our words is constituted by this recognition of the intersection and transcendence of the self and the other in *this* moment. This is what constitutes the prophetic voice and gives people of faith, in general, and the academic theologian, in particular, the right and the space to contribute in the public arena.

4. Echoes of Paul in the Speeches of George W. Bush

Cynthia Briggs Kittredge
Episcopal Theological Seminary of the Southwest

ONE JANUARY DAY IN 2005, I was listening to George W. Bush's second inaugural address on the computer in my seminary office. As the president spoke on this state occasion, I heard in his claims and aspirations the voice of Paul, the apostle. President Bush spoke stirringly of the movement of freedom in the world today:

> There is only one force of history that can break the reign of hatred and resentment, and expose the pretensions of tyrants and reward the hopes of the decent and tolerant, and that is the force of human freedom.

> We are led by events and common sense to one conclusion. The survival of liberty in our land increasingly depends on the success of liberty in other lands. The best hope for peace in our world is the expansion of freedom in all the world.[1]

President Bush's use of the category of freedom in these lines went beyond passing reference to the American ideal of freedom. In describing freedom as a "force of history" opposed to tyrants and to the reign of hatred, the speech was drawing a vivid picture of the world. The portrait sounded true and it resembled closely the worldview in many passages in Paul's arguments, particularly in the letter to the Romans.

As the president's speech progressed and told of successive reigns, struggles, tyrants, and the ultimate victory of freedom, I found that my spirit resonated with the language, while at the same time my mind revolted from the deployment of that rhetoric—grounded ultimately in Paul's rhetoric of slavery and freedom in his letters—to support a particular aggressive foreign policy. To investigate the pattern, background, resonances, and effects of the biblical, particularly Pauline, themes in the speeches allows hearers to engage critically, to question the worldview created by the rhetoric, and to debate the conclusions the speeches lead their audiences to draw.

Orlando Patterson has argued that Paul's opposition of slavery to freedom set the groundwork for the Western political idea of freedom.[2] In this light, Bush's use of this language clearly capitalizes upon that coincidence of ideals. His particular way of portraying a current political conflict comes to appear self-evident; it makes "sense" of the world, in large part because it echoes this Western narrative so closely. As Paul's rhetoric of freedom draws on the cultural matrix of popular philosophical speech about freedom in his own time so Bush's use of the language of freedom effectively resonates with the rhetoric of freedom in the political discourse of this country, for example, Thomas Jefferson's formulation of the rights of "life, liberty, and the pursuit of happiness" in the Declaration of Independence. The allusions to Paul's letter to the Romans, formative in Christian spirituality and in Western culture, combine potently with the democratic political tradition of freedom.

The Contribution of Rhetorical Criticism

To investigate the speech and its relationship with the language of Paul involves a model of biblical studies that critically interrogates the rhetoric of biblical texts and of their reading in contemporary discourse. Developed and described by Elisabeth Schüssler Fiorenza, this rhetorical-critical model of biblical studies consists of a sequence of analytical moves in which the biblical text and its readers are put into conversation with one another.[3] To engage in discussion in the public square, the scholar first employs the analytical tools from her field to illuminate the argument of the biblical text. Then she places the ancient text into conversation with the rhetoric of contemporary public discourse in order to show patterns, make comparisons, and raise questions about public speech that will contribute to the wider intellectual and political discussion of ethics and public policy. I use this model here to investigate the language of freedom in George W. Bush's speeches and to explore how those speeches employ, and transmute, the category of freedom in the letter to the Romans.

When it is conceived as rhetorical-critical biblical studies, this model recognizes that the biblical texts are persuasive texts meant to move, motivate, and give an account of reality. In their ancient context, they were disputed and tested in the public forum of the church, or assembly, the *ekklēsia*. These same biblical texts are called upon and evoked in contemporary political discourse, where their meanings are contested both explicitly and in disguised and hidden fashion.

This model differs from other ways in which New Testament scholarship engages with political discourse by its direct acknowledgement of the rhetorical character of texts and their interpretations. For example, some other socially engaged scholars focus their attention on the meaning of the text in its own time or on the meaning of the author. Then they compare the original meaning of the text, or of its author, with the use made of the text in the history of interpretation. They make their arguments on the basis of that difference or gap between the meaning in its own time and the contemporary readings of it. For example, they might argue that Paul's letters advocate equality between women and men in the *ekklēsia*, against those scholars and pastors who assert that the text meant the maintenance of a relationship of benevolent subordination of wives to husbands. Or, as Richard Horsley has argued so eloquently and persuasively, they might assert, against those who see the letters as accommodations to the elitist values of the Roman Empire, that Paul's texts opposed Roman imperial values. New Testament scholars with a more socially conservative theological orientation might describe the worldview of the first-century text, with its view of female subordination in marriage, for example, and contrast it positively to the individualistic, isolated, consumer, capitalist values of the present.

The rhetorical-critical model I employ here, however, does not depend upon agreement about the original meaning of a text in order to engage that text in ethical and political debates in the present. The original meaning, insofar as it can be reconstructed, does not determine prescriptive meaning for the present. What Paul meant is not the only criterion for contemporary interpretation of the text in the present. Rather, the perspectives of Paul and of other Christ-believers in the community are subjected to investigation, discussion, and debate and placed within broader theological and cultural conversation.

The rhetorical character of biblical commentary is well known to preachers who have more flexibility than scholars in revising, reusing, and reinterpreting texts. As rhetoricians, they find creative ways of putting the language of the Bible into dialogue with current debates about policy. Preachers are more conscious of the rhetorical nature of their activity than are biblical scholars, and they, like presidential speechwriters, know how to harness the authority of the biblical author and the author's rhetoric to move and convince their hearers.

Presidential speeches rarely cite biblical texts, and they do not claim to be presenting correct interpretations of New Testament authors. For this reason, it is not effective for New Testament scholars to take on presidential speeches simply as wrong readings of Paul. But scholars and thoughtful Christian readers can analyze these authoritative utterances for how they draw on and employ patterns of narrative in scripture and in Western culture. The allusions to biblical themes and motifs are not important merely because they may be, as some have argued, "coded language" that speaks to Christian supporters but remains hidden to "those outside."[4] The language of these speeches is also powerful because it evokes these deep patterns in a way that operates below the surface even among those who would not identify themselves as Christian allies. An effective speaker, the president, draws on these patterns and directs them to his rhetorical purposes of arousing passion and patriotism and obtaining rational and/or emotional assent to a particular way of viewing the present time.

However, biblical scholars can and should work in cooperation with intellectuals in other academic traditions—history, political science, rhetoric, sociology—who bring their theoretical tools and their knowledge of history to describe, evaluate, and critique the perspective advanced by the speeches. In vigorous discussion with activists and committed Christian leaders this model of biblical studies will not remain insular and isolated from church and public square, but it will offer its distinctive theoretical tools to the intellectual discussion.

Sampling the Rhetoric of George W. Bush

In the second inaugural address and successive State of the Union speeches since 2001, consistent patterns of thought and a uniform narrative emerge and resonate with the language of Paul's letters. In this narrative, history is a story of energetic and inevitable progress, described with the metaphors of marching or moving from tyranny to freedom: "the advance of freedom is the great story of our time;"[5] "America is always more secure when freedom is on the move."[6] The pathway exists and its endpoint is determined: "The road of providence is uneven and unpredictable, yet we know where it leads, it leads to freedom."[7]

The direction of its trajectory is set, but the story of the progress of freedom is a violent one. The diametrically opposed forces of tyranny and freedom are locked in a dramatic struggle to the death. In the 2007 State of the Union address, Bush described the conflict between terrorism and freedom:

> This war is more than a clash of arms—it is a decisive ideological struggle, and the security of our nation is in the balance. To prevail, we must remove the conditions that inspire blind hatred and drove 19 men to get onto airplanes and come to kill us. What every terrorist fears most is human freedom.[8]

For Bush, the opposite of tyranny and terror is freedom: "the only force powerful enough to stop the rise of tyranny and terror . . . is the force of human freedom."[9] The speeches identify events of September 11, 2001, as the defining episode in this battle: "The attack on freedom in our world has reaffirmed our confidence in freedom's power to change the world."[10] In January of 2003, two months before the Iraq war, the State of the Union address wove Saddam Hussein and his intentions into this story: "Now in this century, the ideology of power and domination has appeared again and seeks to gain the ultimate weapons of terror."[11]

These events have propelled the United States, against its will, to a crisis point. At this critical juncture, a momentous and unambiguous choice must be made about which there can be no ambivalence. On October 7, 2001, a month after the September 11 events, Bush defined the battle:

> Today we focus on Afghanistan, but the battle is broader. Every nation has a choice to make. In this conflict there is no neutral ground. If any government sponsors the outlaws and killers of innocents, they have become outlaws and murderers, themselves. And they will take that lonely path at their own peril.[12]

The second inaugural address restated the choice:

> We will persistently clarify the choice before every ruler and
> every nation. The moral choice between oppression, which is
> always wrong, and freedom, which is eternally right. America
> will not pretend that jailed dissidents prefer their chains or that
> women welcome humiliation and servitude or that any human
> being aspires to live at the mercy of bullies.[13]

The story, told in these excerpts, very powerfully employs the language of
liberation, the transformation from slavery to freedom. The word *liberation*
has positive associations and possesses special appeal to some who would
not otherwise be Bush's natural political or ideological allies. Liberation has
theological resonances. The word for "making free" in the New Testament
is synonymous with the word for "salvation." Bush's speeches describe wars
as wars of liberation: "In Afghanistan we helped to liberate an oppressed
people."[14] "Some in this chamber did not support the liberation of Iraq."[15]
The opposite of freedom is oppression, as negative a word as liberation is
positive. President Bush restates the task of liberation using vocabulary of
call and deliverance: "We accept the call of history to deliver the oppressed
and move this world toward peace."[16] By naming the response to September
11, the invasion of Afghanistan and then of Iraq, as "liberation" and
"deliverance," Bush uses language central to Paul's letters. Bush's rhetoric also
makes a demand for an unequivocal choice between exclusive and opposing
alternatives in a manner that comes close to the way Paul's language works in
the letter to the Romans.

The Rhetoric of Romans

In Romans, Paul, the apostle, uses the emotional and social opposition between
slavery and freedom just as Bush uses the unambiguous choice between
terrorism and freedom. The metaphor of ruling, translated in the NRSV as
"exercising dominion" and of obeying the one who rules, is a way of describing
total bondage, ownership, and lack of autonomy.[17] For Paul, in this passage,
absolute rule is a given; one's only freedom is to choose the ruler one will

serve. For example, in Rom 6:11-18, Paul exhorts believers to transfer their allegiance, described as subjugation, from sin to righteousness:

> So you also must consider yourselves dead to sin and alive to God in Christ Jesus. Therefore, do not let sin exercise dominion in your mortal bodies, to make you obey their passions. No longer present your members to sin as instruments of wickedness, but present yourselves to God as those who have been brought from death to life, and present your members to God as instruments of righteousness. For sin will have no dominion over you, since you are not under law but under grace. What then? Should we sin because we are not under law but under grace? By no means! Do you not know that if you present yourselves to anyone as obedient slaves, you are slaves of the one whom you obey, either of sin, which leads to death, or of obedience, which leads to righteousness? But thanks be to God that you, having once been slaves of sin, have become obedient from the heart to the form of teaching to which you were entrusted, and that you, having been set free from sin, have become slaves of righteousness. (Rom 6:11-18)

The vocabulary of dominion and rule echoes with the language of tyrants and rulers in the way Bush's speeches describe history. History is a succession of different reigns, each characterized by its ruler. Death reigns as a cosmic, coercive power, until a more powerful adversary prevails.[18] Adam and Christ represent antithetical realms, as utterly opposed as terrorism and freedom:

> Yet death exercised dominion from Adam to Moses, even over those whose sins were not like the transgression of Adam, who is a type of the one who was to come. But the free gift is not like the trespass. For if the many died through the one man's trespass, much more surely have the grace of God and the free gift in the grace of the one man, Jesus Christ, abounded for the many. (Rom 5:14-15)

In Romans, the decisive event in the story of struggle is the death and resurrection of Jesus Christ into which believers are baptized: "For the law of the Spirit of life in Christ Jesus has set you free from the law of sin and death" (Rom 8:2). Former slavery is contrasted starkly with freedom: "For you did not receive a spirit of slavery to fall back into fear, but you have received a spirit of adoption" (Rom 8:15).

The liberation of human beings leads to the liberation of all creation. For Paul freedom is responsibly embodied in the natural and social world[19]: "That the creation itself will be set free from its bondage to decay and will obtain the freedom of the glory of the children of God" (Rom 8:21)."

The pattern of sharp dualism, the opposition of good and evil, the division of history into epochs under different reigns are shared in Paul's letter to the Romans and Bush's speeches. Rehearsal of this history precedes the presentation of a moral choice that leads to inevitable consequences of either life or death. Freedom is at once the force for the change and its life-giving result. Both speakers exhort their hearers to choose rightly and to pay the cost.

The Rhetoric of an End

The worldview of apocalyptic Judaism of the first century is the symbolic universe within which Paul argues, and it is the symbolic structure formed by Bush's speeches. History catapulting to its inevitable end, expectation of God's intervention, and intensified moral exhortation are distinctive features of the earliest gospel writer, Mark, and of the earliest New Testament author, Paul.

The imagery of the last battle, the sufferings that precede birth or consummation, and the opposed forces of good and evil have become strikingly pervasive in mainstream political discourse since 2001. Before September 11, 2001, it took a great effort of imagination for college and seminary students in my introduction to New Testament courses to imagine the theological and political situation in which the colorful and violent language of the Markan apocalypse in Mark 13 made sense. Now this form of thinking and expression has become so common in political and in mainstream religious speech as to be taken for granted. Its ubiquity and popularity make analysis and critique even more urgent.

The apocalyptic features of Bush's speeches are mirrored in the rhetoric of Osama Bin Laden. Bruce Lincoln has shown how Bin Laden's rhetoric, too, is structured with these same patterns of thought: "both men constructed a

Manichean struggle, where Sons of Light confront Sons of Darkness. . . ." In Bin Laden's rhetoric, the cosmos is divided between the "camp of the faithful and camp of the infidels."[20] In a comparison of Bush's October 7, 2001, address to the nation with the videotaped address of the same date by Bin Laden, Lincoln shows how the description of a deadly opposition serves to construct and exacerbate that division.[21] Bin Laden's address divides history into periods each divided by a decisive moment: a time of Islamic supremacy that ended after World War II, a time of suffering and victimization by Western powers, and a new period of Islamic counterattack on the West.[22] Both Bush and Bin Laden employ the image of suffering children, and both chastise those who waffle and seek a place somewhere between these radical oppositions.

Bush portrays the conflict between tyranny and freedom as encompassing all reality. For Paul, too, there is nothing outside the opposition between slavery to sin and slavery to righteousness. One can choose only among the options the text constructs. The outcome of the right choice is life itself. Paul's phrase "liberated with respect to righteousness" (Rom 6:20) draws on the language of freedom among popular philosophers and yet subordinates that freedom to the category of righteousness.[23]

Biblical scholars applying rhetorical-critical methods treat rhetoric primarily as rhetoric, rather than by investigating the psychological, autobiographical, or ideological history of the speaker. Psychology and political science are the domains of other public intellectuals who are expert in those areas. The rhetorical critic explores rhetoric as the result of deliberate communicative choices and strategies.

To analyze the skillful deployment of these rhetorical patterns in Bush's speeches requires attention to the cooperative work between George Bush and his chief speechwriter until late 2006, Michael Gerson. Gerson creates the President as an ideal character, shaped by Gerson's own ideal of Bush.[24] His best-known rhetorical formulation is the phrase "axis of evil" to describe Iraq, Iran, and North Korea. He revised "axis of hatred" into the more powerful "axis of evil" in the 2002 State of the Union address. Gerson's skill with words works in a kind of synergy with Bush's political and evangelical fervor in foreign policy.

Educated at Wheaton College, Gerson knows the scriptural texts and narratives and their power to connect with readers emotionally and rationally, and to be rhetorically effective. Gerson, like rhetorical-critical biblical scholars, takes rhetoric seriously: "in times of national grief, the words really do matter. And in times of focusing national purpose, the words really do matter."[25] Rhetoric is not *just* rhetoric, but in its most effective form is indivisible from thought and policy.

Gerson's own reflections show his hermeneutical approach. Ironically, the questions he brings to the political realities of the present are surprisingly similar to the questions feminist and liberation theologians might pose. In speaking of evil, Gerson states:

> We're dealing with these questions, it always occurs to me, How would people who are living in that evil experience it? How would exiles, and prisoners, and the families of the dead describe it? Now that's an element of realism. Are you going to take their side or not? When you talk about women being beheaded in soccer stadiums, or women being stoned for adultery, how would they experience it? I think asking this question is a form of realism. I think one of the ways Presidents and governments and civilizations are viewed is whether they side with this reality or not.[26]

The president's speechwriter expresses self-consciousness about his use of biblical references and allusions.

> There's an idea that we are constantly trying to sneak into the President's speeches religious language, code words, that only our supporters understand. But they are code words only if you don't know them, and most people know them.[27]

Yet, at the same time, Gerson denies the strong implications of his own (the president's) rhetoric that aligns God and Paul with Bush and the Iraq war with freedom *and* also obscures the means by which Gerson's (Bush's) language aligns them. He states:

> The President's views about the universal appeal of liberty come in part from the fact that he is kind of marinated in the American ideal. They come in part from a view that human beings are created in the image of God and will not forever suffer the

oppressor's sword, that eventually there's something deep in the human soul that cries out for freedom. That doesn't mean he believes that God blesses this particular foreign policy or that particular foreign policy.[28]

The Biblical Scholar's Role in the Public Square

The role of the biblical scholar is not to deny the right of the president and his speechwriters to employ biblical rhetoric, but to identify it, analyze how it works, and subject it to critical questions in the public square. This position does not agree with those critics who argue that the use of strongly Christian language in presidential speeches is illegitimate because of its exclusivity. Nor does it interpret the biblical allusions as "dog whistles" for the Christian right.[29]

A biblical scholar can address the authority of the speaker. The orator, Bush, already speaking with the authority of the office, reinforces the authority of his speech by evoking the authority of the apostle Paul and of others like Thomas Jefferson. As this exploration shows, the biblical scholar can point out, for example, how the surface similarities of the language of freedom in presidential speeches and in Paul's letters are supported by the deeper skeletal or structural patterns of apocalyptic thinking. The pervasiveness and power of this deeply engrained pattern makes it very difficult for the hearers to disagree with the argument. Arguing against it requires sketching and elaborating another worldview that is more compelling and crafting arguments within that perspective.

Further work might address the issue of different contexts for the language of Paul and of Bush. While Paul speaks as a leader of a relatively powerless minority sect in the Roman Empire and speaks of liberation by Christ from the powers and principalities, Bush speaks as a leader of the sole political superpower in the twenty-first century. It matters how the persona of Paul is constructed in the latter context. By evoking Paul's rhetoric after two thousand years of interpretation and amplification of the authoritative text, the president takes on the mantle of Western philosopher and ethicist, a persona more powerful now than the tongue-tied charismatic preacher of the gospel in Corinth.

Christian readers, assisted by the work of biblical scholars, might show how Bush's speeches capitalize on certain features of Paul's rhetoric in Romans and not others. For example, in Romans, liberation leads to freedom from fear: "You did not receive a spirit of slavery to fall back into fear, but have received a spirit of adoption" (Rom 8:15). Bush's speeches, however, employ fear in order to heighten the urgency of the choice between freedom and terrorism: "19 men to get onto airplanes and come to kill us"; "the ideology of power and domination has appeared again and seeks to gain the ultimate weapons of terror." Brought to visibility by analysis, the dynamics and paradoxes of Bush's transmutation of Paul's rhetoric of slavery and freedom provide rich material about which we can raise critical questions in public discussion. For example, the language of opposition rhetorically carries its own logic, but what are other ways in which a leader might frame the conflict? As a technique, is terrorism the proper analogy for tyranny? Is not terrorism a certain kind of violence and not an ideology per se, nor the equivalent of the state of slavery? Is total opposition really the most politically effective or ethically fruitful way to describe the events of September 11 and thereafter? Does the language of total opposition deny the possibility of other strategies, such as the realpolitik more characteristic of George H. W. Bush? Does an apocalyptic scenario preclude negotiation?

Speaking in conversation with one another, biblical scholars, political activists, Christian congregations, pastors, and preachers play a vital role in spirited debate in the democratic public square. A rhetorical-critical model of biblical studies raises questions about the way rhetoric works and how it works in particular cases, such as the parallels between George W. Bush's State of the Union and Paul's letter to the Romans. Critical questions are generated and addressed about the assumptions and implications of such patterns of language. In their own communities pastors and preachers, themselves rhetoricians, create other kinds of speech to reuse and renew the images and language of the biblical texts in concert, contrast, or dialogue with the political discourse of the times. Such conversation is one way that freedom is expressed in a democratic society.

5. American Babylon: Days in the Life of an African-American Idea

Allen D. Callahan
Seminário Teológico Batista da Nordeste

Who made Bush president
Who believe the confederate flag need to be flying
Who talk about democracy and be lying

Who the Beast of Revelations
Who 666
Who know who decide
Jesus get crucified

Who the Devil on the real side
Who got rich from Armenian genocide
Who the biggest terrorist

Who change the bible
Who killed the most people
Who do the most evil
Who don't worry about survival

Who have the colonies
Who stole the most land
Who rule the world
Who say they good but only do evil
Who the biggest executioner

Who? Who? Who?
—Amiri Baraka, "Somebody Blew Up America" (2002)[1]

Introduction: "The Beast of Revelations"

In Revelation 18, the figural city of Babylon is declared destroyed ("fallen") and hated because of its rapacious complicity with an interlocking directorate of political and commercial principals who comprise a murderous international regime.

> After this I saw another angel coming down from heaven, having great authority; and the earth was made bright with his splendor. And he called out with a mighty voice, "Fallen, fallen is Babylon the great! It has become a dwelling place of demons, a haunt of every foul spirit, a haunt of every foul and hateful bird; for all nations have drunk the wine of her impure passion, and the kings of the earth have committed fornication with her, and the merchants of the earth have grown rich with the wealth of her wantonness." (Rev 18:1-3)[2]

The audience of this oracle of doom is commanded to escape the condemned city. The addressees are warned that they, too, are in danger of being consumed in the conflagration of divine wrath.

> Then I heard another voice from heaven saying, "Come out of her, my people, lest you take part in her sins, lest you share in her plagues; for her sins are heaped high as heaven, and God has remembered her iniquities. Render to her as she herself has rendered, and repay her double for her deeds; mix a double draught for her in the cup she mixed. As she glorified herself and played the wanton, so give her a like measure of torment and mourning. Since in her heart she says, "A queen I sit, I am no widow, mourning I shall never see," so shall her plagues come in a single day, pestilence and mourning and famine, and she shall be burned with fire; for mighty is the Lord God who judges her. (Rev 18:4-8)

The prophetic oracle delineates a long list of exhibits as evidence of the charges against the evil city.

And the kings of the earth, who committed fornication and were wanton with her, will weep and wail over her when they see the smoke of her burning; they will stand far off, in fear of her torment, and say, "Alas! alas! thou great city, thou mighty city, Babylon! In one hour has thy judgment come." And the merchants of the earth weep and mourn for her, since no one buys their cargo any more, cargo of gold, silver, jewels and pearls, fine linen, purple, silk and scarlet, all kinds of scented wood, all articles of ivory, all articles of costly wood, bronze, iron and marble, cinnamon, spice, incense, myrrh, frankincense, wine, oil, fine flour and wheat, cattle and sheep, horses and chariots, and slaves, that is, human souls. "The fruit for which thy soul longed has gone from thee, and all thy dainties and thy splendor are lost to thee, never to be found again!" The merchants of these wares, who gained wealth from her, will stand far off, in fear of her torment, weeping and mourning aloud, "Alas, alas, for the great city that was clothed in fine linen, in purple and scarlet, bedecked with gold, with jewels, and with pearls! In one hour all this wealth has been laid waste." And all shipmasters and seafaring men, sailors and all whose trade is on the sea, stood far off and cried out as they saw the smoke of her burning, "What city was like the great city?" (Rev 18:9-18)

The cargo manifest that precedes the lament of the rulers and merchants begins with luxury goods, "gold, silver, jewels and pearls, fine linen, purple, silk and scarlet," and ends with slavery. Indeed, the presence of slaves among the itemized commodities is emphasized both by its position as the last item on the list and its epexegetical gloss of *sōmatōn*, "slaves," as *psychas anthrōpōn*, "the souls of human beings."[3]

Babylon is the historical analogue and so the biblical code word for the city the seer condemns, imperial Rome. Babylon, like Rome, was the perpetrator of crimes on a global scale. The Babylonian empire destroyed the Jerusalem Temple and inaugurated the Babylonian captivity of the Israelites; it is Israel's experience of Babylonian imperialism that provides the figural grammar for John's critique of Rome. Roman domination of the Mediterranean, initiated with military conquest, was consolidated with an international army of merchants, tax collectors, and financiers.[4] Provincial elites in Asia Minor allied with Roman imperial power prospered as provincial masses were brutalized and progressively impoverished by a cosmopolitan ruling class and a mercantile economy.[5] Maritime trade, with its big profits and easy taxes, was the vital link in the imperial chain that bound politics and profit. Written near the end of the first century C.E. and in the midst of the economic boom of Rome's Asian provinces, the book of Revelation casts in apocalyptic terms the systemic relation between imperialist politics, global trade, and the murderous oppression of the poor. This book of prophetic vision and apocalyptic language presents empire as inherently inimical to God because it slaughters the people of the world, just as it slaughtered Jesus, the Lamb who was murdered on earth and is enthroned in heaven (Rev 5:6, 12; 13:8).

But in modernity, intellectuals of African descent in the New World have identified not Rome but the United States as the modern Babylon. These thinkers of the African Diaspora, who themselves bore the stain of what the Fourteenth Amendment to the United States Constitution would refer to as their "previous condition of servitude," saw the transatlantic slave trade as the signal feature that showed the United States to be the avatar of the corrupt and corrupting regime condemned in the book of Revelation. In what follows, I offer a rehearsal of emblematic moments in the history of an African-American idea: the American Babylon.

"A Seller of Slaves and the Souls of Men": Maria Stewart

In her reading of Revelation 18, African-American orator Maria Stewart, an abolitionist political philosopher and the first woman to make a recorded public address in America, saw the United States as the new Babylon. In "An Address Delivered at the African Masonic Hall" in 1833 in Boston, Stewart charged, "It appears to me that America has become like the great city of Babylon, for she has boasted in her heart: 'I sit a queen and am no widow, and shall see no sorrow [Rev 18:7]!'" Stewart made the connection between Roman and American slave regimes. The United States "is, indeed, a seller of slaves and the souls of men," Stewart charged; "she has made the Africans drunk with the wine of her fornication; she has put them completely beneath her feet, and she means to keep them there; her right hand supports the reins of government and her left hand the wheel of power, and she is determined not to let go her grasp."[6]

Other Christian critics of the American slave regime would concur with Stewart's interpretation. In the decade following Stewart's denunciations of the American Babylon, several white American abolitionist exegetes cited Rev 18:13 in their biblical arguments against slavery. "John describes in Revelations [*sic*]," wrote I. W. Scribner in 1844, "that among the things that he saw that defiled the Church of God, were multitudes of slaves and souls of men."[7] In the same year, an anonymous tract commented, "The traffic of slaves is recorded as one of the crimes of Babylon the Great. The slave trade naturally accompanies the system of slavery, as shadow does the substance. The history of all slavery proves them to be inseparable."[8]

"To Wake the Nations Underground": The Civil War

Americans slave and free saw the Civil War as a divine judgment rendered against the slave regime. The classic statement, of course, is that of Abraham Lincoln in his second inaugural address: "Fondly do we hope, fervently do we pray, that this mighty scourge of war may speedily pass away. Yet, if God wills that it continue until all the wealth piled by the bondsman's two hundred and fifty years of unrequited toil shall be sunk, and until every drop of blood drawn with the lash shall be paid by another drawn with the sword, as was said three thousand years ago, so still it must be said 'the judgments of the Lord are true and righteous altogether.'"[9]

But what Lincoln admitted as possible, African-Americans affirmed as certain. Former slave W. B. Allen explained, "God was using the Yankees to scourge the slaveholders, just as he had, centuries before, used heathens and outcasts to scourge his chosen people—the Children of Israel."[10] "What God says had got to come to pass, comes," testified ex-slave Jerry Eubanks, speaking of the Union victory. "This is written in the Bible. They says, 'The Yankees done it'—but colored people looks cross years at everything. God did it all."[11] The blood would flow, in the words of the book of Revelation, "even unto the horse bridles" (Rev 14:20).

The slave regime would be brought to a violent end, and the ensign of that violent end would be the martial Jesus of the book of Revelation.[12] This expectation had its most powerful and pervasive expression in the classic music of the slaves, the Negro spiritual. In his reading of the book of Revelation in the light of African-American culture, the biblical scholar Brian Blount has noted the homology between the hymns of Revelation and African-Americans' peculiarly musical response to the antebellum slave regime: "It is no wonder that African Americans faced down their imperial power with the same double-edged sword wielded by the Christians of Asia Minor—Music. In oppressive camps where the powers concentrated against you appear limitless in their scope and evil intent, where, defenseless, you stand with neither ally nor hope, where, though you cannot realistically fight back, you refuse to give up and give in, you can resist. You can sing."[13] In the Negro spirituals, the slave sang of "Jesus, walking down the heavenly road, / Out of his mouth came a two-edged sword."[14]

> They follow their great General
> The great eternal Lamb
> His garments stained in His own blood,
> King Jesus is his name.[15]

As commander of the first Union Army black regiment, the South Carolina Volunteers, the Boston Brahman and Harvard-trained Unitarian minister Thomas Wentworth Higginson became an avid collector of Negro spirituals. In 1867, Higginson published an article in the *Atlantic Monthly* describing the songs that he had heard his black soldiers sing around their watch fires in the camps. "[The book of Revelation], with the books of Moses, constituted their Bible," Higginson writes, "all that lay between, even the narratives of the life of Jesus, they hardly cared to read or hear." But solidarity with Jesus was the fount of the martial valor of Higginson's Union recruits, one of whom explained to his commanding officer the source of his courage.

> Let me live with my musket in one hand the Bible in the other— that if I die at the muzzle of the musket, die in the water, die on the land, I may know I have the blessed Jesus in my hand, and have no fear. I have left my wife in the land of bondage; my little ones they say every night, where is my father? But when I die, when the blessed morning rises, when I shall stand in the glory,

with one foot on the water and one foot on the land, then, O Lord, I shall see my wife and my little children once more.[16]

The soldier describes himself as standing in heaven, "in the glory, with one foot on the water and one foot on the land." He describes the pose of an angel who announces judgment in the book of Revelation: "And I saw another mighty angel . . . and he set his right foot upon the sea, and his left foot on the earth" (Rev 10:1-2). Informed by the rich biblical imagery of the last days, African-Americans have anticipated the return of the militant Jesus as the righteous arbiter of human destiny. His second coming would consummate ultimate deliverance in the consummation of all things at the end of time.

> And I saw a great white throne, and him that sat on it, from whose face the earth and the heaven fled away; and there was found no place for them. And I saw the dead, small and great, stand before God; and the books were opened: and another book was opened, which is the book of life: and the dead were judged out of those things which were written in the books, according to their works. (Rev 20:11-12)

The book of Revelation taught the slaves and their descendents that ultimately the entire world would fall under his sentence. Even death affords no escape: "And the sea gave up that dead which were in it; and death and hell delivered up the dead which were in them: and they were judged every man according to their works" (Rev 20:13).

The last stanza of the Negro spiritual "Judgment" celebrates a forensic Jesus in the apocalyptic imagery of the New Testament:

> *King Jesus sittin' in the kingdom, Lord,*
> *Oh, how I long to go there too;*
> *The angels singin' all round the throne,*
> *Oh, how I long to go.*
> *The trumpet sound the Jubilo,*
> *Oh, how I long to go there too,*
> *I hope that trump will blow me home,*
> *Oh, how I long to go.*[17]

In the Negro spiritual "My Lord, What a Morning," Jesus returns as the judge of the dead as well as the living:

> You'll see my Jesus come,
> To wake the nations underground,
> Look in my God's right hand,
> When the stars begin to fall.
> His chariot wheels roll round,
> To wake the nations underground.
> Look in my God's right hand,
> When the stars begin to fall.[18]

At his return, Jesus will raise the dead—"wake the nations underground"—to face just recompense for their deeds.

The slaves' biblical reflections on the end of the age move from the book of Revelation, the last book of the Bible, back through the teachings of Jesus to the Old Testament prophets, even as far as the first destruction of the world in Genesis. Though the flood is recounted in the first book of the Bible, the African-American associates that ancient cataclysm as a sign of the last days. For the slaves, this sign does not speak of the ancient past but of the future judgment. The anonymous composers of the Negro spirituals compare the cosmic conflagration promised in the last book of the Bible with the global inundation recorded in the first: "God gave Noah the rainbow sign / No more water but fire next time."[19] The cause of the first global catastrophe—the deluge—is likewise that of "the fire next time." As God's righteous outrage against human injustice was the impetus of cosmic catastrophe in the past, so shall it be in the apocalyptic future.

"A Violent End": Theophilus Gould Steward

Following the Civil War, the failure of Reconstruction, and the rise of Jim Crow, African Methodist Episcopal pastor, military chaplain, and university professor Theophilus Gould Steward (1843–1924) argued that the book of Revelation prophetically foretold the destruction of the United States and the ascendant European powers because of their racism and warlike oppression of the darker peoples of the world. "The prophecies [of the Bible]," he wrote, "point to a violent end to those nations which are the legitimate successors of Rome."[20] In his 1888 study of apocalyptic prophecy in the Bible, *The End of the World, or Clearing the Way for the Fullness of the Gentiles*, Steward asserted, "the darker races are excluded from Christianity because the white races who preach it to them have so little brotherly love. . . . The rule holds that white races taken as a whole, have much more clan than Christ, and that clan spirit repels more generally than the Christ-spirit attracts."[21]

But it is these very "excluded darker races" that constitute "that great number which John beheld" who would come into the light of the gospel in the fullness of times.[22] Steward refers to the myriad worshippers pictured in the book of Revelation several chapters before the fall of Babylon: "After this I looked, and behold, a great multitude which no man could number, from every nation, from all tribes and peoples and tongues, standing before the throne and before the Lamb, clothed in white robes, with palm branches in their hands, and crying out with a loud voice, 'Salvation belongs to our God who sits upon the throne, and to the Lamb!' (Rev 7:9-10)." Among this multitude Steward counted Native Americans, whom "combined representatives of all Christendom in America have Christianized . . . off the face of the earth,"[23] and African slaves. Their embrace of Christianity would only be possible—indeed prophetically inevitable, by Steward's lights—after God has annihilated the hindrance of the hypocritical and racist Christendom of the European and American powers: "The writer thinks that the indications point about as follows: 'A great crash of the Christian nations, and a liberation of the Christian idea from the dominance of the principle of clan, and a consequent purification of the Christian Church.'"[24] But of all the Christian nations to fall under divine judgment, Steward singled out the United States for special censure because of its complicity in the transatlantic slave trade and its genocidal decimation of the American native population: "It was Christian America that robbed Africa of millions of her population and committed unheard of horrors on her shores and on the seas."[25]

"The Fall of America": Elijah Muhammad

In the early 1970s, the Honorable Elijah Muhammad, leader of the Nation of Islam, the separatist African-American Muslim movement in the United States, would repeat the charges of Maria Stewart and Theophilus Gould Steward. And he would identify the Babylon of the book of Revelation with the United States. "The 'Mystery Babylon the Great' is none other than America," he proclaimed in his sermons, later transcribed, collected, and published in the early 1970s under the titles *Message to the Blackman* and *The Fall of America*: "You must know," he declares to his followers, "that all of the Revelation, or at least 90 percent, is directed to America."[26]

> It is really because of the evil done to [Negroes] by the American white race that Allah (God) has put them on his list, as the first to be destroyed. The others will be given a little longer to live, as the prophet Daniel says (7:11, 19 and Rev. 19:20). Believe it, or let it alone, the above refers to America. She is the only white government out of the European race that answers the description of the symbolic Fourth Beast [of Daniel 7]. The so-called Negroes are warned to come out of here (America) (Rev. 18:4), though the truth of Daniel and Revelations [sic] could not be told until the time of the end of this prophecy.[27]

Babylon, according to Elijah Muhammad, is indisputably the biblical sign of American military and economic domination. America, he asserts, "was once the greatest slave buyer and seller" with "the greatest merchant marine service."[28]

> This is America, the glory of the world in wealth, sport, and play, with her merchant ships ploughing [sic] the high seas carrying her costly merchandise throughout the population of the nations of the earth. . . . The ships of America can be seen everywhere . . . in every port of the nations of the earth. Her great navy is built to command the high seas. Her decks are mounted with great bristling rifle-barreled guns. The decks of her ships are covered with planes with which to carry deadly bombshells to pour on other nations who dare now to reject her entrance into their waters. The writer, (John), foresaw America threatening and daring the nations to disobey her order to allow her entrance. America's navy planes fly high in the air with their deadly bombs held at ready to drop on the towns and cities of other nations who dare to attack her.[29]

Elijah Muhammad explains,

> The Bible refers to America by the name, Babylon, and teaches us, Rev. 18:2, " . . . Babylon the great is fallen, is fallen, and is become the habitation of devils, and the hole of every foul spirit, and a cage of every unclean and hateful bird." This is true, for America has accepted immigrants of the most evil and lewd character from Europe. America has filled her country with evil and indecency and there is no good in the works of America. America hates the doers of good and seeks to destroy them. This is the cause of the fall of America.[30]

Elijah Muhammad calls special attention to the oracle against Babylon as a warning of judgment already being realized in America.[31] "So the angel notifies us saying, 'Babylon the great is fallen.' Today we are seeing the same thing." Elijah Muhammad's interpretation of the oracle of Babylon's judgment in Revelation 18 calls for the social, political, and economic withdrawal from the American Babylon.

> In the Bible, Rev. 18:4, 5 in the Revelation of John, a people are warned to flee out of her. Here, we get the name Babylon to become modern day people. The voice of the angel warns the people of a certain class to fly out of Babylon. " . . . Come out of her, my people, that ye be not partakers of her sins, and that ye receive not of her plagues. For her sins have reached unto heaven, and God hath remembered her iniquities" (as being an evil people).[32]

Elijah Muhammad, Malcolm X during his tenure as spokesperson for the Nation of Islam, and, more recently, Minister Louis Farrakhan have all advocated that African-Americans develop a nation of their own. Either in the so-called Black Belt of the southern United States or in Africa, this separate, independent nation would allow escape from Allah's divine wrath when America is judged for her crimes.

"Babylon System": The Rastafarians

Revelation 18 shows that the infernal assault on the peoples of the world is a systemic assault. In their traditional exegesis, the Rastafarians (Rastas) of Jamaica have appealed to the Babylon imagery of Revelation to talk about global political economy. In Rasta exegesis, Babylon is a comprehensive sign for domination in the Atlantic world, "symbolic of a complex of oppressive forces represented by slavery, colonialism, imperialism and the systems and ideologies that enforce and sustain them and their aftereffects."[33] In the light of this interpretation of Babylon, Rastas have assumed a posture of cultural, economic, and political resistance to the principalities and powers of globalization that they frequently refer to as "Babylon shitstem" (that is, system).[34] As Bob Marley described it in his 1977 reggae song, "Babylon System":

> *Babylon system is the Vampire*
> *Sucking the children day by day*
> *Me say the Babylon system is the Vampire*
> *Sucking the blood of the sufferers*
> *Building church and university*
> *Deceiving the people continually*
> *Me say them graduating thieves and murderers*
> *Look out now*
> *Sucking the blood of the sufferers*[35]

In their traditional exegesis, the Rastafarians of Jamaica anticipated the interpretation of the contemporary significance of the Babylon imagery of Revelation for global political economy. The Rastas "do not employ biblical figures allegorically or typologically; that is, they do not use the semiotic stuff of the Bible to represent aspects of historical and contemporary experience."[36] Thus for Rastas, Babylon is the biblical and, thus, true name for Jamaica and the regime that dominates the Caribbean.[37] "The slaves who came to Jamaica are the Remnants of an entire people," explains Jamaican scholar of Rastafarianism, Barry Chevannes, "The Remnant is exiled in Babylon, or Jamaica."[38] In Rasta exegesis, Babylon is a comprehensive sign for domination in the Atlantic world, "symbolic of a complex of oppressive forces represented by slavery, colonialism, imperialism and the systems and ideologies that enforce and sustain them and their aftereffects."[39]

In the light of this interpretation of Babylon, Rastas have assumed a posture of cultural, economic, and political resistance to the principalities and powers of globalization. As early as 1971, a Rasta delegate to the ecumenical symposium on development held in Chaguaramas, Trinidad, delineated the following response to the Babylonian captivity of global capital. "The Rasta does not play a part in keeping up Babylon politics but would take part in the development of a just and true politics (a way of running the country), along that of the holy Bible and any other equal and just way that would benefit the people of the Caribbean, Africa and the world."[40]

Babylon became a popular symbol for Rasta resistance to systemic oppression when the Rasta band the Melodians, an enormously popular Jamaican vocal trio during the late '60s and early '70s, recorded a reggae musical adaptation of Psalm 137 titled "By the Rivers of Babylon" in 1969. The song was a great success in Jamaica, but became an international hit when it was subsequently covered by Bonnie Em and was included on Jimmy Cliff's soundtrack for the movie *The Harder They Come*.[41] Some Rastas hold to eschatology realizable in the present when "Jah," that is, God, destroys the Babylon system. Bob Marley and others, however, hearken to an earlier Rasta eschatology that looks forward to total liberation only by being fully repatriated in Africa.

> *Open your eyes and look within*
> *Are you satisfied with the life you're living?*
> *We know where we're going*
> *We know where we're from*
> *We're leaving Babylon*
> *We're going to our Father's land.*[42]

Theologian Nathaniel Murrell explains that "Rastas believe that the expected liberation could come in the here and now if everyone joins in restructuring the political system and adopting the Rastafari social, economic, and political agenda."[43] On the other hand, "In theory, all non-Rastafari are a part of 'Babylon', a part of the oppressive order."[44]

Though Psalm 137 remains a key biblical allusion for anti-Babylon propaganda, the most strident Rasta protests are informed by the imagery of

Revelation 18. "The 'beast' is a recurrent image among the Rastafari and is synonymous for Babylon. It derives from the Book of Revelation."[45] Veteran Rasta composer and vocalist Max Romeo, whose song "Let the Power Fall" provided the slogan of the democratic socialist Michael Manley's successful 1972 campaign for prime minister, recorded "Babylon Burning" in that same year as a critique of "that depressive Capitalist attitude that the government had against us" in the run-up to Manley's electoral victory.[46]

> *Babylon's burning*
> *Babylon's burning*
> *Babylon's burning*
> *But there's no water*
> *Fire, fire*
> *Fire, fire*
> *Fire, fire*
> *But there's no water*

> *All dem a jump and reel*
> *All dem a jump and reel*
> *If dem crawl like snail*
> *Rasta gwaan clip them tail*

> *Babylon's burning*
> *Babylon's burning*
> *Babylon's burning*
> *But there's no water*[47]

The reggae trio, Culture, which has produced a string of Jamaican hits since its appearance in the late 1970s, released "Babylon A Weep" on their 1997 album, *Trust Me*. The title alludes to the opening of the oracle of Babylon's destruction in Revelation 18.

> *The Babylon a weep, weep on*
> *The Babylon a weep, weep on*

Rasta a go tear down Babylon
The Rasta a go tear down Babylon
I, I, I, I a go tear down Babylon
The Rasta a go tear down Babylon

Rasta a go tear down Babylon
Freedom fighters a go tear down Babylon
Revolutionaries a go tear down Babylon[48]

The biblically inspired condemnation of "Babylon shitstem" is a leitmotif in the work of essayist, performer, composer, and webmaster Messian Dread, a contemporary Rasta who has taken his message to the Internet. In Messian Dread's "Babylon," mention of the "whore" who has "slept with every king" clearly echoes the oracle of Revelation 18.

Babylon, let me tell you about Babylon
Let me sing a song about the whore where every king of the
earth has slept with
Babylon, Babylon
Some say she's a mystery but it's clear for all to see
What she's causing is pain and misery
Some say she's a mystery,
But it is not for you and not for me
To co-operate with her in this hurt society
Evil her aims
And what she plays today I can call that games
Cause she is drunk of the sufferer
Who suffered for the name of Jesus
Babylon[49]

In "Jah Seh No," Messian Dread anticipates the destruction of Babylon that is foretold in biblical prophecy: "Babylon will fall yeah bible tell I that (Jah seh so ["Jah says so"]) / Righteous will be taken just no matter what (Jah seh so) / There is not much time left I and I know this (Jah seh so) / Yeshouah [that is, Jesus] return yeah dis world I won't miss (Jah seh so)."[50]

Conclusion: "All Who Have Been Slaughtered"

The unholy union of slavery and capital in the making of the New World has made morality impossible. All who come to market have come to steal, to kill, and to destroy. Interpreters of African descent in the Americas have read Revelation 18 as a text that traces the ties that bind dollars to death, even as those countries are bound to the political and economic influence of the United States. To read the text in this way is to hear a divine condemnation of the demonic powers of the market, the corporation, and government that greedily conspire against humanity in the present world system.

Upon their arrival in chains, African slaves made and were made by the New World. In the person of the Creole born in the slave quarters, producer and product became modalities of the same subject. A subject that was both property and mode of production became a thing, monstrous because the "thingification" could never be complete. Though juridically real, it could never be true. The property was still human, even after being whipped, stripped, ripped open, raped, flayed. Yet as human property, the property relation under capital rendered the humanity of these human beings all but impossible.

Morality, too, was now rendered all but impossible, as all property owners now became enmeshed in the web of slavery's maritime commerce. All property became manifest theft, and, as partakers in a global capitalist order built on the backs of slaves, all property owners became thieves and every merchant guilty of harboring stolen goods. Justice called for nothing short of the complete destruction of the regime, and the slaves, the first victims of the first phase of globalization we call the transatlantic slave trade, recognized in the book of Revelation the call for such thoroughgoing destruction.

Theologian Dwight Hopkins has observed that the "globalization of monopoly finance capitalist culture itself is a religion. Such a religious system feeds on the most vulnerable people in the world theater."[51] Its first victims on the eve of modernity were African "human souls" sacrificed at the transatlantic altar of capital's religion, the market. Then and now, the market stands stained with "the blood of the prophets and saints, and of all who have been slaughtered" (Rev 18:24) in the present regime of global capital—a regime that leads to human thralldom even as it calls for divine judgment.

6. Do Not Fear What They Fear:
A Post-9/11 Reflection on Isaiah 8:11-18

Norman Gottwald
Pacific School of Religion

While we were fearing it, it came,
But came with less of fear,
Because that fearing it so long
Had almost made it fair.
—Emily Dickinson[1]

Fear as a National Way of Life

WE AMERICANS HAVE INDEED BEEN "FEARING IT SO LONG" that while we may not find it "fair" we may be finding it indispensable. We are certainly getting used to it. Fear and the manipulation of fear has been the dominant atmosphere of our national life since the destruction of the Twin Towers in 2001. The consuming passion of our announced public policy has been to prevent such attacks, defensively by Homeland Security measures, and offensively by wars waged in Afghanistan and Iraq, and in a worldwide dragnet to capture and detain thousands suspected of being actual or potential agents of future attacks.

What have been the consequences of this paroxysm of fear?

The panic evoked by the attack, and the subsequent governmental stoking of public fear, has led to several consequences that are doing little to increase our immediate safety while actually putting us in greater jeopardy over the long term. First, the primary response to 9/11 and its aftermath has been to rely almost totally on military power to safeguard us in the future. This military power has been exerted without worldwide support and in the face of much opposition by nations otherwise sympathetic with our losses. Second, very little examination of the motivations of the attackers has been attempted, it being asserted by our

83

national leaders that the reason for the attacks is their hatred of our freedom. So we remain blithely ignorant of the contribution of our policies abroad to the enmity we encounter in the world. Third, in the process of responding to 9/11, the administration has violated the human and civil rights of prisoners, as well as all citizens of this country, by denying habeas corpus and open trials, by secretive wiretapping, and by giving tacit, if not overt, permission to torture.

This national fear of "terrorism" feeds on itself, providing a cover and justification for other political motives and projects. Running as the subtext of our declared antiterrorism posture is the striving of public officials to solidify their grip on political power, flaunt their pretension to empire, indulge their stubborn vanity, make a power grab for Middle East oil, improve the chances for American corporations in the globalization marathon, stoke the profits of arms makers and suppliers of the military machine, and weaken labor unions.[2] So we have invaded and devastated a country uninvolved in the attacks on us. We have killed scores of thousands of its citizens and forced thousands of others into exile. We have killed and maimed thousands of Americans. We have squandered the billions of dollars desperately needed for domestic social and infrastructural services. We have vastly increased anti-American feelings the world over, and we have helped to swell the ranks of jihadists seeking political power and of nationalist insurgents resisting occupation of their country by U.S. forces.

Nevertheless, all the steps taken to secure our safety have failed to lower our fear level. Fear has mushroomed, even to the point of paranoia, attended by corrosive mistrust and cynicism, to the extent that many Americans are now more afraid of what our reckless stubborn leaders are doing to our country than what our foreign foes can do, even if they succeed in carrying out another attack in our homeland.

Fear as a Biblical Theme

Does the Bible have anything to do with this epidemic of fear? We certainly don't need any more pious bromides about America as a Christian nation. We have had far more than we need of ranting about the end of history in which the U.S. and Israel are God's "good guys," and the end of all these end-time wars, from which we should not flinch, will be a kingdom of love and peace for the Christian survivors. Just such poppycock keeps droves of American Christians and Jews from finding in the Hebrew Bible/Old Testament a valuable resource for keeping their emotional and moral bearings. A resource for fortifying their resolve and dissipating the clouds of fear and hatred that presently frustrate every effort to reverse the disastrous course upon which our political leaders are so firmly set.

The biblical resource I have in mind is an opening toward more level-headed and open-hearted reasoning about fear: what to fear, and what not to fear. And, most especially, this resource cautions us against responding to fear in ways that only increase the likelihood that what we fear will come to pass in unintended and unexpected blowback.

It turns out that fear is a major motif in the Hebrew Bible. In the NRSV, several Hebrew terms are translated as "fear," "terror," or "dread" (as nouns and in their verbal, adverbial, and adjectival formations) nearly 500 times. Fear is the first emotion expressed in the Bible, when Adam protests; "I was afraid because I was naked" (Gen 3:10).[3] The imperative "Fear not!" resounds throughout biblical texts both as a command and as a consolation, rising to a crescendo in the prophets. Fear of humans is constantly set over against fear of God. Fear of foreign and domestic foes is met with promises of divine protection and deliverance. Excessive fear of people and circumstances warps sound judgment in nations and individuals and subverts their cherished virtues and values. On the other hand, fear of God, virtually interchangeable with faith in God, is the antidote for debilitating anxiety and fear for our safety and survival.

Isaiah Confronts National Fear

Isaiah of Jerusalem is an excellent exemplar of the dialectic of national fear and faith.

In the latter part of the eighth century B.C.E., the Assyrian Empire was extending its conquests westward toward the kingdoms of Israel and Judah. Israel and nearby Damascus were immediately in the line of the Assyrian advance. They formed an alliance and brought pressure on Judah to join them in resisting Assyria. The ruler in Jerusalem, Ahaz, was resistant, and the allies plotted to depose Ahaz in favor of a monarch who would join the anti-Assyrian alliance. Jerusalem was threatened with siege and, "the heart of Ahaz and the heart of his people shook as the trees of the forest shake before the wind" (Isa 7:2).

Isaiah assured Ahaz that the belligerent kings, Pekah of Israel and Rezin of Damascus, were "two smoldering stumps of firebrands" (Isa 7:4) and would soon be disposed of by Assyria, so there was no need to fear for the outcome of the siege. Even more, however, Isaiah was advising Ahaz of Judah not to surrender voluntarily to Assyria in an effort to shake off Pekah and Rezin.

Ahaz rejected Isaiah's advice and turned to Assyria for help. Isaiah's own take on events was that Judah's best hope for a secure peace was to remain neutral and to carry out programs of domestic social justice on behalf of the poor. The poor were the lifeblood of the nation and greatly in need of relief from heavy debts, taxation, expropriations of their land, and a corrupt system of justice.

Instead of being panicked by fear, Isaiah stood his ground, informed by a clear sense of what he was called to declaim as a prophet of the national deity Yahweh. Having done his best to dissuade Ahaz from alliance with Assyria and having failed to do so, Isaiah withdraws for a time into a company of his disciples, including his wife and sons, and awaits another occasion to speak on public matters when his word might be better regarded.

Amidst the turmoil and panic of the time, in 8:11-18, Isaiah receives this divine reassurance:

> For the LORD spoke thus to me while his hand was strong upon me, and warned me not to walk in the way of this people, saying: "Do not call[4] conspiracy all that this people call conspiracy, and do not fear what it fears, or be in dread. But the LORD of hosts, him you shall regard as holy; let him be your fear, and let him be your dread. He will become a conspirator,[5] a stone one strikes against, for to both houses of Israel he will become a rock one stumbles over—a trap and a snare for the inhabitants of Jerusalem. And many among them shall stumble, they shall fall and be broken; they shall be snared and be taken."

> Bind up[6] the testimony, seal the teaching among my disciples! I will wait for the LORD, who is hiding his face from the house of Jacob, and I will hope in him. See, I and the children whom the LORD has given me are signs and portents in Israel from the LORD of hosts who dwells on Mt. Zion.[7]

Isaiah, the master of vivid metaphors, focuses on "rock" and "stone" in their different aspects, as a symbol of both faith and of fear. There is the rock that impedes travel and must be cleared from the road or pathway. It is an obstacle that, unobserved, becomes a stumbling block. Consumed with dread of foreign conspiracy and neglectful of peace through justice in their own lands, both Israelite states will "stumble" and "fall" over the unyielding demands of God, who is, himself, the actual conspirator against Judah, "one strikes against" (8:14). In another passage, Isaiah pictures "a precious cornerstone" (28:16) as the symbol of a solid foundation on which justice and righteousness can be built in contrast to the refuge and shelter the political leaders have found in lies and falsehood. The treaty Ahaz will forge with Assyria is a "covenant with death" (28:15, 18), but when the Assyrians unleash their might against Judah like the Euphrates River in flood tide (8:7-8), the deceitful treaty to neutralize death will be broken and the refuge of lies will be swept away.

Isaiah as a Weathervane of the Present

Point-by-point analogies that identify each of the biblical parties with contemporary nations or collectivities are not the best way to draw on the Bible for moral discourse. For one thing, the most obvious present-day counterpart of the Assyrian Empire is the American empire, and the states of Israel and Judah are most easily paralleled by small countries throughout the world that are resisting American imperialism. This is the stumbling block that fundamentalist interpreters trip over when they visualize the United States as virtuous Israel threatened by the dark forces of "the axis of evil."[8]

While there is some value in playing with various possible insights that derive from these role reversals, the clearest moral directive articulated by Isaiah, and many other prophets as well, is much more straightforward: The highest priority of a nation or state should be its domestic integrity in pursuing justice for all its people and fairness in relating to other nations. Self-preservation will be best served by adhering to just norms of behavior. The default position for this priority is that God, as the architect of the world, has promised that peace through justice is the absolutely necessary foundation for a world where all people and nations have a secure part to play. This directive translated into secular terms would be to say that the web of human relationships, individually and collectively, is so structured that something like the golden rule is the prerequisite of its proper functioning. Although there are many ways in which that connective tissue can be damaged, the path of repair in each case is to restore justice and fairness to the way humans treat one another.

All states that short-circuit these basic conditions of life by relying on military force and diplomatic and political intimidation to gain their ends will fail in the end. In the process, they will not only severely damage other countries, but they will harm themselves and their peoples. Yet fear and anger continue to ravage the relations among nations. As they battle one another, they flail around in search of strategies that can enable them to achieve their goals. In desperation, the consequences of these ever more reckless and destructive strategies are ignored or denied. Fear and anger, and the hunger for revenge against real or imagined wrongs, prevail over rational thought and human feelings. Political leaders, like the nearly mad King Lear, frustrated with their actual impotence, cry out, "I will have such revenges. . . . I will do such things,—what they are yet I know not,—but they shall be the terrors of the earth."[9]

Isaiah, like many other voices in the Hebrew Bible, cautions us to beware of "shock and awe" methods in human affairs and the attendant fear and panic they incite to little avail, except to trigger another round of vengeful acts. It is more crucial to fear Yahweh, supreme Conspirator and Terrorist, who overturns the plans of prideful men and nations, than to fear frail human conspirators and terrorists.

PART II
Questioning the *Ekklēsia* and the Academy

---

7. Hermeneutics in the American Empire: Toward an Anti-Imperialist Theology

Max A. Myers
St. Andrew's Episcopal Church,
Marble Dale, Connecticut

AMERICAN CHRISTIANS LIVE IN A CRITICAL TIME IN WORLD HISTORY. On the one hand, they live in a society in which they have the wealth of the nations at their feet. They live in a state that has no serious military rivals, whose corporations control the flow of goods and services around the globe, whose culture dominates the subjectivity of virtually all human beings, and whose self-consciousness is at peace with itself. On the other hand, they live in a society that has set itself up as the unilateral global hegemon, a superpower without counterbalance that feels justified in imposing its will as it chooses by "shock and awe" tactics even at the cost of innocent lives. Moreover, this new American empire, as even its defenders now style it, produces and controls the conditions of life for almost all human beings in tandem with its corporations and military, determining not only how well people live but whether they live. Finally, some of the political leaders of the United States government are making plans to ensure that the American empire rules without end by controlling outer space and spying on all people, sending Max Weber's "iron cage" of modernity into its planning stages.[1]

American Christians have a special responsibility in this historical moment. They can, of course, as many do, simply enjoy their position of eminence in the world and thank God for their blessings as Americans. In this humor, American Christians can read the Bible with the Roman and other empires as an already surpassed context without relevance to their own situation in the midst of the American empire. Or, they can look at the American empire through the same lens that the prophets, Jesus, and Paul looked at the empires in which they lived. American Christians are called to decide whether the American empire, as its supporters claim, continues the Enlightenment's emancipatory project of using instrumental reason to organize all of life for individual freedom with the addition of the blessings of the biblical God or whether the liberating God of the Bible calls them to step back from their situation and press for another kind of America.

The Bible and Empires, Old and New

Few biblical scholars have made the case for the latter response with more urgency and credibility than Richard Horsley. In an impressive catalogue of books and articles, Horsley has insisted on reading the message of Jesus and Paul in the prophetic tradition of God's liberation of all of God's creatures.[2] Moreover, Horsley has also kept the contemporary reality of the American empire at the forefront of the reader's consciousness especially as it contradicts the historical trajectory of liberation. This has involved him in an argument with two fronts about the appropriate context in which to read the Bible. On the one hand, Horsley has carried on a long campaign to show how much the context of the Roman Empire shaped and determined the New Testament as an oppositional document, one that carried a critique and a rejection of the dominant culture.[3] On the other hand, Horsley has tried to show that the American empire forms the analogous context for contemporary readers and hearers of the Word. This latter task has often involved providing evidence that the American empire is real and that American imperialism is oppressive and destructive for the poor and wretched of the earth.[4] The assumption in this essay is that, although there are differences between the Roman and the

American empires, there are enough similarities to provide a commonality of context for the reader, or, in Gadamer's image, a "fusion of the horizons" of the text and of the contemporary reader.[5]

The basic outline of social, economic, and religious history on which Horsley relies has become, in large part due to his own work along with that of Norman Gottwald, among others,[6] a widely shared notion, and one that can be summarized briefly. From the foundational narratives of the Hebrew Scriptures until the time of the Second Temple, Yahweh has had a controversy with empires. The basic characterization of an empire is that it is a political, economic, and religious system that is able to define the goals of human action and the means by which those goals are to be realized.[7] As the logic of this system works itself out, some groups have the power to define the way that human life is produced and managed, without consultation with those whose lives are being so shaped. In order to achieve this over time and space, empires have to construct means of domination, and they use the resources of those whose lives they control to support the very means that keep them in thrall. This means that the support and defense of an empire requires the exploitation of the masses. It also means that empires have to continue to grow, in part because as long as there remains a margin of freedom available as an alternative to life in the empire, it cannot feel secure. Religion becomes another means of domination for an empire, since it uses religious symbols to form the subjectivity of life within its power and to be compliant with its aims.[8] The tribes of Yahweh were marked by their refusal to stay within the ideological boundaries of the Egyptian empire and celebrated their God as a God who is outside of such a system of control. It is this theme of liberation that Horsley and others have lifted up as the defining theme of the Bible and, in so doing, have insisted on its anti-imperial character.[9]

Empires Today

Empires have been a constant condition of the political and economic situation of human societies since the development of civilization, that is, since the rise of cities and city states supported by agriculture. Moreover, the actual reality of empires, the way in which they functioned by dominating and exploiting subaltern units of society, tribes, peoples, and nations, was not, and could not have been, thematised by political economists and sociologists until the rise of modern social science in the nineteenth century. In fact, it was not until the waning years of the British empire that a fairly accurate, if crude, analysis was made of the way that European imperial powers operated.

It is with some irony that Lenin, relying for much of his analysis on the work of these capitalist political economists, gave the twentieth century, for better or for worse, the notion of imperialism as the latest stage of world capitalism.[10] In this, Lenin moved Marxist thought to an economic explanation for the movement of European nations to become colonial powers. In this vision, European capitalism moved on to other parts of the world to find raw materials to exploit and new markets in which to sell surplus commodities and to invest surplus capital. This movement led to rivalry between the ruling classes of the various European nations for control over their colonies. Although this rivalry led to the great wars of the twentieth century, it also opened the possibility in Marxist theory of a worldwide proletarian struggle against these imperial powers.

This notion of a global working-class struggle for the freedom of all found fertile soil among the anticolonialist movements in the European colonies of Africa, Asia, and Latin America, in struggles that often took the form of movements for national liberation. It was in these struggles that a practical basis was provided for a more detailed theory of the nature of imperialism, particularly in China. In these countries without a large industrial working class, the anti-imperialist movement had its greatest successes. The irony is that whereas Lenin's work on imperialism had an emancipitory intent, it became a part of the ideology of a new empire, that of the Soviet Union. However, that does not mean that many of the movements that used Lenin's analysis were not genuine in their desire for freedom, nor that their analyses were not based on colonial reality.

As a result of the Second World War, the European imperial powers were in no shape to defeat movements of national liberation in their former colonies and to contain the Soviet Union at the same time. There were some exceptions to this. France, for example, tried to retain control of Algeria and Vietnam, in the face of growing anti-imperialist resistance, with negative results. The British empire apparently accepted the inevitable and was satisfied with the vague relationship of the Commonwealth. Such relationships, together with the growing influence of the United States, signaled the beginning of a new phase of imperialism, dubbed neocolonialism. This phase avoided direct and open control of a colony but worked through more subtle and indirect means with a native elite to retain its former advantages.

Initially, the United States fit rather awkwardly among these imperialist powers. After all, the United States had its birth in the first successful anticolonialist war of national liberation. In fact, the history of the United States has not been consistent with its original republican principles. Aside from the slavery of Africans and the genocide of the Native Americans, the United States has followed a policy that was often self-aggrandizing and exploitative of other peoples. Manifest Destiny and the Monroe Doctrine encouraged the theft of much of Mexico and a sense of entitlement over the western hemisphere. And, as a result of the Spanish-American War, the United States even acquired some real colonies of its own. In general, the policy of the United States was to use its military in order to ensure that its national self-interest was defended and that the economic interest of its larger corporations was safeguarded. Throughout the twentieth century, the United States was ready to intervene militarily, and did in places as far apart as Guatemala and Iran, to enforce its will and even to install regimes judged to be friendlier to its interests. In the course of the Cold War, it became clear to most informed commentators whatever their political bent that the United States had become an imperial power, in defiance of its own founding principles and in contradiction to the biblical teachings that it often professed to follow.[11]

It is difficult for most Americans to admit that their country has become an empire. It goes against not only their civic education but also their deepest sense of self-identity. They do not like to think of themselves as citizens of an empire, even one that may be relatively benign. For decades, many Americans, even progressive Americans, denied, in the strongest terms, that America was an imperialist country or an empire. This reticence had its reasons. Taking on the functions of an empire without officially claiming the name could be very useful ideologically since it allowed the United States to justify its policies and actions not in the name of naked self-interest or domination but in the name of universal peace, justice, and freedom.

After the fall of the Soviet Union, however, America emerged on the world scene as the only superpower. The world had moved from a bipolar to a unipolar world. It was at this point that some, including the so-called neoconservatives, began to claim the title of empire for America.[12] In their view, history had delivered America more power than any challenger, actual or potential, for a purpose. To deny this would be absurd, in their view. It was better, they argued, to grasp this power proudly and to use it boldly. Because of this, the United States could (and should) act unilaterally if necessary when its self-interest dictated it, thereby bypassing the network of international organizations and relationships that had been so painstakingly assembled during the Cold War. At the same time, it could make use of those same organizations to promote its goals when it was convenient to do so, and thus maintain the pretense of collaboration.

Faith in Empire; Faith against Empire

The view of the American empire put forward by these neocons was colored by traditional American exceptionalism. All empires, they argued, tend to destroy democracy and to place ever narrower limits on freedom, except the American empire. The American empire uniquely carries through, they claimed, on the promises of all former empires; what had been pretense in others, became practice in the American empire. The fact that such a claim could be taken seriously is a tribute to the power of official American ideology that draws on both biblical and Enlightenment sources to legitimate its rule.[13] Like the Bible, the Enlightenment can also be read in various ways. The tradition of the Enlightenment can be seen as part of an ideology of formal freedom in all spheres of life without regard to content, or it can be interpreted dialectically as an early, but one-sided attempt to bring rationality, justice, and freedom to bear on all of societies' institutions. It must be said that the formal, non-dialectical mode of understanding the Enlightenment has usually won out in American culture. Because of this ambiguous history entwining biblical interpretation with the presuppositions and formalistic ideology of the Enlightenment in the legitimation of American power, these two traditions of the Bible and the Enlightenment have always been uneasy partners, sometimes even conflicting with each other, while they both serve to legitimate the American empire.[14]

Beyond issues that are embroiled in high-profile political struggles, such as the teaching of some version of creationism alongside the theory of evolution or the distribution of condoms by government agencies around the world to combat HIV/AIDS and promote health, there are other major issues where the fundamentalist position has policy implications of great consequence. Two of the chief issues are a policy on the state of Israel and Jerusalem, driven by a particular Christian eschatology, and global warming. The way that both of these issues play out in the future will have an enormous, potentially catastrophic, effect on the nature of the American empire and life on earth itself. On both of these issues, the fundamentalist and Enlightenment sides have diametrically opposed positions. For fundamentalists, the basic position on Israel is the need to defend the state of Israel and to rebuild Jerusalem and its temple, because these are prime components of fundamentalist end-time theology. For policy makers based more squarely in the Enlightenment tradition, on the other hand, the goal is to treat Israel as one state among others and to help the Palestinian people regain a home and a state of their own in order to restore a peaceful equilibrium. At the very least, the fundamentalist position guarantees more war and conflict in the Middle East. At the worst, it may instigate a broader regional war, even one with nuclear weapons.

The effects of not developing clear policies based on the scientific evidence for global warming are obviously dangerous for all people, even for all creatures who dwell on the earth. Once again, fundamentalist Christianity has played a major role by distracting public consciousness and public discourse from the real ecological disaster unfolding around us with its own prophetic script. In this, it is joined by some major corporations and oil companies who are willing to trade their own profits for the future of the planet.[15] In place of reliance on science, many fundamentalist Christians focus on the fantasies of the end-times mediated by prophetic timetables and sadistic fiction such as the Left Behind series of novels.[16]

It is important, therefore, that Christian theologians, ethicists, and biblical scholars help contemporary readers of the Bible find a rational, responsible, and credible hermeneutic to counter this religious ideology legitimating the American empire. Richard Horsley's work on Jesus and Paul has shown the all-pervasive presence of resistance to the Roman Empire and its ideology in the New Testament. His work has also shown the development of early Christian assemblies as alternative communities of freedom and mutual love in the midst of an exploitative empire. At the same time, Horsley urges the reader to see the analogy between the Roman Empire, against which Jesus and Paul struggled, and the American empire in which contemporary American readers of the Bible live.[17]

An important contribution of Horsley's hermeneutic is to challenge the modern separation of religion and politics by pointing out the political power of the emperor cult in Rome and analogous popular icons of consumerism in contemporary America.[18] On the other hand, Horsley's work shows that when Jesus speaks of the kingdom of God, he is not speaking only of an inner state, a pious heart, or an existential attitude. Rather, the kingdom of God is, as the Lord's Prayer has it, where God's will is done on earth including in the realms we call political, economic, and social. And God's will, as Jesus' life and teaching shows, is for all creatures to experience health, well-being, justice, and love. Religious symbols, like the kingdom of God, have both symbolic, ideal functions and real, material, effects. That is why our modern, post-Enlightenment presupposition that religion is one thing and politics is another skews our interpretation of Jesus' message. When Jesus says that his kingdom is not of this world, we tend to hear that as if he meant that it is located in some sort of nonhistorical, private realm far away from the public, political world in which we actually live out our daily lives. What we should hear Jesus saying, however, is that in God's kingdom relationships are different than those that we find in an imperial society. In God's kingdom, the great do not lord it over the weak, and the one who serves others is the greatest of all. Where God reigns, the child, the woman, and the marginalized are honored and helped, not exploited. What God wills are nonhierarchical, egalitarian, and mutual relationships among all people, the reverse of the sort of top-down control based on wealth and power typical of an empire structured on the basis of a system of patronage.[19]

Horsley's strategy for reading the New Testament is not satisfied with pointing out the role of biblical religion as a negative response to oppressive power in the past, but goes on to point out the way that we are called to respond to analogous manipulation and oppression in our own day. Horsley urges contemporary readers of the New Testament to look around for those points in their own situation where the same God, whose kingdom Jesus and Paul proclaimed, is calling us to resist, to protest, and to discover alternatives. It is just here, however, that I would like to make a suggestion meant to augment Horsley's position. In order to confront and to challenge the imperial system of domination and control, I would argue that one needs an anti-imperialist theology. A responsive reliance on the prophetic tradition is good as far as it goes, but I think that there needs to be a positive vision and some account of where that positive vision comes from and how it may serve the future. It is not enough to have an agenda to demand change from an imperial system, there must be some notion of a dynamic source of value at the center of this nonimperialist vision. This dynamic source of value and energy must be capable of providing future ideals that change with the changes of history and yet remain faithful to a liberating vision.

This anti-imperialist vision, itself, as Horsley articulates it, is scattered throughout his work, but enough is said to make clear its basic outlines. In the first place, the new world order is actually producing a world in disorder. We cannot here rehearse all of the destabilizing features of our world, especially since the attack on the World Trade Center in 2001. Many of these features have already been mentioned above. Others point directly to our consumer society because it uses the earth's resources and human labor to produce wealth, in an unsustainable way, for a very small percentage of the world's population while leaving the vast majority of people in deepening poverty. At the same time, the need for oil by the American empire drives politics and even causes war, all the while forcing those same societies deeper into debt. Partly because of that debt, the United States has tried to have an empire on the cheap. It has reduced the size of its military and thus has shirked one of the main responsibilities of historic empires, providing security and peace to those under its umbrella of defense. This reduced military, by failing to protect the subjects of the empire, allows determined armed groups who oppose it to strike and create insecurity and fear.

One challenge for Christians is to organize nonviolent democratic movements for peace and justice in such a way that the resentments and injustices on which armed opponents thrive may be blotted out. These movements must be local, diverse, in communication with one another but not hierarchically organized. As opposed to the Platonic thesis that there must be one dominant ideal vision, there should be an encouragement to each movement to imagine its own ideal without censorship. In this way, the promise that many saw in the emergence of the Internet might be realized. At any rate, it does seem that we are entering a period of postnationalism, or post-Westphalian political organization.[20] It may be that the European Union provides a workable model that relegates the older, modern, nationalism to a secondary level and might challenge the hegemony of the American empire, probably along with other regional organizations. Through such organizations, it may be possible to let the marginalized multitudes sometimes living in chaos, sometimes living under domination by local or foreign elites, have an opportunity to create a better life for themselves through local democracy. This seems to be the best hope for a multiplicity of equal subjects to replace the global domination and hegemony of any unilateral power. It also seems to be the best hope for replacing current disorder with a harmonious and peaceful order by allowing movement from below based on the principle of subsidiarity, that is, dealing with problems on the most local level possible, as in liberation theology and process theology alike.[21]

God "from Below"

Any interpretation of the Bible that hopes to offer ideals and values for human action and that attempts to provide some coherent and adequate account of the universe must ground those ideals and values in ultimate reality and also give a reason to think of creativity, novelty, and diversity as both real and valuable. If we do not give such an account, we run the risk of making the biblical text we are interpreting an interesting but irrelevant document from the past. It seems to me that process theology, namely, that theology based on the philosophical system of Alfred North Whitehead, comes closest to satisfying these demands and providing an understanding of God that can fit nicely with the anti-imperialist hermeneutic recommended here. Whitehead, as a mathematician/logician interested in the philosophy of modern science, set forth a system that was based on an organic and temporal interpretation of all of reality, self-consciously incorporating but going beyond the Enlightenment tradition. Although Whitehead himself did not lay out an explicit hermeneutical position, his philosophy certainly is most compatible with a contemporary historical, realistic, and context-sensitive reading such as that offered by Horsley and many others. Process theology has the further advantage of grounding the values of justice, peace, and freedom in God's vision of the future, even as it insists on the power of self-determination and creativity for each actual entity.

It also seems to me that process theology could provide a highly systematic basis for the critique of imperialism and for its remedy in local democracy discussed here. Whitehead's metaphysics requires pluralism and egalitarianism and explicitly endorses the love ethic of Jesus, at the same time as it gives an account of reality that is based on relationships between actual entities. Moreover, as he distinguishes between the prophetic ethics of Jesus and the traditional Christian doctrine of God, Whitehead makes a very sharp critique of those traditional views of God because, as he puts it, they worship a God made in the image of an emperor ("the Divine Despot"), and the world of such a God is a "slavish world."[22] Whitehead, that is, starts with an explicitly anti-imperialist God and goes on to eliminate or reformulate traditional attributes of deity, such as omnipotence, impassivity, immutability, omniscience, and nontemporality.[23] In Whitehead's view, God does not control every event but seeks to influence them by the persuasion of goodness and beauty. Accordingly, in the process vision, all creatures are free, and the future is truly open and unknown, even for God. God in process thought is responsive to every event and provides a constantly revised and renewed vision of future possibilities leading to the deepest, most intense, and most harmonious satisfaction of every creature. In offering this vision of the future to be accomplished, in the process view, God does not coerce the creatures but depends upon persuasion and the intrinsic appeal of a peaceful, just, and harmonious future. This vision, therefore, works in precisely the opposite way to the way of empire, which works through force, even terror and awe.[24]

The notion of God that is developed in process thought is remarkable for its consistency with the religious ethics implicit in Jesus' life example and teaching.[25] Because God is working toward a commonwealth of creatures, not by coercion, but by sympathy and the lure of future beauty and justice, so we should imitate God by similar relationships with other people and with nature. The more orthodox doctrine of God fits rather poorly with such a vision insofar as it does not allow God to feel sympathy with creatures and seek the common good of all beings in a truly open future. This future is one in which all beings are called to cooperate to make actual a just and harmonious democracy for all.

In process thought, religious belief and doctrine must be coherent with other modes of knowledge, including natural and social science. I think that the humility that process thought urges on theology and ethics and the demand it makes to respect and accommodate other ways of knowing is vitally important for the contemporary world. Many voices today counsel a choice between a nonreligious scientism and a pietistic form of evangelical Christianity that denies science. What is needed, I would argue, is a science with religious, ethical, and aesthetic depth that is able to challenge the American empire with a transformative vision.[26]

If it were just a matter of theoretical concern that leads me to urge an engagement with process thought, it might not be that important. My contention, however, is that a concern with an adequate doctrine of God is more than merely theoretical. Without such a revised doctrine of God, this anti-imperialist way of reading the Bible, in the context of both the ancient Roman Empire and the contemporary American empire, is open to misunderstanding and attack by those who oppose such a hermeneutic politically and religiously. Perhaps, more importantly, those who are learning this way of reading and interpretation may be left without a clear notion of the religious source of the values and ideals that can inspire their resistance and their attempt to construct an alternative to empire. The possibility that such a lack of a clearly religious account of this way of reading the Bible may obscure and limit the critical response to the American empire by contemporary Christians should lead us all to widen and to sharpen our theological discussions.

8. Contending with the Bible: Biblical Interpretation as a Site of Struggle in South Africa

Gerald O. West
University of KwaZulu-Natal

Introduction

SINCE ITS ARRIVAL IN SOUTHERN AFRICA, the Bible has been a site of struggle, though the parameters of the struggle have changed as our context has changed. In this essay, I will examine a number of case studies, covering a period of nearly two hundred years, in which the Bible is contested. This journey transverses scholarly and ordinary African engagements with the Bible and brings us to the present moment, where, after liberation in South Africa, the Bible remains a contested site.

My first case study is located among the BaTlhaping people of southern Africa in the early 1800s as they probe the Bible and related artifacts brought by the missionaries to their community just beyond the boundary of the nascent Cape colony; my second focuses on Isaiah Shembe, the founder of an African Independent Church, who deliberately "steals" the Bible from the colonial powers of the early 1900s so that he may use it to build his dislocated peoples into a new community; my third draws on the women (and a few men) who courageously live "positively" with HIV and AIDS in the face of stigma and discrimination in present-day South Africa; the fourth is a brief examination of the type of contestation in South African Black Theology; and I conclude with a brief fifth case study which analyzes President Thabo Mbeki's current use of the Bible in the public sphere.

Our president's public engagement with the Bible signals a return of the Bible to the public sphere. This is a significant development, for after a long history of the Bible's very public presence in all spheres of South African life, the post-1994 liberation period was one in which the Bible was less apparent. An analysis of the *Kairos Document*, this essay argues, may shed some light on these more recent developments.

Contested though it has been since its arrival in South Africa, the Bible has become an African book, central to the lives of the vast majority of South Africans. And yet contestation remains an indelible attribute of the Bible's presence among us, and so it should remain, for without ongoing public contestation, the Bible will increasingly be co-opted by neoconservative forces both internal and external to our context. The tendency by prophetic forces in church and society to abandon the Bible must, I will argue, be resisted. The Bible must remain a site of struggle.

And so the Bible's journey of contestation begins, with the arrival of the Bible among indigenous South Africans nearly two hundred years ago.

The BaTlhaping

In 1812, when the missionary John Campbell and his companions came among the Tlhaping people, who then occupied territory to the north and beyond the boundary of the Cape colony, one of the items they brought with them as a potential object of exchange was the Bible.[1] Campbell's vision was to gain the support of Chief Mothibi and his people, representing, as they did to Campbell, the southernmost part of a number of related clans who shared a similar language (what we now speak of as Tswana). Campbell's interest in a chain of language-related clans was predicated on his primary interest in proclaiming the gospel to these related peoples and translating the Bible into their common language. Campbell, therefore, used every opportunity he could to "instruct," emphasizing the merits of the written word over the oral word, explaining to the Tlhaping "how knowledge, conveyed by means of books, was more certain than that conveyed by memory from father to son."[1]

While there was considerable interest in the Bible on the part of the Tlhaping, including the query by Mothibi's uncle (one of the most senior members of the community), "if they should be taught to understand books,"[2] others in the community were more circumspect, already beginning to contest this newly arrived item. Among these is "an old man," Campbell reports, "who is averse to our sending teachers," and who went on to say "he did not need instruction from any one, for the dice [bones or bola] which hung from his neck informed him of every thing which happened at a distance [one of the properties of written text propounded by the missionaries]," adding that if the Tlhaping "were to attend to instructions, they would have no time to hunt or to do any thing."[3]

This "old man" is almost certainly a "ngaka" (an indigenous doctor/diviner/healer), given that he is wearing a "dice," one of the elements among the bones, shells, and other materials making up the "ditaola," the collection of items used in divining.[4] It is clear from the context of Campbell's report that this indigenous diviner is referring directly to the Bible, in particular, and to books in general. This ngaka was not only concerned about how the Bible might undermine traditional knowledge, he was also resisting the time schedules and modes of production of established mission station, church, and school routines to the south, in the Cape colony, whose "notions of time, work, and self-discipline were drawn from the natural lineaments of the industrial capitalist world."[5] In sum, he was contesting both the instruction regime associated with books and the Book.

Later on in the visit, Chief Mothibi reiterates his ngaka's concerns. This takes place during their first formal meeting, for Mothibi had been away when Campbell and his party had arrived. After the formal exchange of gifts, Campbell gets to the heart of the matter, from his perspective, stating the real purpose of his visit, namely, "to instruct the nations of Africa."[6] Mothibi's initial response to this request was to object, saying that "his people had no time to attend to their instructions, because they had to attend to their cattle, to sowing, reaping, and many other things," and "'besides [said Chief Mothibi, being quoted by Campbell], the things which this people teach are contrary to all our customs, which the people will not give up.'"[7]

But Mothibi must have known that he must negotiate with the colony and the colonial powers represented by Campbell, for he immediately continues, according to Campbell's narrative, to say that "'It would not do for them [missionary teachers] to live at Lattakoo [Dithakong, the capital], but should they be willing to live at a distance, I should have no objection to send some of the children to them to learn the Dutch language.'"[8] Mothibi was to hold his ground, quite literally, for many more years, giving his people time and space to work out what they would do with the Bible and other items of empire.

Ibandla lamaNazaretha

A hundred years later a semiliterate laborer on the Durban docks founded what is still today a large and thriving African Independent Church in South Africa. Isaiah Shembe had not set out to establish his own church in opposition to the European mission, encouraging those he healed and converted to join established mission communities. However, "as a consequence of the 1910 Union, the effects of the iniquitous 1913 Natives Land Act, and the pleas of his followers,"[9] Isaiah Shembe did eventually construct a "hybrid religious community from the substance of archaic Nguni and biblical beliefs."[10]

Baptised by a black Baptist minister, William Leshega, in 1906, Shembe embarked on a ministry of preaching and healing, largely outside the influence and controls of missionary Christianity.[11] Shembe's African Christianity is primarily a product of three strands of discourse. The first is his African cultural and religious heritage. The second is the immediate sociopolitical flux and instability that characterized this time, including the Anglo-Zulu War, the Anglo-Boer War, the Bambatha Rebellion, the formation of the Union of South Africa. And the third is missionary Christianity, particularly the Bible. While a hundred years before, Chief Mothibi and the Tlhaping were not sure they wanted to transact with the Bible, Isaiah Shembe quite deliberately appropriates the Bible.

This is clear in the account of Petros M. Dhlomo, the great collector and historian of Isaiah Shembe's life and ministry,[12] who recounts a sermon by Shembe in the home of Nldlovu, "the headman of Zibula at Lenge, in the year 1933,"[13] in which Shembe tells the story or "the parable of the liberating Bible":

> In olden times there were two might[y] nations who were fighting over a certain issue. In their war the one conquered the other one and took all their cattle away. They took even their children captive and put them into the school of the victorious nation.[14]

The story continues with a focus on three of these children, "three sons of the same mother." Among the tasks given to these children was that they "had to sweep the houses of their teachers and the house of the Pope."[15]

Shembe goes on to narrate: "All these children made good progress in school and passed their examinations well. Then they were trained as bishops." However, Shembe goes on immediately to recount how there was a certain book that was locked away from them. The implication is clear. Children of the conquered nation had limited access to the texts of the victorious nation, thereby allowing them to rise to a level no higher than that of bishop. The Pope alone had access to one special text. This was the Bible: "In the house of the Pope there was a Bible which was kept under lock by him and only read by himself."[16] However, Shembe goes on to relate,

> On a certain day he [the Pope] had to go for a few weeks to another place and he forgot to lock the Bible up at home. When the boys were sweeping his home they found the Bible unlocked. When they began to read it they discovered that their nation which had been demolished so badly by the war could never be restored unless they would get a book like this one, and they considered what to do.
>
> When they came back from school they bought a copybook and copied the whole Bible. When they had finished their work, they returned the Bible to its place. Thereafter the Pope came back and saw that he forgot to lock his Bible in. He called the boys who worked in his house and asked them whether they had opened this book. They denied it and said that they did not see that it had not been locked up. Then he forgot about it. The boys considered how they could bring this book to their parents at home.
>
> At another day, they went and asked permission to visit their parents at home. They were permitted to go and they were given a time by which they must be back. When they came home, they did not stay there, rather they went from home to home and preached about this book until their time of leave was over and policemen were sent to look for these boys. Then they left this book there and returned to school.[17]

Shembe's sermon moves in another direction at this point, but leaves us with a stolen, valued, copied, and appropriated Bible, which, in the remainder of the story, comes to be the benchmark for all that is written in the Shembe tradition.[18] In stealing the Bible from the victorious nation Shembe not only appropriates it for the conquered nation, he also effectively separates the Bible from the "Pope's" dominant form of Christianity, allowing for a whole host of appropriations not activated or anticipated by that form.

Siyaphila

A hundred years after Isaiah Shembe another group of South Africans, in the same province, are also taking up the Bible quite deliberately. In the midst of a devastating HIV/AIDS pandemic, a group of mainly African women who are HIV-positive have formed themselves into a support group known as "Siyaphila," which means "We are alive!" Every two weeks, in collaboration with the Ujamaa Centre for Community Development and Research, based in the School of Religion and Theology at the University of KwaZulu-Natal, they meet for contextual Bible study. This is part of a weekly program in which they meet and share resources to build their resilience, biologically, socioculturally, economically, and pyscho-theologically.

Confronted daily, in their families, churches, society at large, with biblically based stigma and discrimination, Siyaphila members reappropriate the Bible for life. Contextual Bible study, in which scholarly and ordinary community-based resources for biblical interpretation are shared, places the Bible and its interpretations in the hands of those who are HIV-positive. An important constituent element of the contextual Bible study process is reflection (as part of the praxis action/reflection cycle), allowing members of the Siyaphila group an opportunity to articulate among themselves how they understand the Bible.

In discussing with them their attitude toward the Bible before and since they joined Siyaphila,[19] the Ujamaa Centre found that the dominant metaphor used to describe the experience of the Bible of most Siyaphila members prior to their joining in the contextual Bible studies was one of distance. The Bible was there, but far off. Not one of the members portrayed the Bible in a negative manner. Distance was the issue, not negativity. Related to this image of distance was the image of place. The Bible was located in particular places, mostly in the church, but also on the shelf at home. In only one instance did the Bible have a place in the life of a participant prior to their membership of Siyaphila. As one person expressed it, the Bible "was opened and closed in church."

A related image used was that of belonging; the Bible belonged to others. For most, the Bible belonged to the minister/pastor/priest. For some, the Bible had some sense of belonging in their homes, usually with a parent or grandparent. But even in these few cases, the Bible belonged predominantly in the hands of the professionals. Closely related to this image was that of its relative silence. As one member put it, the Bible required a preacher to make it speak. What she wanted to convey in saying this was that the Bible was a holy book and could, therefore, only be made to speak by those whose task it was to do so. As one person put it, it was a book "handled" by others. In fact, this person reported, she has been expressly forbidden to touch the Bible, given that she was HIV-positive! Only holy people should "handle" the Bible. And when the Bible did speak to them personally, it was used negatively. As we have already said, there was no sense that the Bible itself was negative, but there was general agreement that the Bible was used in a negative way to speak about people like them, namely, those living with HIV and AIDS.

There was also general agreement that the Bible was not about ordinary life, let alone about their predicaments. As one said, the Bible "is just a book, talking about things that do not touch me." She certainly could not bring her questions or reality to the Bible. It was about other things, unrelated to her context. These comments prompted others in the group to say that church leaders seemed to be selective in what they allowed the Bible to say.

All of these damaging experiences of the Bible had been reversed by their membership of Siyaphila. What was far off had become close; what had no place now had a place; what belonged to others now belonged to them; what had nothing relevant to say now spoke directly to their condition; what could not be touched or made to speak by them was now in their hands, and they could make it speak; what had brought judgment, stigma, and discrimination now brought healing, hope, and life.

The Bible was no longer far off. It affected them personally, dealt with daily issues, and challenged them. As one person described, it affirmed to her that she was made in the image of God and supported her in her inner struggles. The Bible also belonged in a new way. As one person put it, now that she actually owned a Bible, she was aware of how much the Bible was used selectively in church by the church leadership. She now understood the wider context of the Bible.

One of the most startling changes was that the members had come to see that the Bible dealt with real-life issues. The Tamar Bible study (on 2 Samuel

13) more than any other had contributed to this new perception. They were amazed to discover that things that were happening in their contexts are "in the Bible." The many connections between their lives and the Bible astounded them. In addition to the Tamar example, another text that resonated with their reality was the story of the workers waiting to be hired for a day's work (Matt 20:1-16). The existence of this text was further proof, one person noted, of how selective the church was in its use of the Bible. Here was an obviously relevant text, and yet she had never heard it read or preached on.

Closely related to this new understanding was their sense of control. Through the contextual Bible studies they had realized that they did not need anyone else to interpret the Bible; they could do this for themselves. Another aspect of this control was the sense that they could critique or interrogate the Bible. As one member put it, the Bible itself gave you permission to probe its stories, referring to the Job Bible study (in which Job contends with his friends and God) as a particular example. This was especially empowering, she continued, for it enabled her to talk back at those who used the Bible to say that HIV is a punishment for sin. She could now affirm that God loved her and take the issue deeper. Another member had actually felt secure enough in her newly found sense of ownership of the Bible that she had confronted her own minister about the way he was using the Bible against people like her.

In collaboration with the Ujamaa Centre, Siyaphila group members have taken control of their own biblical interpretation, having both adapted the contextual Bible study process used by the Ujamaa Centre and quite deliberately chosen their own preferred texts. The texts they choose are those texts where the good news for them is clearest; texts in which Jesus takes a clear stand against prevailing social perspectives and dominant theologies in favor of those who have been pushed to the margins by these perspectives and theologies. In declaring another perspective and another theology, the texts they choose articulate their incipient sense of God's presence with them.

Black Theology

Given our colonial and apartheid history in South Africa, it is not surprising that the Bible has been a particular site of struggle. In many respects, apartheid was built on the Bible, and so was the liberation struggle. So our history is profoundly one of the Bible as a site of struggle. However, while this contestation was predominantly characterized by both sides' belief that the Bible was on their side, within South African Black Theology the Bible has been also been contested in a quite different way, reminiscent of Chief Mothibi's ngaka.

Within the first phase of Black Theology (in the 1970s), the Bible was predominantly appropriated by the side of the liberation struggle. But in the 1980s, a second phase of Black Theology raised serious questions about this. Takatso Mofokeng was to insist that there are numerous "texts, stories and traditions in the Bible which lend themselves to only oppressive interpretations and oppressive uses because of their inherent oppressive nature." What is more, he continues, any attempt "to 'save' or 'co-opt' these oppressive texts for the oppressed only serve the interests of the oppressors."[20] Young blacks in particular, Mofokeng argues, "have categorically identified the Bible as an oppressive document by its very nature and to its very core," and suggests that the best option "is to disavow the Christian faith and consequently be rid of the obnoxious Bible."[21] Indeed, some "have zealously campaigned for its expulsion from the oppressed Black community," but, he notes, with little success.[22] The reason for their lack of success, Mofokeng claims, is

largely due to the fact that no easily accessible ideological silo or storeroom is being offered to the social classes of our people that are desperately in need of liberation. African traditional religions are too far behind most blacks while Marxism is, to my mind, far ahead of many blacks, especially adult people. In the absence of a better storeroom of ideological and spiritual food, the Christian religion and the Bible will continue for an undeterminable period of time to be the haven of the Black masses par excellence.[23]

Given this situation of very limited ideological options, "Black theologians who are committed to the struggle for liberation and are organically connected to the struggling Christian people, have chosen to honestly do their best to shape the Bible into a formidable weapon in the hands of the oppressed instead of leaving it to confuse, frustrate or even destroy our people."[24]

Itumeleng Mosala would go on to elaborate a hermeneutic by which the Bible would become "a formidable weapon in the hands of the oppressed."[25] And writing within the third, and current (from the 1990s to today) phase of

Black Theology, a phase that refocuses on African religion and culture and raises the question of whether the Bible might be replaced in Black Theology by African Traditional Religion,[26] Tinyiko Maluleke concludes that he doubts whether "pragmatic and moral arguments can be constructed in a manner that will speak to the masses without having to deal with the Bible in the process of such constructions."[27] So the consensus in South African Black Theology is that the Bible has been and remains a site of struggle.

The Bible after Liberation

More than a decade into our political liberation, we have fairly good evidence to support Mofokeng and Maluleke. The vast majority of South Africans still turn to the biblical silo for sustenance and continue to base their moral arguments on the Bible. Today, whether for Mothibi's people, Shembe's community, or Siyaphila groups, the Bible is a significant resource. The real change, however, after liberation, is that the Bible no longer occupies the same kind of place in the public realm.

Indeed, religion, in general, has receded to the private sphere. Part of the impetus has been self-imposed. Having partially provided the platform for resistance to apartheid while the liberation movements were banned, religious institutions have readily conceded this territory to the liberation movements and political parties. And part of the impetus has been driven by our secular state and constitution. The effect on prophetic religion has been substantial.

What the *Kairos Document*[28] referred to as "State Theology" is gratefully gone. Our state is resolutely secular, and the Constitution, not the Bible, is its inspired text. "Prophetic Theology" has diminished, with many of its practitioners now in government or para-statal structures, implementing the policy of the African National Congress (ANC) led alliance (which includes the Confederation of South African Trade Unions [COSATU] and the South African Communist Party [SACP]) under the guidance of the Constitution and Bill of Rights. What the *Kairos Document* called "Church Theology," however, is on the upsurge. The space created by the demise of State Theology and the diminishing of Prophetic Theology has been filled by new forms of Church Theology.

Church Theology is best characterised in my view by what Walter Brueggemann describes as a theology of "consolidation which is situated among the established and secure and which articulates its theological vision in terms of a God who faithfully abides and sustains on behalf of the present ordering."[29] Our current moment, however, and the constellation of forces that have led to the resurgence of Church Theology after liberation warrant a fresh analysis of this theological phenomenon and its appropriation of the Bible.

The *Kairos Document* is, itself, an illuminating example of where we find ourselves. The product of theological activism and reflection in the wake of the 1985 State of Emergency,[30] the *Kairos Document* "came straight out of the flames of the townships in 1985," as the Dominican priest Albert Nolan put it.[31] In the words of the *Kairos Document*,

> The time has come. The moment of truth has arrived. South Africa has been plunged into a crisis that is shaking the foundations and there is every indication that the crisis has only just begun and that it will deepen and become even more threatening in the months to come. It is the KAIROS or moment of truth not only for apartheid but also for the Church.[32]

In profoundly insightful but deeply controversial analysis, the *Kairos Document* identified the three aforementioned kinds of theology in the church and called for a move towards a "Prophetic Theology," a theology that "speaks to the particular circumstances of this crisis, a response that does not give the impression of sitting on the fence but is clearly and unambiguously taking a stand."[33] It is surprising, therefore, that no sooner had we achieved our political liberation than one of the architects of the *Kairos Document* stated publicly that the prophetic sector of the church could now "go back to being the church." The church in South Africa has by and large settled back into various forms of what the *Kairos Document* called "Church Theology." A prophetic strand within the church continues to strive to read the signs of our times and to do theology with the poor, working class, and marginalized, but, once again, we are in the minority. Almost everyone, it would seem, is content with Church Theology.

Ironically, our democratic government, which includes large numbers of theologians who drafted or supported the *Kairos Document*, exerts considerable pressure on the religious sector to stay within the confines of Church-type Theology. The whole moral regeneration movement is an excellent example of this. Morality is narrowly defined as about condoms, crime, and corruption, and faith-based organizations are told to remain within this terrain. We are rebuked if we argue that our government's economic and HIV/AIDS policies may be immoral. It is not our place, we are scolded, to be prophetic about matters like these.

But it is not only the state that prefers the current predilection for Church Theology. Conservative forces in the churches are revelling in the space that an unlikely consensus over the preference for Church Theology is providing. Church leaders who were vocal proponents of Church (and even State) Theology in the 1980s now share platforms with government officials, nodding their heads together and looking pious and worried about the moral state of our nation—and they do not mean the neoliberal capitalist Growth, Employment and Redistribution economic policy[34] or the mismanagement of HIV and AIDS.

Civil society, too, seems content to see religion almost exclusively within the ambit of Church-type Theology. Celebrating the demise of State Theology and its hold on civil society, civil society has relegated all religion to the margins. Though not surprising, given the evils of Christian National Education and other heresies, the bracketing of religion—or being embarrassed by religion—in a society like ours simply compounds the problem, relegating it to the sphere of Church-type Theology.

Even the academic sector is feeling the pressure of the pull of Church Theology. There are growing indications that the churches desire to reassert their control over those university departments that have traditionally served their constituency. There is even talk of a new reformation in the corridors of the academy, signaling a return to a piety-centered Church Theology.

Just as the *Kairos Document* was a sign of its times, so the passing of its twentieth anniversary last year with little notice is a sign of these times.[35] We have all, it would seem, settled for a benign, cloistered form of Christianity. But Prophetic Theology is not dead. Indeed, there are clear signs that the struggle against HIV and AIDS and global capitalism is awakening many from their slumbers. Church Theology does not have the resources to deal with these signs of our times. Those who are infected and those who are unemployed know that it is bankrupt. Uncomfortable as it may be for the state, the church, and civil society, Prophetic Theology may be regaining its voice.

What the *Kairos Document* got wrong was its analysis about the Bible and its conclusion that, "It hardly needs saying that this kind of faith and this [Church

Theology] type of spirituality has no biblical foundation."[36] Unfortunately, as biblical scholars know, Church Theology does in fact have a substantial biblical foundation. This was the very argument of Mofokeng and Mosala, one that the *Kairos Document* failed to grasp (to our current cost). It is not only the church and theology that are sites of struggle, so, too, is the Bible.

The Legacy and the Task

This legacy of a publicly contested Bible is a profound resource. The tendency of left-leaning, ex-prophetic theologians to abandon the Bible in our current postliberation context is understandable but dangerous. Church Theology is gobbling up the Bible at a rapid rate; having been on the defensive briefly in the wake of liberation, it has now regrouped, with the Bible as its domain. The prophetic sector has exchanged the Bible for the Constitution. Though the Constitution is a worthy document with which to take forward progressive projects, separating it from the Bible is counterproductive,[37] particularly as the Bible remains not only a silo for the masses but also regularly has a place in the public realm. Even our South African president, Thabo Mbeki, cites it.

This is not the occasion for a detailed analysis of how Mbeki uses the Bible, but it is instructive to note that Mbeki's use of the Bible has increased during his presidency. While Mbeki has also been fond of and adept at using classic literature, ranging from local African poetry to Shakespeare, in his speeches, he has increasingly cited the Bible, recognizing that the masses are more likely to connect with the Bible than almost any other literature. So, for example, in his recent presentation at the Fourth Annual Nelson Mandela Lecture,[38] he cites the Bible directly and repeatedly in addressing the issue of corruption, concluding that:

> We must therefore say that the Biblical injunction is surely correct, that "Man cannot live by bread alone" [Matthew 4:4; Luke 4:4] and therefore that the mere pursuit of individual wealth can never satisfy the need immanent in all human beings to lead lives of happiness.

Clearly the Bible is in the public realm. But how is it being used? Is Mbeki's use of it simply politically instrumentalist, or is it a variant of Church Theology?

While many of his allusions to the Bible seem instrumentalist, his more recent substantive appropriations sound like variants of Church Theology. However we understand his use of the Bible, what is clear is that Mbeki has increasingly engaged with it, publicly.

Mbeki seems to be bucking the trend advocated by others, not least of whom is Cedric Mayson, long-time liberation theologian and currently National Coordinator of the African National Congress Commission for Religious Affairs. In an occasional document circulated for discussion among colleagues (including myself), Mayson canvasses for "liberating religion." [39] Like me, he notes the demise of any serious theology since the *Kairos Document*, and he laments the failure of religious leaders in taking up Nelson Mandela's initiative "to discover an inter-faith theology of transformation."[40] He then offers an incisive analysis of the tendency of institutionalized religion, whatever its form (including African Traditional Religion), to usurp the "prophets of peace and harmony, service and compassion" in whose memory it was established.[41] Our current moment, Mayson argues, calls for "Secular Spirituality" (and the uppercase is his).

> We need to liberate religion into a new secular spirituality [lowercase this time] which drives away superstition and fear, and empowers millions of agnostics and believers who are seeking a spirituality not wrapped in colonial religions. It means a new evangelism, a unity in diversity of people seeking values which change society, a new prophetic context which sees politics and economics as godly spheres.[42]

While I am sympathetic to Mayson's project and would look for ways to collaborate with it, I worry about our abandoning the established religions and, particularly, the Bible.[43] For what the decade after liberation has made abundantly clear, as I have argued, is that Church Theology (and similar theological forms in other religious traditions, including African Traditional Religion) will co-opt whatever we do not claim and contend for.

This is why socially engaged biblical scholars, among whom I include Richard Horsley (a comrade to whom this essay is dedicated), must contend for the Bible for all we are worth. I invoke Horsley here because he is an excellent example of a socially engaged scholar who refuses to allow the mainstream academy, let alone the church, to dictate the Bible's meaning. His long commitment to actual struggles for liberation and life provides him with what Mosala referred to as "eyes that are hermeneutically trained in the struggle for liberation today to observe the kin struggles of the oppressed and exploited of the biblical communities in the very absences of those struggles in the text."[44]

My own work with the Ujamaa Centre provides collaborative opportunities to work with each of the sectors I have mentioned as preferring forms of Church Theology. So, we in the Ujamaa Centre can collaborate with the South African Communist Party (SACP) and the Confederation of South African Trade Unions (COSATU) in the struggle for a more socialist economic vision. We can collaborate with civil society in a host of projects, particularly the campaign for a Basic Income Grant,[45] the ongoing work of resisting violence against women and children, and the many projects connected to HIV/AIDS. We can collaborate with prophetic forces in the church and other religious traditions in contending for the souls of our faiths. Finally, we can collaborate with socially engaged scholars in the academy in transforming biblical studies and incorporating it into an emancipatory project.

Conclusion

The case studies I have used in this essay are part of the legacy we have received in contending for the Bible and in recognizing that the Bible is a site of struggle. As long as the Bible is a (if not, the) silo of the masses, socially engaged biblical scholars, pastors, and laypeople cannot afford to neglect it, for when we do, we simply multiply the space of Church Theology to co-opt the Bible for its purposes.

That South Africa's president has had to treat the Bible more substantively, even if it is for Church Theology-type purposes, is a clear indication that the Bible remains a significant resource for most South Africans. Our task, as socially engaged biblical scholars together with all those who work with the Bible for liberation, transformation, and life, is to serve them by contending for the prophetic and emancipatory potential of the Bible. Like Jacob, we will wrestle with it until it blesses us.

9. The Blessings of Hegemony: Poverty, Paul's Assemblies, and the Class Interests of the Professoriate

Steven J. Friesen
University of Texas at Austin

RICHARD HORSLEY HAS BEEN EXHORTING BIBLICAL SCHOLARS for many years to examine the biases of our discipline. Whether the topic is Jesus, Paul, the first-century assemblies, or modern believers, Horsley has persistently urged us to question our received wisdom, and has provided us with other ways to envision the history of the followers of Jesus.[1] In that spirit—and in his honor—I offer this brief analysis of some ways in which Western New Testament scholarship has consistently ignored and marginalized the topic of poverty in Paul's churches. I argue that twentieth-century interpretation of the Pauline assemblies went through three phases in its attempt to avoid its own conclusion that most of the members of those assemblies were poor. I also suggest a possible explanation for this contorted history of interpretation: the class interests of the interpreters. But first I must deal with some widely disseminated misinformation about the history of interpretation.

A History of the "Cross-Section Consensus"

Most New Testament scholars who address the social status of Paul's churches today assert some version of the following: While earlier interpreters held that the members of Paul's assemblies came only from the lower classes, only recently scholars have realized that these assemblies included a cross-section of social strata. The following two quotes illustrate the tendency. They both come from popular textbooks that are used widely throughout North America.

> In the past, many historians thought that the first Christians largely belonged to the lower socioeconomic ranks of Greco-Roman society. Recent analyses of Paul's Corinthian letters, however, suggest that early Christians came from many different social classes and represented a veritable cross-section of the Hellenistic world.[2]

> The majority of Paul's converts were evidently from the lower classes, as he himself reminds them: "Not many of you were wise by human standards [highly educated], not many were powerful, [influential in the community], not many were of noble birth" [in the upper classes] (1:26). Recent scholars have observed, however, that at least some of the Corinthian converts must have been well-educated, powerful, and well born, or else Paul would not have said that "not many" of them were. Indeed, if we assume that some members of the community came from the upper classes, we can make better sense of some of the problems that they experienced as a group.[3]

The idea that the cross-section consensus (my term) only emerged in the second half of the twentieth century first appeared in a monograph from 1977. In that year, Abraham Malherbe wrote:

> It appears from the recent concern of scholars with the social level of early Christians that a new consensus may be emerging. This consensus, if it is not premature to speak of one, is quite different from the one represented by Adolf Deissmann, which has held sway since the beginning of the century. The more recent scholarship has shown that the social status of early Christians may be higher than Deissmann had supposed [in the early twentieth century].

Malherbe went on to describe the agreement in this way: "Representatives of the emerging consensus on the social status of early Christians view the church as comprising a cross section of most of Roman society."[4]

A more detailed study from 1983 supported this conclusion. Wayne Meeks wrote, "The 'emerging consensus' that Malherbe reports seems to be valid: a Pauline congregation generally reflected a fair cross-section of urban society."[5] Meeks also described the history of this alleged emerging consensus.

> The prevailing viewpoint has been that the constituency of early Christianity, the Pauline congregations included, came from the poor and dispossessed of the Roman provinces.
>
> Within the last two decades, however, a number of scholars have looked at the evidence afresh and come to conclusions very different from Deissmann's about the social level of the first-century Christians.

Despite this widespread and distinguished support, the idea that a new consensus emerged in the 1970s is inaccurate. In fact, most Western scholars have supported the cross-section consensus throughout the twentieth century. Even Deissmann himself accepted it.[6] The standard view during the twentieth century was that most of Paul's converts came from the lower social strata with some converts from further up the social hierarchy.

Since my claim flies in the face of what one reads in the secondary literature, it requires support. My method for defending my claim is to provide a series of representative quotes from a broad spectrum of New Testament introductions published throughout the twentieth century. The goal of such books is normally to provide a responsible summary of scholarly opinion, and so they give us a window into the academic consensus about the economic standing of the Pauline believers. I include publication dates for orientation. Note that these authors all make their point casually, because the cross-section consensus was never a contested issue among them.[7]

1904 (translation of an earlier German publication): "It [the Corinthian church] was composed for the most part of poor and uneducated folk, many of them, as might be expected, slaves; yet, as the presence of individual members of good position may be inferred even from this passage, so the existence of considerable difference of social standing among the Corinthian Christians follows from [1 Corinthians] xi. 20 f."[8]

1906 (translation of an earlier German publication): "During Paul's stay of a year and a half in Corinth he had founded a church there which consisted almost exclusively of former heathen, and for the most part of people of the lowest classes."[9]

1909 (translation of 1906 German original): "There are a number of things which account for this condition [that is, for the relative peace of the Corinthian congregation], e.g., the mixed character of the population of a great commercial city, where men are constantly coming and going from all parts of the world, . . . the impartiality in religious matters of the proconsul in whose term of office the Church became established . . . , the social standing of some of the members of the Church, and the prominent place of others even in the government of the city . . . "[10]

1921: "Apparently the lower classes of Corinth were chiefly converted by Paul (I Cor. 1:26-28 and 7:21), and the world of fashion, wealth and intellect was sparingly represented, although Gaius (I Cor. 1:14; Romans 16:23), and Erastus, treasurer of the city of Corinth (Romans 16:23) belonged to the latter class."[11]

1924: "Most of the members were from the lower walks of life (I Cor. 1:26), though there were also a few wealthy and cultivated persons (Chloe, Aquila and Priscilla, Crispus, Erastus, Tertius)."[12]

1936: "The Christian community at Corinth was, it must be remembered, a large one, the members of which were drawn from very different social levels."[13]

1946: "The membership of this first house-church was recruited largely from among humble people, although some differences in social status probably existed."[14]

1958 (translation of 1956 German original): "In eighteen months he [that is, Paul] succeeded in establishing a considerable Christian community which was mainly recruited from the Gentiles . . . though it had a Jewish element also. . . . Most of the members belonged to the lower classes, but there were also converts from the upper classes and well-to-do people."[15]

1965 (translation of 1959 French original): "He stayed there [Corinth] for a year and a half (Acts 18, 11) or longer (18, 18), founding a community whose faithful were enlisted principally—but not solely (I Cor 1, 16; 11,

17-34)—from the lower strata of the populace."[16]

1966: "First, there were some people of means (Paul, Barnabas, Erastus, Gaius) so that the wholly proletarian origins of the early Church must not be overemphasized."[17]

1971: "The church probably represented a cross section of the local inhabitants. In the main they were not distinguished for learning or position (I Cor. 1:26ff.), although the very language of this passage suggests that there were exceptions such as Sosthenes (Acts 18:17; I Cor. 1:1) and Erastus (Rom. 16:23)."[18]

1975 (translation of 1973 German original): "After a year and a half of Paul's ministry (Acts 18:11) there was a flourishing community, which consisted of Gentile Christians (I Cor 12:2), mostly from the lower classes (I Cor 11:7ff), but the Jewish-Christian element was also represented (Acts 18:4; I Cor 7:18), as were the upper social and economic levels (11:21 ff; Acts 18:8; Rom 16:23)."[19]

If these quotes seem repetitive or even monotonous, then they are demonstrating one of my points—that the twentieth-century mainstream consensus on economic issues in the Pauline assemblies was tedious. There was little progress on the topic and little curiosity about it. The quotes also demonstrate that it is factually wrong to claim that a new consensus emerged in the 1970s. Mainstream writers throughout the twentieth century thought that Paul's assemblies were a cross section of Roman imperial urban society, coming mostly from the lower classes but containing a few upper-class individuals.[20]

Whatever Happened to All those Poor Folk?

As a specialist in New Testament interpretation, it is embarrassing to me that we have misrepresented the history of twentieth-century interpretation. But another facet of this topic takes me beyond embarrassment. It should be deeply troubling to us that for at least a century, poverty, and economic inequality have not been important topics in Pauline studies, even though we have agreed that most of the early believers were poor. A survey of twentieth-century New Testament introductions also sheds some light on this absence of reflection on economic inequality, showing three distinct phases in the marginalization of first-century poor people in twentieth-century scholarship. In other words, the cross-section consensus held up throughout the twentieth century, but the ways in which scholars avoided discussing economic inequality shifted.

The first phase covers the period from about 1900 to the end of the Second World War. During the first half of the twentieth century, the main way in which scholars marginalized poverty was by ignoring it completely: It was common to write about Paul and his assemblies without any serious discussion of economic issues.[21] Those writers who did mention economic factors usually did so briefly in the context of discussing "social status."[22] These discussions were short and normally had no effect on the interpretation of Paul's writings.

A second phase began after World War II. From approximately 1950 to 1970, this new phase included some descriptions of Paul's churches as part of a booming urban economy. Many specialists still ignored economic issues but in the late 1950s and through the 1960s, at a time when the Western economies were expanding after World War II, we encounter assertions that the Roman imperial economy of the first century was also expanding. Some writers during these decades extolled the economic success of Roman imperialism and asserted that the blessings of Roman hegemony permeated all levels of society. These writers admitted that poor people still had less than the aristocracy, but they maintained that the poor had plenty to eat and must therefore have been satisfied with their lot.

The following two examples of this prosperous-empire theme from the 1950s and 1960s give us a sense of this tendency in the interpretation of Pauline assemblies.

> At the beginning of the Christian era, the Empire was at peace and, in general, order reigned securely within its frontiers. Hence it was, that this period was marked by an extensive growth in economic life and particularly in commerce. The artisans in the cities, the farmers in the country, the merchants in the urban centers, the traffickers in the interregional markets and all business men enjoyed prosperity; people got rich quickly. Almost everywhere there sprang up temples, gymnasia, basilicas, theaters, market-places, and porticos. State and city banks had abundant resources at their command; their officers encouraged and financed public works; the newly rich played

the role of Maecenases; the common people had work and, by the same token, a sufficiency of bread.[23]

Syria-Palestine, Asia Minor, and Greece all enjoyed the benefits of imperial peace and security. Long linked together by Hellenistic culture and the Greek language, they now formed part of the same noble state offering centralized control and security. Such unity created favorable circumstances for the spread of the community of Christ throughout the world.

However, the solidarity of the empire was not maintained by brute force. Roman law was highly developed and protected the state, the citizen, and private and public property. Equity was of increasing concern and the status of women and slaves had begun to improve. All peoples and areas in the empire benefited from Roman law that did not, however, supersede local law when the latter was just. Penalties for breaking the law were sometimes vindictive and harsh, especially for public offenses, but for the most part Roman law made significant contribution to the integrity and stability of the Roman state.[24]

In these quotes, we see quite clearly the second phase in the marginalization of poverty and poor people in the secondary literature. This tendency to portray the Roman Empire with a booming economy led some scholars to trivialize oppression by assuming that the poor would be satisfied if they simply had enough to eat. In some writing of the 1960s, we even see scholars suggesting that the poor were *better off* than the rich because the poor were allegedly happy with their subsistence lifestyle while the rich had great anxiety about the possibility of losing their vast wealth.

Generally speaking, life of the lower and lowest classes was quite tolerable, especially in the absence of advertising and the invention of new products for mass consumption. The rich were very rich, but their position was often insecure because of demands made upon them by emperors and other officials. They did not have to cope with an income tax, graduated or otherwise, and the inheritance tax was very low (five per cent); at the same time, it was quite possible for them to lose everything by political misadventure.[25]

So in the 1960s, we see new ways in which poverty in the Roman Empire was dismissed as an irrelevant topic. Instead of simply ignoring economic issues, during that decade there was a new trend in some New Testament introductions to portray the Roman imperial economy in glowing terms. According to those writers, the growth in commerce made everyone's life pleasant (except Judeans, in some formulations[26]), and poor people were satisfied because their low wages allowed them to buy enough food to fill their bellies.

Beginning in the 1970s, economic interpretation of Pauline communities began to shift toward a third phase, a phase that still persists. The prosperous-empire theme began to fade away in the secondary literature,[27] and writers tended to return to the earlier practice—either silence on economic issues[28] or short summaries of the cross-section consensus.[29] With either approach, scholars still paid little or no attention to the impoverished majorities in the early churches.

By the end of the 1970s, there was a noticeable trend toward more description of social issues, but, as I have argued elsewhere, this trend actually led to the marginalization of poor people in two new ways. One way was for scholars to focus on social status in a way that allowed them to pass over economic issues quickly and to dwell on other noneconomic factors that might influence social status. In the process, economic inequality was never thoroughly explored.[30] The second way in which poor people in the first-century assemblies were marginalized was a new tendency that began in the 1970s whereby scholars focused their attention on the few individuals from Paul's churches who might have been wealthier than average while still ignoring the bulk of the believers who can be described as poor.[31]

The shift that began in the 1970s did result in some important progress. The increased attention to social status led to more consideration of house-church relationships, the Lord's Supper, Jews and Gentiles, and gender.[32] Throughout the 1980s and 1990s, the elaboration of social-status issues continued. By the early years of the twenty-first century, it became standard expectation that an introduction to the New Testament would have some sort of overview of the

Roman Empire as a political and social unit, sometimes with several pages devoted to issues of social status in the Pauline assemblies.[33] Material from 1 Corinthians dominated the discussions, with marked increases in the topics of the Lord's Supper as a meal, households as a social unit, patronage practices, and even Paul's manual labor.[34]

Economic inequality, however, never gained a foothold as a significant topic of discussion. Justin Meggitt addressed the issue directly, but his reformulation has not gained acceptance.[35] I have also attempted to bring economic issues to the fore from other angles, but this has, apparently, not made a dent in the mainstream of Pauline scholarship.[36] At this point, the discipline as a whole still locates itself within the trajectory of twentieth-century scholarship, which found (at least) three different ways not to discuss poverty in the Pauline assemblies. From 1900–1950, poverty was ignored as irrelevant; from 1950–1970, there were some attempts to describe poverty as insignificant because of alleged expansion of the Roman imperial economy; and from 1970 to the present, scholars have deflected attention away from poverty by focusing on social status or on the exceptional individuals who might have been richer than most.

Why This Particular History?

This overview of introductions—a survey of surveys!—provides a general orientation to the history of twentieth-century interpretation regarding the socioeconomic standing of Paul's assemblies. While these introductions do not provide detailed argumentation, they do illuminate the findings that the discipline presented to the world as reliable. In the process, they also raise questions about the strange history of interpretation regarding poverty and wealth in Paul's assemblies. Specifically, why would a century of scholarship be so persistent in its avoidance of the question of economic inequality?

A partial explanation comes from other histories of Western universities in the twentieth century, which point out the way that economic trends have affected higher education. In his exploration of the development of disciplines in American universities, Louis Menand noted the same three periods I have highlighted. There was a formative period between 1880 and 1910, when most of the current disciplines took shape. The years 1945–1975 were a "Golden Age" for higher education when the baby boom and a growing domestic economy resulted in unprecedented expansion. In addition, the Cold War dramatically increased funding for science, technology, and area studies, with some funding trickling down also to the humanities as a necessary part of a well-rounded curriculum. This Cold War university system began to show fissures by about 1975, however, for several reasons. The Civil Rights Movement, women's liberation, and the Vietnam War all raised questions about the alliance between higher education and national security. As the national economy sputtered in the 1970s, however, there was less funding for higher education and more pressure for universities to soften their social critiques.[37]

Menand's study is helpful because he provided economic and political contexts for developments in American higher education. Richard Ohmann, however, has built a broader critique that helps fill out the picture. Ohmann argued that we need to take the class interests of professors into account in order to understand the history of twentieth-century scholarship. The primary function of the American professoriate in the twentieth century, according to Ohmann, was to train members of the professional-managerial class. His point was that teaching and research are linked to the reproduction of social relationships within a particular historical setting.

Ohmann noticed the same three phases in higher education that I have noted in Pauline studies, and he attributed these developments to changes in the history of capitalism. According to Ohmann, the decades around 1900 saw the formation of the professional-managerial class, a new middle class that was necessary for the maintenance of "Fordist" capitalism.[38] This form of capitalism was characterized by giant corporations that required layers of specialists who were organized hierarchically. Universities were restructured to produce such specialists, and professors were put in charge of the training process.[39] This economic system went into overdrive after World War II, for the reasons noted by Menand, but it came to an end around 1970 with the crisis in global capitalism that brought the period of Fordist capitalism to an end.[40] The development of an "agile capitalism" (also known as "globalization," "turbo-capitalism," or "the knowledge society") in the 1970s created new pressures for higher education. This reconstitution of American capitalism around 1970 forced educational institutions to become more like business, which also provides a growing proportion of the funding for the creation of knowledge. As a result, the critique of oppressive social relations that came to the fore in the 1960s and 1970s (especially the analysis of race and gender) is being de-funded, as government resources for research decrease, and the creation of knowledge is placed in the custody of market forces.

Ohmann's class analysis of the American professoriate within twentieth-century capitalism could help us understand the odd history of mainstream Pauline studies in that same period. The resulting reconstruction would look something like this. During the first half of the twentieth century, Pauline studies ignored poverty because it was in the class interests of New Testament scholars to reproduce the existing socioeconomic relationships of Fordist capitalism. In that context, higher education taught future professionals to accept and to overlook economic inequality, and Pauline studies did so as well. Most New Testament scholars taught their students that Paul's assemblies were made up of a cross section of society, mostly poor people but also a few well-to-do. These scholars did not make poverty an issue, however, and focused the attention of their students on other issues (soteriology, eschatology, and so on). In the 1950s and 1960s, the post-war economy expanded to produce a new form of hyperconsumption and higher education experienced explosive growth. In this setting, most New Testament scholars continued to point their students toward noneconomic topics, although some specialists began to imagine that the Roman Empire also experienced an economic expansion that would have made poverty irrelevant. Poverty, of course, has never been irrelevant, either in the ancient world or in ours. Inequality persists, and dominant society finds new ways to rationalize this persistence.

As the 1960s wore on, Fordist capitalism began to show its age. Various social movements in the West criticized domestic inequalities and foreign imperialism. These threads of critique made a lasting contribution to the academy, where they were woven into the fabric of higher education and into Pauline studies as well. But these critical voices never became dominant in the academy.

As a result, the narrative of higher education, in general, and of Pauline studies, in particular, during the last decades of the twentieth century suggests re-entrenchment rather than progress. The dominant discourse in Pauline studies discusses individual social status, not structures of economic inequality. Theories of oppression are relegated to "politicized" studies on the margins of the discipline. Paul is still portrayed as a thinker, not as an activist.

All of this raises many questions about the future of New Testament studies in the twenty-first century—a topic dear to the heart of Richard

Horsley, who has sought in his own scholarship to foreground precisely these issues. Specifically, this raises questions about the vocation of a practitioner of Pauline studies. What benefits will studies of Paul's first-century assemblies offer to twenty-first-century audiences? Will such studies be bound to the class interests of the professoriate? Or will they make substantive contributions to our understanding of religion and economic inequality? It remains for biblical scholars to create the answers.

10. "Nobody Tasted Blood in It": Public Intellectuals Interrogating Myths of Innocence in Biblical Studies

Abraham Smith
Perkins School of Theology

Introduction

THE TRANSCENDENTALIST RALPH WALDO EMERSON (1803–1882) is hailed as a public intellectual for a variety of reasons. He advocated informed civic engagement on the issues of his day. He laid the groundwork (later taken up by the classical American pragmatists Charles Sanders Peirce, William James, and John Dewey) for the "American evasion" of analytic philosophy and, thus, for a move toward viewing philosophical study as social criticism, not simply as a strict academic exercise.[1] He offered outspoken praise for the abolitionist John Brown (who had raided Harper's Ferry). He opposed the "'removal' of the Cherokee [Indians] from Georgia in 1835" and wrote a letter of protest to President Martin Van Buren. He contested the Fugitive Slave Act of 1850.[2]

Emerson is also lauded as a public intellectual because he brought critical exposure to those U.S. citizens (including those in his beloved New England) who failed to see the death-dealing that stood behind the commodities they purchased and the comforts they enjoyed. In response to an invitation by the Women's Anti-Slavery Association, he stood on a platform with Frederick Douglass at the Concord Courthouse on August 1, 1844, and delivered a speech titled "On Emancipation in the British West Indies." Emerson proffered a stirring rebuke to his fellow citizens for their complicity with the whole machinery of sugar production—the forcing of enslaved women to construct the cane holes, the throwing of enslaved men into boiling vats of sugar as punishment, and the larger traffic in human cargo that exploited the labor of thousands of enslaved Africans.[3] For Emerson, U.S. shoppers saw no further than the walls of their neighborhood shops, safe from the fitful cries of lives wrecked and families ruined for the sake of the sweet taste of sugar. Referring to the sugar, Emerson inimitably, aptly, and stingingly quipped: "Nobody tasted blood in it."[4]

In the spirit of Emerson, many public intellectuals in our own day seek to demystify myths of innocence: that is, they seek to *interrogate* institutions, cultural formations, and cultural productions that appear "innocent" but, in fact, participate historically and discursively in death-dealing, or otherwise in the subjugation of one or more parts of God's creation.[5] How would biblical studies look were it to take up this role? What if biblical scholars no longer saw the larger part of our professional task as what it has been almost exclusively from the Enlightenment until the recent decades, namely, examining a biblical text's sources, stages of production, or final form as the text came to be used by one or more ancient audiences, or even those various readers/auditors themselves?[6] What if we saw our task fundamentally as the interrogation of myths of innocence, and in so doing, as Mary Ann Tolbert argues, we expose the full panoply of power arrangements for "each site of writing, reading, or theorizing by carefully investigating the specific historical, cultural, political and social matrix that grounds it?"[7] These are indeed the types of questions prominently raised in the scholarship of Richard A. Horsley, a biblical historian whose stellar oeuvre is an incarnation of the aforementioned public intellectual's interrogationist mode.

In order to address these questions, I will first sketch the contours of a field within biblical studies in which I can now see this interrogationist mode taken up seriously. Then I will interrogate a myth of innocence about Luke-Acts, a myth that often prevents us from seeing the whole machinery of domination associated with a textual product that is otherwise lauded for its claims of inclusion, a myth that prevents us from tasting the blood in the sugar.[8] In the conclusion, I will return briefly to the spirit of the aforementioned questions with comments on the need for a new self-understanding of biblical studies professionals in the face of empire.

"Empire Studies" and the Interrogation of Myths of Innocence

An emerging feature of biblical scholarship is an interest in the historical and discursive forces of "empire."[9] Whether the trend emanates from postcolonial and diasporic studies,[10] a heightened desire for thicker historical analyses and disciplined access to the submerged histories of biblical peoples,[11] an honest attempt to address critically and responsibly the most recent growth of transnational corporations and the most recent wave of U.S. military aggressiveness,[12] or a combination of all the above, what cannot be denied is that "empire" studies is one of the signs of the times in recent biblical studies.

With this "interrogationist" mode, the adherents in part focus on the Bible's own embodiment of colonial postures. Although biblical texts have perennially been used as resources to resist colonialism, these cultural products are not innocent. Instead, many of these texts themselves actually support oppression and repression, running the gamut from the annihilation of indigenous peoples,[13] to negative depictions of "femaleness,"[14] to the subordination of women.[15] And although these texts are now canonized, and thus deemed sacred to certain religious communities, they are no less oppressive and repressive. Rightfully, then, Cornel West has seen the embrace of patriarchy in these texts and warned that "without the addition of modern interpretations of racial and gender equality, tolerance, and democracy, much of the [biblical] tradition warrants rejection."[16]

"Empire studies" adherents also interrogate the "innocence" of biblical studies, thus bringing scrutiny to the discipline's own role in maintaining or subverting hegemonic structures of oppression.[17] That is, questions are raised about the emergence of biblical studies roughly at the same time that discourses of domination arose in the so-called Enlightenment to justify "the political position of imperial Europe."[18] For example, D. F. Strauss's two-volume *Life of Jesus* (1835–1836), reaction to which set off a spate of "lives" of Jesus, was motivated by German nationalism.[19] As Halvor Moxnes observes, Strauss wrote the book "as a part of a national, German program."[20] Similarly, Ernest Renan, a specialist in philology, wrote his own life of Jesus (*Vie de Jésus*, 1863) in the context of official trips to Palestine supported by the French government.[21] As Moxnes also notes, "Renan's travels to the country of the Gospels were immersed in a context of *empire*, with *French* military and political presence and domination in the area."[22]

Yet, discourses of domination in biblical studies did not end with its emergence. It is now well known, for example, that members of the discipline of biblical studies were directly involved in the propaganda efforts in support of Nazi Germany. For example, Johannes Hempel, professor of New Testament at the University of Berlin, wrote in *Zeitschrift für alttestamentliche Wissenschaft*, "The opposition between the Third Reich and the Jews is a struggle for life and death."[23] Similarly, Walter Grundmann, professor of New Testament at the University of Jena and a member of the prestigious Societas Novi Testamenti Studiorum, was the director of the infamous Institute for the Study and Eradication of Jewish Influence on German Religious Life, which sought to "de-judaize" the New Testament.[24]

Furthermore, questions are now also raised about the shadow of "empire" latent behind the acceptable reading practices and foci of the discipline.[25] That is, the dominant reading practices of a profession are neither natural nor innocent. Such practices, whether those of the American Historical Association, the Modern Language Association, the American Academy of Religion, or the Society of Biblical Literature, both organize knowledge and create a professional, expert class in contrast to a so-called nonexpert class, as general studies of professional societies by Emile Durkheim, Talcott Parsons, and others have shown.[26] The net effect of this distinction in reading practices, moreover, is a power arrangement, an arrangement that reinscribes dominant reading practices while it disavows those that are not dominant.[27]

Interrogating a Myth of Innocence in Luke-Acts

These general reflections on the myths of innocence in biblical discourse aside, let us now take a sustained look at a specific mythic production of biblical literature and the issue of "empire."[28] My thesis is that Luke's motif of cosmopolitan beneficence is not innocuous, despite its otherwise alluring appeal. Rather, it draws on the discursive machinery of domination to negotiate prestige within the power complexes of the Greek East. To support this thesis, I first sketch the motif's presence in Luke-Acts and then expose the discursive machinery of domination that renders the motif a myth of innocence.

The Motif of Cosmopolitan Beneficence in Luke-Acts

It is well known that Luke-Acts highlights the theme of inclusion, especially given Luke's emphasis on the inclusion of women, the poor, the socially ostracized, the Gentiles, or some mixture of the above.[29] For example, Luke frequently mentions women (particularly in the Gospel according to Luke), with several women paired with men "either in the immediate context or in the larger structure of the gospel."[30] Likewise, Luke, following the Septuagint, appears to laud the poor and chastise the rich,[31] as can be seen in the contrast between the two groups in the so-called Sermon on the Plain (Luke 6:20-21; 6:24-25; see, by way of comparison, Luke 1:53). Moreover, in what is touted as Luke's programmatic statement (Luke 4:16-30), Jesus envisions his ministry as one in which he is sent to proclaim good news to the poor (Luke 4:18; see, by way of comparison, Luke 7:22).[32] And, in Acts, Luke continues to feature a concern for persons in need, as with the depiction of the early church as a virtually idyllic community of caring and sharing (Acts 4:32–5:11; 6:1-7; see, by way of comparison, Acts 11:29-30).[33] In the Gospel according to Luke, the openness of Jesus (the deity's chief mediating broker) extends to many others including those who are marginalized by virtue of their "occupation (toll collectors)," or their "moral and religious failure ('sinners')."[34] Luke's interest in the inclusion of Gentiles is also clear. As John T. Carroll has noted, "the direction of movement in the narrative is significant. Both Luke and Acts begin with scenes in Jerusalem, but the narrative ends in Rome, with Paul's assurance that the word of salvation will be heard among Gentiles (Acts 28:23-31)."[35]

To the extent that both volumes endorse the spread of the deity's good news and benefactions everywhere, moreover, Luke's theme of inclusion also highlights cosmopolitan beneficence. Accordingly, in the Gospel according to Luke, John and Jesus are cast as mediating brokers who herald their deity's claim to be the universal patron or benefactor.[36] And, in the book of Acts, that role is assigned to the twelve, the seven, or to Paul, all of whom are cast as powerful figures who make possible the propagation of the good news of Jesus' resurrection from Jerusalem to the imperial center, and, thus, they demonstrate the cosmic influence of their deity over every level of the society.[37]

As the deity's mediating brokers, moreover, the leading characters in both volumes are cast as philosophically virtuous, marking them as wise, just, courageous, and self-controlled representatives for the deity and as persons who are willing to suffer in order to share their deity's good news and benefactions, even in the presence of the most powerful local, regional, and imperial figures of that world.[38] Accordingly, in the Gospel according to Luke, John, like other philosophers, emphasizes sharing (3:10);[39] speaks against pretentiousness (3:8-9);[40] offers individuated counsel (3:10-14);[41] and, most importantly, dies at the hand of a tyrant (3:19-20; see, by way of comparison, 9:7-9).[42] And, Jesus, like other philosophers, is precocious in his childhood;[43] endures rigors;[44] speaks powerful sayings;[45] cultivates keenness of insight in his adult ministry;[46] and, most importantly again, is calm, innocent, and paradigmatic before two tyrannical figures at his death.[47]

Likewise, in Acts, the protagonists are depicted with the boldness (*parrēsia*, 9:27; 13:46; 14:3; 19:8; 26:26) of sages, with Stephen and Paul palpably drawn as exhibitors of self-mastery, a well-known philosophical ideal.[48] And, in the depiction of Paul's visit to Athens (Acts 17:16-34), Luke's allusions to Socrates (whether that of Paul's dialogical style of debate, *dielegeto* [17:17];[49] or Luke's reference to the "marketplace" [*agora*], which "imparts a Socratic flavour to the scene";[50] or the charge that he proclaimed foreign deities [17:18], which was "one of the two charges that the Athenians leveled against Socrates"[51]) all contribute to the casting of Paul in the guise of a philosopher.[52] According to Loveday Alexander, moreover, Paul's initiation of the "debate in the *agora*," in contrast to the usual pattern of going first to a synagogue, signals a venture toward a non-Jewish civic space, the ultimate examples of which will occur later when he is on trial, when Paul—like a Socrates—can state and demonstrate his readiness to die for his beliefs (20:22-24; 21:12-14).[53] Thus, clearly the motif of cosmopolitan beneficence resounds in both volumes, as the leading characters face increasingly more significant figures of that world with philosophical wisdom, boldness, and self-control.

The Motif's Problematic Discursive Machinery

Understandably, then, many modern (or postmodern) interpreters are attracted to Luke because the two volumes underscore the theme of inclusion, whether of women, the poor, the socially ostracized, or Gentiles on the one hand, or, relatedly, because the volumes emphasize the offering of God's good news and beneficence everywhere on the other. Given the long history of exclusion in the U.S. and elsewhere on many fronts, it is not difficult to see why many would find Luke's writings attractive.

For women interested in "dignity studies," that is, in the recovery of "positive examples [of women] from the past,"[54] the mention of women frequently might appear as a reason to praise Luke's writings. For those still reeling from the exploitative blows of the European "scramble for Africa"[55] or of the United State's own expansionist version of the "white man's burden,"[56] the Lukan perspective on the poor (concomitant with Lukan perspective on the proper use of possessions) would mark these volumes as laudable texts. And, for many whose histories in the U.S. are sullied with the soot of racist social marginalization, as would be true for many black and womanist theologians, the prominence of the role given to Africans (and/or black-skinned figures) among Luke's *dramatis personae* would commend Luke-Acts, and that not discounting the problems of a "hermeneutics of return."[57]

Acknowledgement of Luke's inclusiveness or cosmopolitan beneficence, though, should not lead to the conclusion that Luke-Acts is innocuous. Various parts of a culture may appear relatively benign until the underlying assumptions of those products are exposed.[58] That is, biblical texts may initially appear to be relatively benign until their underlying assumptions are shown to harbor demeaning images. As indicated in the examples that follow, Luke's motif of inclusion is replete with "double messages," which—even if explained in the light of Luke's strategic cultural reproduction of the past—are troubling and damaging in their effects.[59] So, although Luke certainly mentions women frequently (again, particularly in Luke), neither the Gospel according to Luke nor Acts assigns women the important role of being public leaders of the idyllic community.[60] As Turid Seim has noted, Luke gives a "double message,"[61] and accordingly, "'dignity studies' must be balanced by insight into mechanisms and structures of oppression and silencing."[62] As well, Luke's interest in the poor, while still present in Acts, wanes as a palpable concern as the narrative shifts from Jerusalem to the rest of the *oikoumenē*. Furthermore, the openness of Jesus to the socially marginalized often seems staged to pit Jesus against other "stylized" leaders who wish to exclude categorically toll collectors and sinners as dining partners.[63] And, neither the Gospel according to Luke nor Acts critiques slavery. As Mitzi J. Smith has shown, slaves in Luke-Acts are expendable (as with the slaves in the parable of the tenants, Luke 20:9-16), subject to another's command (as with the centurion's slave, Luke 7:1-10), and even comical (as with Rhoda who leaves Peter knocking at the outer gate, Acts 12:13), thus reinforcing the "social reality of the paterfamilias."[64] Within Acts, moreover, beyond the early Jerusalem scenes, the protagonists largely encounter persons of status, for example, the Ethiopian official (8:26-40), the centurion (10:1–11:18), leading women and men (13:50; 17:4; 12; 34; see, by way of comparison, 24:24; 25:13), and various magistrates (as with Felix, 24:16, and Agrippa II and Festus, 26:1-32). And, although Luke emphasizes the *inclusion* of Gentiles, none of the protagonists in either the Gospel or Acts are Gentiles.

So, we must ask: What then accounts for these multiple 'double messages'? And, notwithstanding the allure of Luke for our times, we must now also explore the whole machinery of discourse behind Luke's cosmopolitan beneficence to determine the extent to which this motif is not innocent but problematic. To proceed, we will need to understand the imperial context in which Luke wrote and the politics of respectability he likely adopted.[65]

Luke's Imperial Context

Luke-Acts is a cultural production written within an imperial context. Luke's earliest auditors likely not only felt the historical coercive pressures of Rome, marked by massive military forces and the extraction of taxes from colonized nations.[66] They likely also reckoned with the discursive ideological pressure of Rome's visible symbols of world domination, along with its divine expansionist claims, autoethnographic literary strategies, and scripted rendering of its own ethnic group as morally superior to all others.

In Rome, visible symbols of world domination included maps that listed all of the nations conquered or controlled by Rome,[67] triumphal monuments (for example, the Arch of Titus or Trajan's Column) to commemorate victories or campaigns over foreign nations, triumph celebrations in which "prisoners and spoils were paraded through the streets of the city,"[68] and coins with the goddess Roma either "holding a globe or with her foot upon the globe."[69] Yet, even beyond Rome, symbols of world domination were acknowledged, for Rome's citizens populated the cities; Rome's magistrates sat on tribunals, often with "a glint of legionary armour in the background";[70] provincial coins, calendars, and inscriptions honored Augustus and his successors;[71] "hymns, encomia and plays" gave homage to Roman military commanders;[72] and the imperial cult, which the local elites initiated for themselves, proliferated itself through a variety of media and public spaces (temples and games, public festivals, statues, and so on).[73]

Furthermore, Augustan propagandists were "capable of retrieving and manipulating the tradition [of the past] on a grand scale."[74] Thus, in the *Aeneid*, Virgil retrieves the distant past to cast Aeneas as "the executor of a divine universal plan which did not become visible until Virgil's time," namely, in the imperial reign of Augustus.[75] Rome is depicted as divinely ordained to rule an "empire without end,"[76] and Augustus is depicted as a descendant of Aeneas and a long-awaited restorer of peace.[77] That Aeneas's own journeys are drawn to parallel those of Odysseus, moreover, is Virgil's way not simply of depicting Aeneas as an epic-hero type, one capable of facing tests and perils without losing focus, but also Virgil's way of showing the divine protection of the hero in the face of the tests and perils.[78]

Moreover, the retrieval of history also reconfigures Rome's past shame to fit its present glory.[79] So, although Rome's story, as told by Virgil, is set against the backdrop of shame (which was a part of *The Odyssey*'s depiction of Rome), the *Aeneid* reconfigures the story of the Romans (or the ancient Trojans in *The Odyssey*) to overcome that "record of shame."[80]

Rome's claims of superiority also entailed a gendered elitist ethos. For elites in ancient Mediterranean societies, a contrast between austerity and self-control on the one hand and decadence on the other "represents an ethnocentric attempt on the part of Greeks and Romans to project and explain the relative positions of themselves and other peoples within the world by recourse to explanatory frameworks of competition, success, and failure appropriated from classical Athens of the fifth and fourth centuries B.C.E."[81] Furthermore, both austerity and self-control were viewed as *masculine* traits or virtues in opposition to decadence, which was viewed as *feminine*.[82] Accordingly, with misogynist rhetoric, ancient Mediterranean societies claimed these virtues to justify their right to rule and they denigrated various "others," whether "foreigners, slaves, [or] animals," as feminine and thus full of decadence.[83] Likewise, elite Romans (or their supporters) could also exploit the gendered contrast to justify the right of one Roman elite to rule as opposed to another—a point made vividly clear in the competition between Octavian and Antony.[84]

Luke, the Greek East, and Its Politics of Respectability

Given this imperial context and the gendered discursive strategies deployed by Rome's elites, Luke, like other elites in the Greek East during the consolidation of Rome's empire in the Flavio-Trajanic period (70–117 c.e.),[85] negotiated within the various "webs of power" that intermeshed at the "local, regional, imperial, and cosmic" levels.[86] Luke, thus, negotiated a politics of respectability.

What were the religio-political appeals in the Greek East in the Flavio-Trajanic period to ensure a politics of respectability? In brief, as Douglas Edwards has averred, such negotiations for power and prestige often stressed a group's links to antiquity or to venerated traditions,[87] the designation of certain leaders of a group as virtuous "cosmic power brokers" who were able to mediate power from a deity to the deity's adherents, and the travel of the group's leaders to indicate the spread of a group's influence (as seen in the ubiquity of shrines to its deity).[88]

With respect to antiquity and venerated traditions, for example, the whole of Luke-Acts is saturated with nods to antiquity, and it is likely that the nods negotiated ethnic pride for the Jesus movement. The account of the census (Luke 2:1-3), for example, is usually read as a sign of Joseph's obedience to the Roman order, and perhaps, in part, it should be so read.[89] The marked emphasis on the first occurrence of the census, however, may well also signal the relatively recent arrival of Roman power in contrast to the ancient venerable Jewish nation of which Bethlehem, the city of David, stands as a testament. Furthermore, the depiction of Jesus' birth as a part of a promise made long ago to Abraham (Luke 1:55, 73) also bespeaks the power and faithfulness of the Jewish deity. In Luke's retrieval of history, this deity has not just recently begun to care for generations. The deity's mercy has long aided the lowly and still does so (Luke 1:50-52). Pontius Pilate, with others, may have been the agents for Jesus' death, moreover, but the sordid spectacle of Jesus' trial and death, avers Luke, was a part of an old plan (Acts 2:23; see, by way of comparison, Acts 4:28), something God "announced beforehand by the mouths of all the prophets" (Acts 3:18; see, by way of comparison, Luke 24:26-27, 44), and, thus, not a result of Rome's imperial force.

With respect to the mediation of power, Luke portrays John the Baptist and Jesus (in the Gospel according to Luke) and Stephen, Peter, and Paul (in Acts) as "Septuagintal prophets," that is, as prophets who resemble in their powerful words and deeds the venerable Spirit-filled prophets or cosmic power brokers of the Septuagint: Moses, Elijah, Elisha, and so on. On the one hand, and in accordance with Jesus' prediction (Luke 21:15), the words of these cosmic power brokers are irresistible (Acts 6:3, 10). Their speech, moreover, is open and bold, and, as we have noted, on the order of philosophers (Acts 2:29; 4:13, 29, 31; 9:28; 14:3; 18:26; 26:26; 28:31).[90] On the other hand, the cosmic power brokers perform signs and wonders (*terata kai sēmeia megala*, Acts 2:19, 22, 43; 4:30; 5:12; 6:8; 7:36; 14:3; 15:12), which again makes them appear like the venerable Moses (Deut 7:19; 11:3; 28:46; 29:2).

With respect to the spread of the Jesus movement's influence, Luke honors Jerusalem as a "powerful geographical symbol" from which the idyllic community proceeds to the rest of the *oikoumenē*.[91] So, on the one hand, Luke connects the idyllic community to Jerusalem because the antiquity of Jerusalem, its worldwide fame (as noted, for example, by Josephus, *Jewish War*, 6.442; *Against Apion*, 2.79), and its status as the *omphalos* of Jewish life (also noted by Josephus, *Jewish War*, 3.52) brought a measure of prestige and power even if by Luke's time the city (and its temple) lay in ruins. On the other hand, Luke's protagonists, as adumbrated in Luke 24:47 and explicitly narrated throughout Acts, travel throughout the nations, an action that shows the spread of the movement and thus that "the movement has universal and worldwide significance."[92] Also, unlike the earliest Greek novels (Chariton's *Chaereas and Callirhoé* and *An Ephesian Tale* by Xenophon of Ephesus) that created a "Rome-free landscape," Luke creates a landscape more closely consonant with the political realities of the first century C.E.[93] Yet, within Luke's "mental map," even Rome, itself, would be conquered, as would any place where Jesus' followers would gather in worship to their deity.[94]

Why did Luke negotiate within the web of the aforementioned politics of respectability? One possible motivation was the rehabilitation of the image of Jesus given the ignominious character of his death, that is, death on a cross. Yet another motivation, as noted by John Lentz, was "to build up the status of the Christians so that the faith . . . [would] be attractive to the cosmopolitan, status-conscious world."[95] The effect of Luke's portraits of the Jesus movement, then, is that Luke's key characters are drawn as morally responsible and even superior characters "suitable for the public and civic forum" by virtue of their ideals.[96] As Penner and Vander Stichele have noted, though, such ideals "were inextricably linked to elite male performance in the ancient world."[97] Thus, in his efforts to gain respectability for the Jesus movement, particularly in the light of the ignominious character of Jesus' death, Luke negotiates within the "webs of power" by means of gendered discursive features that were already being deployed by other elites in the Greek East.

Conclusion

Thus, the well-known motif of inclusion (of women, the poor, the socially marginalized, and even of Gentiles in Luke-Acts), or cosmopolitan beneficence, is not an innocent offering of God's beneficence to all people. Rather, it is a gendered and elitist power play given sacral character as a part of a divine plan, and a legitimation motif for a minority group struggling to exert some form of prowess before the formidable presence of the Roman imperial complex. With the motif Luke, thus, mimics "empire."[98]

It should not go unmentioned, moreover, that the similarities some have seen between Luke's writings (the Gospel according to Luke and Acts) and ancient novelistic literature also mark Luke's agenda as one of an exertion of prowess, for the ancient Greek novels and ancient Jewish novelistic literature were all designed to "capture a sense of ethnic pride and competitiveness."[99] All of these works, then, employ a "hermeneutics of return" to express ethnic prowess in the face of Roman power. Thus, even if the intent is to oppose the colonizers, these writings do so through neocolonial discursive means. So, on the one hand, beneficence to all everywhere seems appealing. On the other hand, Luke's emphasis on cosmopolitan beneficence appears to be in competition with the Roman Empire's claims of worldwide benefaction. The motif of cosmopolitan beneficence subscribes to a Manichean, asymmetrical dichotomy that pits one group as superior to another, thus providing a basis for later colonizers who thought they were divinely appointed to bring "light" to "others" who—in their estimation—were "sitting in darkness" (Luke 1:79).[100] It defines salvation in exclusivistic terms (see, by way of comparison, Acts 4:12). It is linked to the imperialistic strategy of placing cities throughout the oikoumenē in a list to indicate implicitly the power of the movement over those cities.[101] It also construes its "ideals" as masculine.[102]

In my judgment, therefore, the motif of cosmopolitan beneficence is not innocent. When interrogated for its machinery of domination, the motif is dangerous. And, as examples from more recent times would bear out, the motif leads many benefactors to assume that they are divinely authorized to offer the beneficence and at whatever costs, whether the aid was requested or not.[103]

To return briefly then to the spirit of the questions first posed in this chapter, I suggest that the questions bespeak the need for a change in the self-understanding of biblical studies professionals. That is, when "empire" is taken seriously, professional biblical scholars must not view themselves simply as *interpreters* of biblical texts. Rather, they become *engaged public intellectuals* who seek also to evaluate the biblical texts, to examine the reception of the biblical texts in the formation of human subjectivity, and to proffer hermeneutics that would rewrite the history of the silent and oppressed voices of the biblical texts.[104] In the end, this interrogation and its concomitant professional self-assessment may make it possible for us never again to look at the biblical texts simply as "sacred" texts, unrelated to discourses of domination from the past or the most recent present. Rather, as engaged public intellectuals like Ralph Waldo Emerson and Richard A. Horsley have done, we must interrogate the whole machinery of domination behind what otherwise seems to be alluring and beneficial. To do otherwise is to fail to "taste blood in it."

11. Jesus' Subversive Victory Shouts in Matthew 27: Toward an Empowering Theology of the Cross

Robert Ekblad
Tierra Nueva and The People's Seminary

I WRITE THIS ESSAY AS DIRECTOR OF TIERRA NUEVA, an ecumenical ministry to immigrant farm workers from Mexico, prison inmates, and ex-offenders in Burlington, Washington. I serve as part-time chaplain to inmates in a county jail and as a pastor to people on the margins, especially immigrants, many of them undocumented. I also hold a degree in Old Testament, keeping a foot in the door of the academy through some research and writing and in graduate-level teaching through offering one course per semester here at The People's Seminary. I also lead retreats and teach seminars to leaders who work with people on the margins in different parts of the world. As a Bible scholar and pastor, in my particular ministry contexts, it is almost impossible not to be politically engaged (though not necessarily in a partisan way).

Reminders of barriers to liberation are in my face daily, forcing me to read scripture in search of true hope. The inmates, with whom I read, are up against impending deportation, charges that could lead to years in prison—often with no effective legal representation. In addition, they face ongoing addictions, chronic pain, incurable diseases like Hepatitis C and HIV/AIDS, restraining orders, relationship breakups, estrangement from children, exclusion from the church, loss of housing, and confiscation of property, together with heavy burdens of guilt, shame, self-hatred, and sadness.

Most of my insights come through a narrative reading of the biblical text rather than through a sociohistorical emphasis. This is not because I do not value perspectives gained from the disciplines of history and sociology; rather, I long to see people who feel hopelessly distanced from scripture, because of minimal education and functional illiteracy, empowered to find fresh, hopeful news in the lone tattered Bible to which they have access. I usually begin my Bible studies with an opening prayer. I invite someone to read the text, then ask questions that help people see parallels between their own lives and the scriptures. We conclude our reflections with some concrete enactment of whatever is most relevant to people's lives from the text.

The "hermeneutic of the street,"[1] as I encounter it among inmates and immigrants, is much closer to that of first-century interpreters than to modern scholarship in that scripture from anywhere is used to enlighten the text in hand. While I often model and even attempt to teach people on the margins how to read texts in their immediate literary contexts, I do not insist on sticking to one book. Freedom to transgress religious (or academic) rules must be cultivated among people who are already insecure before printed matter and sacred writings. They can learn the values of critical distance later, after having first become comfortable enough to enter into honest dialogue without fear of sanctions.

Real hope for transformation here and now is what caused the masses to follow Jesus. That is the picture depicted in the gospels, as well as in Richard Horsley's many studies on the life of Jesus and Paul.[2] Horsley's tremendous sensitivity, as a historian and exegete, to the effects of the sociopolitical realities of first-century Palestine on the struggles of ordinary people has inspired and encouraged me as a Bible scholar in the trenches of ministry. His own sensitivity to the plight of marginalized people in North America undoubtedly rightly influences his research, helping him see how Jesus offered real hope to the masses in his preaching of the kingdom of God.

Looking Again at the Cross

For many years, I sought solace in a theology of the cross that elevated Jesus' death beside us in weakness, and his apparent fruitlessness at the end of his ministry as a comfort. A gospel emphasizing God's willingness to become fully humble and downtrodden in Jesus, even to the point of renouncing glory, as well as God's effective power over "the powers" here and now, helped me stay in the trenches with the disinherited for years, despite seeing only very few of the most oppressed people break free. At the same time, I now realize that my version of a theology of the cross served as an apologetic for not seeing much real transformation among the most broken—the users of methamphetamines, crack cocaine, and heroin, perpetrators of domestic violence, and sex-offenders at the top of the list. I am no longer content with a theology that elevates the cross apart from the resurrection. Nor does it work for me to focus on Jesus' life of resistance as something to contemplate from a distance, with little expectation of seeing "greater things than these" among the damned here and now. I believe in death-defeating power unleashed through weakness, and I see it in Matthew's crucifixion account.

The hopelessness of many inmates and immigrants in crisis has pushed me to look more closely at the darkest passages of scripture, the passion narratives, for the possibility of hope. I have led a Bible study on Matthew 27, including an enactment of Jesus' two cries from the cross, on numerous occasions with immigrant farm workers, inner city activists, and graduate students of theology taking my course "Breaking the Chains: Biblical Perspectives on Resisting Personal and Structural Evil." This chapter is an adaptation of that Bible study, and I offer it in the hope that the "hermeneutic of the street" will open up new vistas for readers.

Looking for Hope in Unusual Places

Because we are searching for hope in the crucifixion, let us consider some of Paul's lines affirming power through weakness. In 1 Cor 1:18-25, Paul writes how the crucified Christ, the weakness of the cross, and God's weak-looking chosen ones bring down the strongholds of this world:

> For the message about the cross is foolishness to those who are perishing, but to us who are being saved it is the power of God. For it is written, "I will destroy the wisdom of the wise, and the discernment of the discerning I will thwart." Where is the one who is wise? Where is the scribe? Where is the debater of this age? Has not God made foolish the wisdom of the world? For since, in the wisdom of God, the world did not know God

through wisdom, God decided, through the foolishness of our proclamation, to save those who believe. For Jews demand signs and Greeks desire wisdom, but we proclaim Christ crucified, a stumbling block to Jews and foolishness to Gentiles, but to those who are the called, both Jews and Greeks, Christ the power of God and the wisdom of God. For God's foolishness is wiser than human wisdom, and God's weakness is stronger than human strength.

Paul hails Jesus' death on the cross as, itself, unleashing the power of God. How could the power of God be manifested in Jesus' death?

Let us bear in mind the larger context of Jesus' relationship to the powers in Matthew. According to Matthew's Gospel, Jesus exercised his authority as the Son of God in a way that made him free from the constraints put on him by the official authorities. This threatened the authorities (in Matthew, the high priests, scribes, and Pharisees), leading them to do everything possible to crush and, in every way, repress this announcer of the kingdom of God. While Jesus ignores their moves to stifle him, in the end he is depicted as knowingly submitting to their plots to destroy him. Jesus shows an awareness of the powers he is up against.

> Behold, we are going up to Jerusalem; and the Son of Man will be delivered up to the chief priests and scribes, and they will condemn him to death, and will deliver him up to the Gentiles to mock and scourge and crucify him, and on the third day he will be raised up. (Matt 20:18-19, NASB)

Later in Matthew, Jesus warns his disciples of trials that await them and him.

> Then they will deliver you up to tribulation, and will kill you, and you will be hated by all nations on account of My name. (Matt 24:9, NASB)

> You know that after two days the Passover is coming, and the Son of Man is to be delivered up for crucifixion. (Matt 26:2, NASB)

Readers accustomed to debilitating penal notions of the atonement that attribute Jesus' suffering to God[3] are surprised by what they find in the actual narrative. Many people on the streets have been exposed to the idea that Jesus had to die because God needed someone to pay the price so that God's demand for justice could be satisfied. This notion suggests that Jesus is actually sacrificed to God. In Matthew's account, however, it was *Judas* who "delivered Jesus up," and to the *chief priests* and *elders* (Matt 26:14-16, 47), not to God. The religious authorities had Jesus arrested (26:47) by a crowd. The chief priests and council falsely accused him before the high priest (26:59-64), who charged and convicted him (26:65), and condemned him to death (26:66). They went on to accuse him and hand him over to Pilate (27:2, 11-26) who had him beaten and delivered him over to the soldiers to be crucified (27:26). Matthew describes Jesus being sacrificed to the *Romans*; Matthew describes Pilate offering Jesus up to the Jewish authorities and their manipulated masses to satisfy them and their need for a scapegoat. But Matthew does not suggest that Jesus is offered up as a sacrifice to *God*. Rather, God is the assumed subject who raises Jesus up on the third day.

In Matthew's account, we see the religious authorities going to extreme measures to do away with Jesus' threat. They even put his tortured, dead body in a prison cave, sealing it and leaving armed guards, as we read in Matt 27:62-66:

> The next day, that is, after the day of Preparation, the chief priests and the Pharisees gathered before Pilate and said, "Sir, we remember what that impostor said while he was still alive, 'After three days I will rise again.' Therefore command the tomb to be made secure until the third day; otherwise his disciples may go and steal him away, and tell the people, 'He has been raised from the dead,' and the last deception would be worse than the first." Pilate said to them, "You have a guard of soldiers; go, make it as secure as you can." So they went with the guard and made the tomb secure by sealing the stone. (Matt 27:62-66)

No doubt, readers can name situations they are facing in their own lives or ministries that seem like no-exit situations. *What situations are you facing in your life or ministry that seem equivalent to Jesus' tortured, penalty-inflicted, bloodless body sealed in a heavily guarded stone tomb?* Men in the county jail mention the legal and prison systems; crack, methamphetamines, and alcohol addictions; unemployment; incarceration. Ministry practitioners who work with people at the margins mention some of these same forces, but add HIV/AIDS, the war in Iraq, global economic systems that keep peasants from a sustainable life in Mexico, racism, the military-industrial complex, the Israeli-Palestinian conflict, despair, consumer capitalism, species extinction, global warming, and other forces.

Let us consider Matt 28:1:

> After the Sabbath, as the first day of the week was dawning,
> Mary Magdalene and the other Mary went to see the tomb.

This is like us when we go and face problems that appear insurmountable. For some people involved in ministry in the face of the powers, going out to the drug corner, the jail, or their parish is analogous to the women going to see the tomb.

What reaction do you have when you are made especially aware of apparently insurmountable barriers to liberation? What do you feel in your gut as you stand before the equivalents of the sealed tomb?

People have mentioned emotions like anxiety, fear, anger, rage, despondency, and sadness. Some talk about a feeling of paralysis and hopelessness before what seems like a growing darkness and chaos. Despair before the obstacles to life and ministry overcomes any reasons to hope.

Yet, what the women find at the tomb leads to a surprising event. Let us consider Matt 28:2-4:

> And suddenly there was a great earthquake; for an angel of the Lord, descending from heaven, came and rolled back the stone and sat on it. His appearance was like lightning, and his clothing white as snow. For fear of him the guards shook and became like dead men.

Despair or nostalgia before death is interrupted by a great earthquake. Matthew's narrative unashamedly depicts help coming from heaven in the form of an angel, who descends to overcome all human attempts to keep Jesus dead and in every way repressed. These happenings strike such fear into the soldiers assigned to guard the dead man that they, themselves, become "like dead men." The angel makes sure that the women know that the event is not to terrify them, but, rather, to fill them with joy.

We continue by discussing the narrative of Matt 28:5-10:

> But the angel said to the women, "Do not be afraid; I know that you are looking for Jesus who was crucified. He is not here; for he has been raised, as he said. Come, see the place where he lay. Then go quickly and tell his disciples, 'He has been raised from the dead, and indeed he is going ahead of you to Galilee; there you will see him.' This is my message for you." (Matt 28:5-7)

The women respond to the good news by running away from the grave to announce to the disciples the incredible news. Then the risen Jesus, himself, meets the women, encouraging them not to be afraid, and sends them off to tell the disciples to go back to the place where they had experienced good news in Galilee, expectant of an encounter with someone on the other side of death.

> So they left the tomb quickly with fear and great joy, and ran to tell his disciples. Suddenly Jesus met them and said, "Greetings!" And they came to him, took hold of his feet, and worshiped him. Then Jesus said to them, "Do not be afraid; go and tell my brothers to go to Galilee, there they will see me." (Matt 28:8-10)

When might this power that led to the earthquake and opening of the tomb have been unleashed? This question shifts our attention to the crucifixion scene itself. *Is there any other time this kind of power is described as being released?*

According to Matthew's narrative, at Jesus' moment of greatest weakness, as he hangs upon the cross, power is released. This is when Jesus cried out with a loud voice, which actually happened two different times. This loud voice is literally a *phōnē megalē* (from which we derive our English word "megaphone"), which could be translated as a "great" or "big voice" or "noise." Each cry is important, reflecting two distinct symbolic actions on the part of Jesus.

The first cry happens in Matt 27:46.

> And about three o'clock Jesus cried with a loud voice, "Eli, Eli, lema sabachthani?" That is, "My God, my God, why have you forsaken me?"

I suggest that this cry represents Jesus' total solidarity in weakness with human beings who feel God's distance in their suffering. In fact the Greek verb here, *anaboan*, occurs only here in the entire New Testament.[4] This verb occurs in the Septuagint in Ezek 11:13, where the prophet falls on his face and cries out with a loud voice, in solidarity with the people: "Alas, alas, O Lord! Wilt thou utterly destroy the remnant of Israel?"

Here in Matthew, Jesus' cry given in a Greek transliteration of the Aramaic shows his identification with the common people, under Roman occupation, who were oppressed by the very ones who were crucifying him. This cry shows Jesus as humanly present, suffering alongside others. God's suffering presence in Jesus brings comfort to sufferers, much like ministries of presence and solidarity among the marginalized do today.

What would it mean for us to enact or actualize Jesus' cries in our own contexts, based on our reflections on the text? What would it mean for us to join with Jesus in his shout, "My God, my God, why have you forsaken me?" in solidarity with all who feel God's distance, and even abandonment, in the midst of suffering? We might all agree that we should cry out together with Jesus, but first we do well to ponder silently Jesus' anguish and that of others today who suffer from depression, loneliness, grief, or other afflictions. Together we cry out with Jesus. The shout feels almost blasphemous, but potent.

But this cry, alone, is not enough. People in bleak, no-exit situations also need God to come in power. Ministries emphasizing solidarity and presence alongside those who are suffering are essential, but they must also come to appreciate and embrace Jesus' second cry that releases power.

After a period of silence in Matthew's narrative, as people try in vain to bring relief by offering the dying Jesus sour wine, Jesus cries out with a loud voice a second time and releases his spirit:

> Then Jesus cried again with a loud voice and breathed his last [literally, released his spirit]. (Matt 27:50)

Jesus' second cry can be interpreted as a loud cry of victory or possibly even a war cry—but in a way different from a triumphalistic cry. This cry is followed by his releasing of his spirit.[5] The Greek term here, *aphiēmi* (to forgive, let go, release, drop) signals that Jesus' loud cry and the release of his spirit accomplish many powerful things on behalf of people.

Consider Matt 27:51-54:

> At that moment the curtain of the temple was torn in two, from top to bottom. The earth shook, and the rocks were split. The tombs also were opened, and many bodies of the saints who had fallen asleep were raised. After his resurrection they came out of the tombs and entered the holy city and appeared to many. Now when the centurion and those with him, who were keeping watch over Jesus, saw the earthquake and what took place, they were terrified and said, "Truly this man was God's Son!"

Jesus' loud cry achieves five significant liberations:

1. The veil in the temple is torn in two from top to bottom (27:51), suggesting God's removal of the separation between what we might call "clergy" and "laity," the religious leaders and the masses, the holy God and the profane people, the heaven and earth.[6] God rips the curtain from top to bottom, showing that this separation can only be lifted as a divine act.
2. The earth shook (27:51), showing how Jesus' cry represents a revelation of the glory of God as at Sinai (Exodus 19).
3. Rocks are split, showing that some of the hardest elements of this world are busted apart at this moment of God's total weakness.
4. Tombs were opened and many bodies of the saints that had fallen asleep were raised.
5. Finally, the centurion and others keeping watch, the executioners who work for the powers, are terrified and come to recognize Jesus' true identity as the Son of God as they recognize the power of Jesus' loud cry.

Consider other scriptures that support this reading of the loud cry as a victory cry. Read Josh 6:20, for example, where the same term occurs in the Septuagint:

> So the people shouted and the trumpets were blown. As soon as the people heard the sound of the trumpets, they raised a great shout, and the wall fell down flat; so the people charged straight ahead into the city and captured it.

In the Gospel according to John, Jesus follows being deeply disturbed in his spirit (John 11:38) before the death of his friend Lazarus with a loud cry: "'Lazarus, come out!' And the dead man came out" (John 11:43-44, NRSV).

Read the account of Paul's healing of a man crippled from birth that illustrates how crying out with a loud voice releases physical healing.

> In Lystra there was a man sitting who could not use his feet and had never walked, for he had been crippled from birth. He listened to Paul as he was speaking. And Paul, looking at him intently and seeing that he had faith to be healed, said in a loud voice, "Stand upright on your feet." And the man sprang up and began to walk. (Acts 14:8-10)

Crying out with a loud voice represents pledging a counterallegiance, an allegiance to Jesus contrary to that demanded by the powers and principalities.

> After this I looked, and there was a great multitude that no one could count, from every nation, from all tribes and peoples and languages, standing before the throne and before the Lamb, robed in white, with palm branches in their hands. They cried out in a loud voice, saying, "Salvation belongs to our God who is seated on the throne, and to the Lamb!" And all the angels stood around the throne and around the elders and the four living creatures, and they fell on their faces before the throne and worshiped God, singing, "Amen! Blessing and glory and wisdom and thanksgiving and honor and power and might be to our God forever and ever! Amen." (Rev 7:9-12)

A loud voice is heard from heaven announcing Jesus' victory over death and all the powers in Rev 12:10-12:

> Then I heard a loud voice in heaven, proclaiming, "Now have come the salvation and the power and the kingdom of our God and the authority of his Messiah, for the accuser of our comrades has been thrown down, who accuses them day and night before out God. But they have conquered him by the blood of the Lamb and by the word of their testimony, for they did not cling to life even in the face of death. Rejoice then, you heavens and those who dwell in them! But woe to the earth and the sea, for the devil has come down to you with great wrath, because he knows that his time is short!"

A multitude in heaven echoes this voice, celebrating the judgment of the great whore Babylon.

> After this I heard what seemed to be the loud voice of a great multitude in heaven, saying, "Hallelujah! Salvation and glory and power to our God, for his judgments are true and just; he has judged the great whore who corrupted the earth with her fornication, and he has avenged on her the blood of his servants. (Rev 19:1-2)

Finally, the loud cry is associated directly with a roar, which unleashes God's work in the world in Rev 10:3:

> He gave a great shout, like a lion roaring. And when he shouted, the seven thunders sounded.

In light of these readings, let us again consider the many obstacles to life and liberation that people are confronting today. At first, we may resist getting personal, mentioning only the larger structural obstacles: indebtedness, the war in Iraq, racism, HIV/AIDS, global warming, poverty. But then we may begin to share obstacles to healing and liberation that are closer to home. People mention cancer, addiction to methamphetamines, alcohol, painkillers, and other drugs. Depression, addiction to pornography, jealousy, anger, hatred, and lust are also vocalized, along with many other things.

Imagine setting ourselves against these things as we prepare to join Jesus in his final shout. I suggest that our shout, like Joshua's before the walls of Jericho and Jesus' before the tomb of Lazarus, is powerful because of the Holy Spirit of God that is released.

Together we shout, as loud as we are able. Some people shudder and even cry after this shout. The shout breaks a dam, opening people in extraordinary ways. People report emotional release and even healing; others report a revival of hope. The shout is an act of radical faith in God's superior power, released in the moment of greatest weakness and vulnerability. The kingdom of God is released as the Holy Spirit is released over the earth, where it hovers over the darkness and chaos, awaiting the word: "Let there be light"; and God's response: "There was light!" Life from the dead.

I conclude with a poem, written by Brita Miko after she participated in this same Bible study.

The Scream[7]

There is the scream. The scream so loud it will be the last word.
The scream so loud it will render the man mute. The scream
so loud the man will die. You cannot release such a cry and
survive. You can only release such a cry if it is the last thing you
do. You can only release such a cry if all things are done.
It is the cry of death.
It fills the whole earth. The very earth shudders. The very earth
splits. The very earth might not survive. The very earth tears.
The very rocks tear.
And history tears. And all stories tear. My story tears.
And the cry is more than volume, more than decibels, more
than sound. The cry is the power of death. The cry is the power
of life. The cry releases power.
There is the moment of the cry. There is the moment the man
dies. But what is released in his cry and what is released in his
death is life.
The dead rise.

The dead walk.
The dead are given a way through.
Because his spirit, which exits his body, fills the very earth. And
the earth cannot hold still. And the dead spill out like salt, like
salt pouring out through the millions of tiny holes torn in the
earth. The dead spill. They rush back into life like children into
their mothers' arms, like babies carried by a river on, like an
infant sailing through the air. His exiled spirit fills this earth
with life.

Life.
Like bread.
Like wine.
Like what you always longed to ingest.

Life.
Like hope.
Like a future.
Like a meaning you always wished to believe.

Life.
Like jumping.
Like floating.
Like a body you actually belong in.

Life.
Like peace.
Like grace.
Like everything old and stupid and done being forgotten.

Life.
Like joy.
Like laughter.
Like children climbing into your heart.

Life.

Like energy.
Like voltage.
Like light so comforting you don't miss the dark.

Life.
Like miracles.
Like magic.
Like fairytales becoming truth.

Life.
Like blood.
Like water.
Like all that flows within you.

Life.
Like breath.
Like spirit.
Like inhaling the love of God.

And in the scream, life left his body and entered ours. And in the scream, one boy with black hair dies and another boy with black hair comes back to life.

Life.
Like change.
Like difference.
Like your dead son returning home.

PART III
Prospects for Politically Engaged Biblical Studies

———————◆———————

12. Reading Scripture in the Context of Empire

Elisabeth Schüssler Fiorenza
Harvard Divinity School

THIS COLLECTION OF ESSAYS HONORS RICHARD HORSLEY who has consistently attempted to draw connections between ancient texts and contemporary political meanings. In the past several years, his work has focused on empire[1]—the Roman and the American—and assessed the contributions of postcolonial theory to biblical studies.[2] Hence, it is appropriate that the editors have invited us to reflect in his honor on the question as to what it would mean for biblical scholarship to take the Bible into the public square.

Since the Moral Majority in the 1970s and the Christian New Right in the 1980s and 1990s have used biblical language for legitimating the militaristic politics of the U.S. as a global superpower,[3] the language of religion, in general, and scripture, in particular, has played a major role in public discourses. Hence, it is important that biblical scholars and biblical readers critically assess the rhetorical power of scripture,[4] which is claimed to be the authoritative revealed, sacred word of G*d.[5] Those who want to take the Bible into the public square and to read the signs of the times, need not only to critically assess the Bible's function in public discourse but also to enable readers to question its authority, which has been understood throughout the centuries in analogy to imperial power. Such power of empire is wielded by a few and demands the obedience and submission of the many, either in the name of G*d or in the name of patriotism.

Hence, biblical scholars have to explore not only how the power of empire has historically shaped and affected Christian scriptures, but also how it continues to shape cultural and religious self-understandings today. Christian scriptures and interpretations, I argue, could and can rightly be used in the service of empire, colonialist expansion, and heterosexist discrimination because they have been formulated in the context of Roman imperial power.[6] Therefore biblical language is determined by this rhetorical-political imperial context. If people do not become aware of the language of empire at work today, they internalize the ethos of empire: violence, exclusion, and submission to G*d, the almighty King and Christ the Lord, in and through the process of reading scripture.

In order to avoid such internalizations of the ethos of empire, scholars need to develop an understanding of scripture that will allow people to deal critically with the scriptural language of empire rather than compel them to repeat and reinscribe it today. Historically, the language of democracy has provided an alternative discourse to imperialism and domination. Although democracy has different shades of meaning that are not always liberating, democracy, through the times, has been and still is the discourse that sets the terms for critique of imperial power and institutions and creates the basis for their change.[7] Radical democracy that I have called the *ekklēsia* of wo/men[8] offers the language and space for the imagination to develop a public religious discourse, "wherein justice, participation, difference, freedom, equality and solidarity set the ethical conditions."[9]

The challenge for biblical scholars today, then, is to develop modes of interpretation that can not only recognize imperial biblical language but also are able to trace languages and imaginations of radical democratic equality, which are different from those of empire, inscribed in scripture and Christian discourses. Since Christian fundamentalism draws on the language of empire inscribed in Christian scriptures, progressive biblical scholarship needs not only to critically make such inscriptions conscious but also to articulate elements of a radical-democratic-egalitarian vision that is also inscribed in Christian scriptures. This is not just an inner-Christian problem, but is a challenge to all those who seek to change the cultural-political ethos of empire today, and it becomes more and more pressing at a time when, in the name of G*d and the Bible, antidemocratic tendencies are on the rise.

To explore this problem more fully, I will *first* discuss the contemporary context of our reading of scripture. In a *second* step, I will reflect on the rhetorical power ascribed to scripture and, *finally*, indicate an approach to scripture that is able to recognize the inscriptions of empire and free us from their internalizations of subordination.

Empire as the Context of Scripture Today

In recent years, New Testament or, as I would prefer, Christian Testament[10] scholarship has rediscovered or reemphasized the Roman Empire and its impact on early Christian life and literature as an important field of study. Such studies of the Roman Empire have emerged in the biblical academy at the same time as publications on contemporary forms of empire and its exploitations have been discussed widely.

While the study of the Roman Empire has always been part and parcel of historical Christian Testament scholarship, such studies have often tended to either celebrate Rome's accomplishments as a great civilizing power in the Mediterranean world of the first century c.e., or they have narrowly focused on the persecution of Christians by the Roman authorities. For instance, in the 1980s a debate ensued in scholarship on the book of Revelation between scholars of liberation theology who read the book's symbolic language as anti-Roman and other scholars who denied that harassment and persecutions of Christians were at work, at all, at the time.[11] Those scholars praised the benevolent cultural impact of imperial Rome for the citizens of Asia Minor, reading the anti-Roman symbolic language of this book as expressing the "resentment" of the author. In contrast, the new scholarship on empire and scripture tends to read such language as critical of the Roman Empire without pointing out the inscription of empire in and through the Bible into public discourse and religious ethos.

This renewed focus of early Christian scholarship on the Roman Empire and its exercise of power has been invigorated by new approaches in the field of classics, such as the study of Roman imperialism and cultural studies. It also has benefited from inspirations from postcolonial biblical studies and their forerunner, liberationist biblical studies. However, like all malestream studies, it has not much engaged with or learned from critical feminist studies. This new approach has left its footprints in diverse areas of early Christian studies, but it has especially sought to change Pauline studies, which have focused on Paul, the great individual, and his religious opponents rather than on Paul's sociopolitical context, the imperial power of Rome.

Nevertheless, such studies often still proceed in an apologetic fashion. Studies of the gospels, the Pauline literature, or other Christian Testament writings and their attitude toward the Roman Empire have tended to argue that these writings were critical of Roman imperial power and resisted its structures of domination. Yet, such an argument overlooks that even resistance literature will reinscribe the structures of domination that it seeks to overcome. For instance, writings like the book of Revelation transfer the titles of the Roman emperor to G*d and Christ when they describe G*d as a great monarch and Christ as King of Kings and Lord of Lords. Although Revelation uses imperial language as anti-language, it still reinscribes the ethos of empire so that Bible readers are convinced that G*d sits on a throne or Christ is Lord and King.

The gospels also function as apologetics of empire insofar as they displace the responsibility for the execution of Jesus from the Roman imperial representatives to the Jews and, thereby, continue to engender anti-Judaism in and through their proclamations. The Pauline literature, in turn, fosters imperial subordination, insofar as it interprets the execution of Jesus as dying for our sins, which, according to 1 Timothy, were brought into the world by a wo/man. The stress of the post-Pauline literature on the subordination and obedience of slave and freeborn wo/men as well as of the whole community to kyriarchal (that is, emperor, lord, slave-master, father, husband, propertied free male) authority fuels the Christian Right's rhetoric on family values and same sex marriage.

In short, if one does not consciously question the language of imperial domination in which early Christian texts remain caught up, one can not but internalize it either in cultural or religious terms. For instance words such as "gospel" or "*parousia*" are derived from the ideology and propaganda of the Roman Empire. "Gospel" meant first the "good news" about the emperor and, in an analogous way, also the "good news" of G*d. It announces the glad tidings brought about by Roman imperial power and, in an analogous way, the glad tidings brought about by G*d. *King* and *lord* are first titles of the emperor, celebrating his power of domination and, in an analogous way, construe the power of G*d in imperial terms.

In attempting to rescue early Christian scriptures as anti-imperial literature, scriptural apologetics tends to overlook that the language of empire and its violence, which is encoded in Christian scriptures, has shaped Christian religious and Western cultural self-understanding and ethos throughout the centuries, and still does today. Hence, today this language is understood as legitimating a culture of domination, even if in its original setting it was used as anti-language. Such language of domination, subordination, obedience, and control is not just historical language. Rather as sacred scripture, it is performative language that determines Christian identity and praxis. It does not need just to be understood, but must be made conscious and critically evaluated.

However, academic biblical scholars are, for the most part, not trained to investigate and study the interplay of biblical imperial language and ethos with contemporary public discourses. The historical-philological bent of the field and the defense of biblical writers such as Paul as anti-imperial have prevented critical exploration of the workings of scripture texts and language in public discourses today.

True, this new interest of biblical scholars in the study of the Roman Empire has been engendered by public discussions of the U.S. or globalization as an imperial, political, and cultural power, but, for the most part, it has not focused on how the discipline needs to change to equip biblical readers to read "the signs of the times." The intellectual context of such studies, moreover, has not just been the renewed popular and academic interest in empire but also the arrival of postcolonial criticism,[12] although postcolonial studies have tended to see themselves as the more sophisticated replacement of liberation theologies. Because of their location in the academy they are less equipped to move out of the academy and into the public square.[13] Finally, the growing political influence of biblical and other religious fundamentalisms around the world has sparked renewed interest in religion. Religious violence has become a topic of intense discussion in the universities, but less so in biblical studies.

In the past few years, a stream of books has appeared indicting the U.S. as empire or conceptualizing globalization in terms of empire. Some of these books discuss the rise and fall of the American empire. Others argue that China will be the next empire in the global market. Again, others elaborate the moral and economic price to be paid for being an empire. While the American people fervently believe that the U.S. is a democracy, some historians argue that it has always been an empire.

As in earlier instances, so, also, the present expansion of the capitalist globalization of empire is secured by the American military-industrial complex. In his book *American Empire*, Andrew Bacevich, a former military officer, quotes Theodore Roosevelt who, in December 1899, stated, "Of course, our whole national history has been one of expansion," and Madeleine Albright, who in February 1998, remarked: "If we have to use force, it is because we are America. We are the indispensable nation." To quote Bacevich:

> Bill Clinton interpreted the end of the Cold War as signifying the "fullness of time"—a scriptural allusion to the moment when God choose to transform history. . . . As the bloody twentieth century drew to a close, God's promise of peace on earth remained unfulfilled; it was now incumbent upon the United States, having ascended to the status of sole superpower, to complete God's work—or as members of a largely secularized elite, preferred it, to guide history toward its intended destination.[14]

The present expansion of capitalist globalization is secured by the military-industrial complex and justified also in Christian religious terms. As Kim Yong-Bok observes:

> The emergence of the Global Empire provides the new global context of theology. This context is ecumenical and universal. No theological reflection can avoid this context. All faiths and religions are bound to deal with this context. There may be different starting points, depending on the locus of the faith community. Whether one is at the seat and center of the empire or at its periphery, one is not outside of the empire.[15]

Economic globalization[16] has been created with the specific goal of giving primacy to corporate profits installing and codifying such market-values globally. It was designed to amalgamate and merge all economic activities around the world within a single model of global monoculture. Neocapitalist globalization of the economy, which keeps profits high by outsourcing and reducing labor costs, has engendered a redistribution of wealth from the middle and working classes into the hands of the top ten percent of the population. Such capitalist and militarist globalization conceived in terms of empire threatens democracy and human rights.

Yet, globalization also presents possibilities for a more radical democratization worldwide. It narrows geographical distances between people, fosters their growing interdependence, makes experientially available the interconnectedness of all beings, and engenders the possibility of communication and solidaristic organization across national boarders on the basis of human rights and justice for all.

Consequently, religious communities and biblical studies face a theo-ethical choice today: We can strengthen global capitalist dehumanization, or we can support the growing interdependence of people; we can spiritually sustain the exploitation of capitalist globalization, or we can engage the possibilities of radical democratization for greater freedom, justice, and solidarity. Religion can either foster fundamentalism, exclusivism, and the exploitation of a totalitarian global monoculture, or it can advocate radical democratic spiritual values and visions that celebrate diversity, multiplicity, tolerance, equality, justice, and well-being for all. Such an ethical either-or choice does not reinscribe the dualisms created by structures of domination, but struggles to overcome and abolish them.

Yet, in the public square, the religious right and the emergence of global cultural and religious fundamentalisms claim the power to define the true nature and essence of religion. Right-wing religious movements around the globe have insisted in the past decades on the figuration of emancipated wo/men either as signifiers of Western decadence or of modern atheistic secularism, and, at the same time, they have presented masculine power as the expression of divine power. The interconnection between religious antidemocratic arguments and the debate with regard to wo/men's place and role is not accidental or of merely intrareligious significance.

Christian religion and scriptures have been used consistently for legitimating Western expansionism and military rule as well as for inculcating the mentality of obedience and submission to the powers of empire. The Bible and biblical studies are clearly implicated in empire since they are associated with Western colonialism. This is aptly expressed in the pithy saying usually ascribed to Archbishop Desmond Tutu: When the missionaries arrived they had the Bible and we had the land. Now we have the Bible and they have the land.

The form of biblical and religious legitimization most closely associated with colonialism has been monarchical Catholicism and biblicist Protestantism, both of which are oriented toward the salvation of the soul and profess an individualistic theology, which preaches personal submission to the authority of scripture or to the pope. In contrast, critical biblical studies, at first glance, seem not to be aligned explicitly with Western imperialism because they allegedly are driven by scientific rationality and objectivity. Yet, anyone studying the history of biblical scholarship will recognize that it has been articulated for the most part not only by elite, Western-educated clergymen but also in the interest of imperial, cultural, and political power. In recent years, critical feminist and postcolonial biblical studies have amply documented this function of positivist biblical scholarship in the interest of empire, whereas feminist studies have shown that the majority of those dehumanized by global imperialism are wo/men and children dependent on wo/men.

In many respects wo/men are suffering not only from the globalization of market capitalism, but also from the sexual exploitation instigated by it. However, the scriptural roots of systemic inequality, abuse, violence, discrimination, starvation, poverty, neglect, and denial of wo/men's rights, which afflict the lives of wo/men around the globe, are still not taken seriously by biblical scholars but seen as an unacademic special-interest issue of middle-class white wo/men. However, a glance at statistical data on wo/men's situations around the world will easily show that wo/men as a group are disadvantaged worldwide in and through the processes of globalization. Wo/men still earn, in most parts of the world, only two-thirds of what men in similar situations earn; the majority of people living in poverty are wo/men; violence against wo/men and genocide, that is the killing of wo/men, is on the increase; sexual trafficking, various forms of forced labor, illiteracy, migration, and refugee camps spell out globally wo/men's increasing exploitation. Rose Wu sums up this situation:

> The borderless societies that the global economy promotes continue to exploit women by selling them as "wives," forcing them into prostitution or engaging them in other kinds of exploitative work, such as working in sweatshops or working as domestic labour. . . . Women displaced from farms and collapsed domestic industries because of trade liberalisation have been forced to seek survival by migrating to foreign lands

where they often suffer abuse and harsh treatment at the hands of their recruiters and/or employers. Many become victims of sex trafficking.[17]

Wo/men's struggles for survival and well-being must therefore remain at the heart of all discussions of global empire and its death-dealing violence. The question of feminism and scripture, I argue, must become central to any discussion of empire, globalization, and religion since, according to fundamentalist voices, feminism equals godless humanism and Western decadence. Because the authority of the Bible as the "word of G*d" has been and still is used to justify the violence of empire against wo/men, it is necessary to investigate more closely what kind of power scripture develops in the public square.

Power and Scripture

To bring notions of scripture and empire together has an irritating, upsetting, and disturbing effect on people's minds; it jars religious imagination and sensibilities. Whereas scripture is believed by many to be the authoritative sacred word of G*d, empire evokes the notion of domination, conquest, and subjugation. If scripture is understood as demanding unquestioned obedience and submission, it is conceived in terms of empire. At the same time, it is claimed that scripture is the liberating word of a just and loving G*d. This understanding of scripture is contradictory to and clashing with the rhetoric of empire that advocates domination and submission. Hence, it is necessary to learn how to distinguish the sacred power of scripture from the power of empire if biblical readers are to be able to resist the global exploitation of empire.

Such an adjudication is possible because power can be seen and exercised not only as "power over," as power of domination and rule, as control and command, as the power of empire. Power also can be understood as "power for," or as "power to," as capacity, energy, and potential,[18] as energizing, enabling, and transformative power, as creative activity and strength.[19] The power of scripture can be wielded only by a few to dominate the many, or it can be seen as energizing everyone, as enriching, creative possibility for community and justice.[20]

If power always has this dual connotation, then biblical readers must learn to adjudicate in a process of critical evaluation what kind of power each scriptural text espouses and authorizes, since Christian scriptures share in the rhetoric of "power over" and in the "power to." In light of these two definitions of power, scripture can be understood as "power over" in terms of the imperial command-obedience, superordination, and submission structure inscribed in scripture, or it can be seen as enabling and energizing power.

The power of the Word to exclude and to legitimate wo/men's second-class citizenship and, thereby, to reinscribe the "power over" of empire is explicit, for instance in the following Pauline injunction:

> As in all the *ekklēsiai* [assemblies] of the saints,
> the women should keep silence in the *ekklēsiai* [assemblies].
> For they are not permitted to speak,
> but should be subordinate, as even the law says.
> (1 Cor 14:33b-34, my translation)

Not all scriptural texts are so obvious in promoting imperial power relations, but all of them must be carefully analyzed and critically assessed as to what kind of power they advocate. Insofar as the power of the Word and the authority of scripture as "power over" are understood as divinely sanctioned, the authority of scripture has been understood in analogy to imperial power that is exercised by a few and demands submission and obedience from the many. Biblical interpretation, therefore, can not but reinscribe the rhetoric of empire as divine rhetoric if it understands scripture as the direct word of G*d.

Scriptural language symbolization and rhetoric call for critical feminist assessment and theo-ethical evaluation in contemporary rhetorical situations of empire. Such a critical ideological evaluation is necessary because the symbolic world of scripture is not only a theo-ethical model of its own sociopolitical-religious world but also serves as a theo-ethical model for sociopolitical-religious life today. The scriptural language and metaphors we use shape our perception of the world in which we live. The uncritical fundamentalist or positivist reinscriptions of the rhetoric of empire as the word of G*d do not simply misunderstand or misconstrue Scripture. Rather, they are correct because the Roman and other Near Eastern empires are, as the context of scripture, historically constitutive of it.

Nevertheless, inscribed in scripture is not only the rhetoric of empire as "power over," and its demand for submission, suffering, obedience, and control. We also still can find traces of an alternative rhetoric of power that understands power as "power to," as creative, liberating "power for." Hence, all language of power inscribed in scripture must be carefully explored and critically assessed in terms of what it does to those who submit to its sacred power of imagination: whether it advocates imperial "power over" or radical democratic "power to." What the Spirit says today to our own particular sociopolitical situations must be assessed in an ethical practice of rhetorical analysis and critique of ideology that can trace G*d's power for justice and well-being both in the Bible and in today's political struggles against the domination of global empire.

Sacred Scripture and Its Interpretation

However, biblical readers are not taught to engage in such a critical reading of scripture. Biblical readers, early on, learn to develop strategies of textual valorization and validation rather than hermeneutical skills to critically interrogate and assess scriptural interpretations and texts along with their visions, values, and prescriptions. In order to foster the ability of spiritual discernment, cultural and religious education needs to enable readers to take a critical stance toward all human words, especially to those that claim the unmediated power and authority of G*d. Whereas historical and literary biblical scholarship has flourished, biblical studies has generally neglected its critical-theological or ideology-critical task. Hence, neither biblical scholarship nor biblical readers are able to understand the authority of scripture as inviting them, in a critical process of discernment, to liberate the words of scripture from their inscriptions of empire.

Instead of giving the power of interpretation to so-called popular audiences or common readers, biblical scholarship and preaching generally do not give people the tools for investigating the ideologies, discourses, and knowledges that shape their religious self-identities and determine their lives. Instead of empowering Bible readers as critical thinkers, education in general and biblical education in particular often contributes to their self-alienation and adaptation to the values of imperial society and religion.

An objectivist scientific academic ethos neglects the spiritual desire for the sacred that has brought many students to the university and to the study of the Bible.[21] bell hooks reflects on this experience, saying that she knew when she went to Stanford University from her small town that there would be no "discussion of divine spirit." Her years of teaching at elite universities confirmed the knowledge "that it was only the mind that mattered, that any care of our souls—our spirits—had to take place in private." However, as a student and later as a faculty member she continued to "reclaim the sacred at the heart of knowing, teaching and learning." Hence she asserts: "It is essential that we build into our teaching vision a place where spirit matters, a place where our spirits can be renewed and our souls be restored."[22]

A feminist-emancipatory, radical-democratic model of biblical reading seeks to inhabit this visionary space "where spirit matters," a space that I have called the "open house of wisdom."[23] In this space, biblical studies no longer serve to internalize kyriarchal biblical teachings and malestream scientific knowledges, but they seek to foster critical thinking, ethical accountability, and intellectual self-esteem. The basic assumption is that knowledge is publicly available to all and that everyone has something to contribute to religious knowledge. Such an ethos seeks to engender radical democratic thinking, which requires a particular quality of vision and civic imagination.

Feminist postcolonial biblical studies are, thus, best understood in a radical democratic Wisdom key insisting that all wo/men are competent biblical interpreters. They seek to facilitate wo/men's critical readings by fostering examination of our own presuppositions and social locations. Radical democratic Bible study searches for freedom from cultural bias and religious prejudice and seeks to replace them with critical arguments that appeal to both reason *and* the emotions. It wants to foster the ability to ask what it would be like to be in the shoes of someone different from oneself and to see the world from the point of view of another who is not like oneself, but still much like oneself.

Instead of looking to "great books" and "great men," a radical-democratic model of biblical reading/learning in the open house of Wisdom engages in critical questioning, exploration, and debate in order to be able to arrive at a deliberative judgment about the Bible's contributions to the "good life," to democratic self-determination and self-esteem. It is about choice, deliberation, and the power to take charge of our own life and thought, rather than about control, dependence, obedience, and passive reception. Its style of reasoning is not combative-competitive but deliberative, engaging in conversations about values and beliefs that are most important to us rather than retreating into positivism, dogmatism, or relativism that avoids engagement with differences.

In this Wisdom model of learning, thought and study are problem-oriented rather than positivistic or dogmatic, perspectival rather than relativistic; they are contextual collaborative, recognizing that our own perspective and knowledge are limited by our social-religious location and that differences enrich our thought and life. Truth and meaning are not a given fact or hidden revelation but are achieved in critical practices of deliberation.

To be able to achieve a constructive engagement with religious difference and diversity inscribed in the Bible and in contemporary reading contexts, biblical readers need to become aware of the pitfalls of one-dimensional thinking that strives to find in the Bible definite answers and final solutions. As the Jewish feminist Alicia Suskin Ostriker so succinctly puts it:

> Human civilization has a stake in plural readings. We've seen this at least since the eighteenth century when the notion of religious tolerance was invented to keep the Christian sects from killing each other. The notion of racial tolerance came later. . . . Most people need "right" answers, just as they need "superior" races. . . . At this particular moment it happens to be feminists and other socially marginal types who are battling for cultural pluralism. Still, this is an activity we're undertaking on behalf of humanity, all of whom would be the happier, I believe, were they to give up their addiction to final solutions.[24]

Because of the all-too-human need to use the Bible in an imperialistic way for bolstering our identity over and against that of others, because of our need for using the Bible as a security blanket, as an avenue for controlling the divine, or as a means for possessing revelatory knowledge as an exclusive privilege, we are ever tempted to use scripture as a weapon to keep others in line: the homosexuals, the feminists, or the terrorists.

To understand the Bible in the paradigm of the open, cosmopolitan house of Divine Wisdom allows one to conceptualize scripture as an open-ended prototype rather than as an archetype that has to be repeated in every generation. It enables one to understand the Bible as a site of struggle over meaning and biblical interpretation as debate and argument, rather than as transcript of the unchanging, inerrant Word of G*d. It requires that we rethink the notion of struggle, debate, and argument that is usually understood in terms of battle, combat, and competition. Within the radical democratic space of Wisdom-Spirit, struggle can be recognized as turning conflict into opportunity and debate and argument as fostering difference and respect for a multiplicity of voices.

Wisdom teaching holds out as a promise the fullness and possibility of the "good life" and encourages a search for justice and order in the world that can be discerned by experience. Wisdom teaching does not keep faith and knowledge apart; it does not divide the world into religious and secular, but provides a model for living a mysticism of the everyday. In short, the educational space of Wisdom is debate and discussion, public places and open borders, nourishment and celebration. Divine Wisdom provides sustenance in the struggles for justice and cultivates creation and life in fullness.

The open cosmic house of Divine Wisdom needs no exclusive walls or boundaries, no fortifications and barricades to separate and shut up the insiders from the outsiders, the Bible from its surrounding world. Wisdom imagination engenders a different understanding of the Bible.

> Wisdom has built Her house
> She also has set Her table.
> She has sent out Her wo/men ministers
> to call from the highest places in the town . . .
> "Come eat of my bread
> and drink of the wine I have mixed.
> Leave immaturity, and live,
> *And walk in the way of Wisdom.*"
> (Proverbs 9:1, 3, 5-6; my translation)

Wisdom's inviting biblical table with the bread of sustenance and the wine of celebration is imagined here as set in a temple with seven pillars that allow the spirit of fresh air to blow through it. This image seeks to replace the understanding of canonical and scholarly authority as limiting, controlling, and exclusive authority and "power over," which demand subordination. To approach the Bible as Wisdom's dwelling of cosmic dimensions means to acknowledge its multivalence and its openness to change. It means to give up using it as a security blanket or as an instrument of violence; it means to recognize that the free spaces between its seven pillars invite the Spirit to blow where it wills. Biblical authority and biblical studies renewed in the paradigm of Divine Wisdom will be able to foster such creativity, strength, self-affirmation, and freedom of the sacred in the public square.

13. Coded Resistance: A Proposed Rereading of Romans 13:1-7

Sze-kar Wan
Perkins School of Theology

ANY DISCUSSION OF PAUL'S VIEW ON CIVIL GOVERNMENT must begin with a consideration of the enigmatic Rom 13:1-7. Throughout the ages, the passage has been the subject of intense scrutiny, and results have ranged from Paul advocating civic submission to political authorities, to mission, to quiet engagement of society.[1] Besides being notoriously difficult to interpret, the passage is also fraught with dangerous implications. Historically, it has been used to justify acquiescence to, even compromise with, unjust regimes, or at the very least retreat from or limited engagement with the state.[2] As such, it has become the classical locus for formulating a church-state relation in the New Testament. Ethically, it displays a glaring double standard. While elsewhere, even in Romans, Paul denies power to all earthly authorities because of his apocalypticism, here he seems willing to acknowledge the superiority of the civil government.[3] In Phil 3:20, for example, since our "citizenship" (*politeuma*) is in heaven, we should not keep our minds on earthly things, for the end has drawn near when Christ will deliver the kingdom to the Father by demolishing "every ruler and every authority and power" (*pasa archē kai pasa exousia kai dynamis*, 1 Cor 15:24).[4] The use of *exousia* ("authority") in this connection is especially relevant for the consideration of Rom 13:1-7. The problems with the passage so exasperate scholars that some have even resorted to dismissing it as a non-Pauline interpolation.[5]

Only recently have scholars begun to investigate Paul the writer more self-consciously as a subject in "the imperial situation" under the terms of Pax Romana.[6] For the first time, we are made aware of the imposing influence of the imperium on writers of the New Testament, especially Paul.[7] Closely aligned with this insight is a postcolonial hermeneutics that reveals Paul as constructing a discourse that, at once, mimics and subverts his colonial overlords. Such a discourse discloses an ambiguity that is best explained by Paul's own hybridity as a Greek-speaking, diaspora Jew living in the empire. The best evidence for this ambiguity is the prevalence of terms and concepts capable of double meanings: one to outsiders, the ruling elite, who would like nothing more than to have their own values reaffirmed; the other to insiders who would enter into the discourse as disadvantaged subalterns compelled to resist colonial power. While the insiders would share the coded language of Paul's discourse, it must be disguised before the powers that be, so that Paul's rhetoric would give the appearance of advocating submission and docile subservience, which, in turn, reinforces the overlords' view of themselves as the dominant class of society and reassures them that no revolution is afoot, no social upheaval is being fomented. To insiders conscious of their own powerlessness, however, the passage is capable of being read as a subversive text. It discloses to those in the know the underlying structure of reality: namely, the God of their faith is the final arbiter of all authorities, including civil powers. The message thereby helps the underclass to make sense of their lowly status in society and to hope for the eventual triumph of the God of Jesus. How readers from these two groups, the rulers and the ruled, the oppressors and the oppressed, the dominant and the dominated, enter into the discourse depends on their station in society, which, in turn, influences how they understand key terms of the discourse. A proper reading of Rom 13:1-7 invites us to take into account the two simultaneous discourses encoded in the same text.[8]

Reading from the Top Down

It is instructive to begin with a thought experiment by speculating how a local official, or someone sympathetic to the government, overhearing Paul for the first time, might have understood the rhetoric of this passage. The passage opens with a general call for "every soul" to submit itself to "governing authorities":

pasa psychē exousiais hyperechousais hypotassesthō (Rom 13:1). *Exousia* has a wide range of meanings, from "freedom" to "capability to perform an action" to "authority." Since "authority" implies power, be it legal, political, or military, the word is closely aligned with *dynamis* ("power"). From this is derived the sense of "authoritative position" or "office of state," even "office-bearers" or "rulers" when the word is used in the plural.[9] The common phrase *hoi en exousiais* means "those in office" or "those in positions of government."[10] Since the term does not denote government or the state in general, there is ample reason to reject the common tendency to base a grand, universal theory of church-state relationship on this passage.[11] In view of common usage outside the New Testament, it seems prudent to assert with virtually all commentators that most first-century readers without the benefit of Paul's other writings would take the plural *exousiai* to refer to local magistrates.[12] It follows, then, that the uniquely Pauline expression *exousiai hyperechousai* would be taken in the same way. The plural participle *hoi hyperechontes* (from *hyperechein*, literally, "to hold over," but with a transferred reference to social and political prominence[13]), like *exousiai*, can similarly be used to refer to government officials. Hence, concludes Robert Jewett, "Their redundant combination here has a cumulative sense that encompasses a range of officials placed in superior positions of political authority, duly appointed to their tasks and currently exercising their power."[14] This is evidently how the later author of 1 Peter understood a similar phrase as well.[15]

With the opening line safely co-opted thus, the elite hearer could then place the rest of the passage in the context of local Hellenistic administration.[16] *Hoi archontes* (Rom 13:3) in that case would be understood to be referring to "the public officials,"[17] and *agathon ergon* and *kakon ergon* in the same connection would be interpreted not as moral deeds but as political conducts.[18] *Theou diakonos* (literally "deacon of God"), used in the singular twice in Rom 13:4, would likewise be seen as a natural reference to local political authorities. Though service in general was roundly disdained, especially by the Sophists, service acquires a higher value only when it is rendered to the state, and then only voluntarily without remuneration.[19] "Hence the statesman rules as *diakonos tēs poleōs* ("deacon of the city"), not for the sake of ruling nor for the sake of his own desires, but for the sake of the service laid upon him, which consists supremely in the education of good citizens."[20] At any rate, *diakonos* as a civic official or functionary is well attested already in the Septuagint (*Esth*

1:10; 2:2; 6:3).[21] When read through the ruling optic, *leitourgos* (Rom 13:6) would be considered a close synonym.[22] Robert Jewett finds Paul's calling tax ministers *leitourgoi theou* ("servants of God") surprising,[23] but lexical data would seem to dispute that. The title was first used in Athens and ancient Greece in connection with the collection of taxes, which is the exact context of Rom 13:6. It was then extended to include services of all kinds to a political body.[24] The same secular sense is attested in the Septuagint (2 *Sam* 13:18; 1 *Kgs* 10:5; *Sir* 10:2).[25]

The verb *hypotassesthai* (Rom 13:1a, 5a) and its cognates, *tassesthai* (Rom 13:1c), *antitassesthai* (Rom 13:2a), and *diatagē* (Rom 13:2a), are used liberally throughout this passage. *Tassesthai*, literally "to be ordered or appointed," is a military term denoting the arrangement of the rank and file for battle, and officials are *tetagmenoi eis tini* ("appointed for something").[26] The same word is used in the Septuagint to refer to political appointment (for example, 2 Sam 7:11; Tob 1:21).[27] In Rom 13:1b, readers could therefore find justification for the view that officials are appointed and ordered by God: *hai de ousai hypo theou tetagmenai eisi* ("those that exist are instituted by God").[28] The use of *hypotassesthai* ("to submit oneself" or "to be submitted") thus acknowledges the supremacy of the *hyperechousai* ("governing") authorities.[29] The use of *diatagē* ("instruction, ordinance, direction"[30]) and *antitassesthai* ("to oppose") in Rom 13:2a would, therefore, be understood in the same way: Namely, the authority comes from God, and anyone who opposes the authority opposes the ordinance of God.[31]

That foreign leaders can be used by God to fulfill divine purpose is a common enough attitude in the Bible, and anyone familiar with Jewish culture would know that. But just as God would institute mortals to be sovereigns, God could just as easily depose them. The kingdom of powerful King Nebuchadnezzar, for example, exists at God's pleasure (Daniel 4). Such a view is especially prevalent in the Wisdom tradition (for example, *Sir* 10:4; *Wis* 6:1-11).[32] For unsuspecting Roman officials, however, this subtlety is probably lost on them.[33] For them, it is enough that the passage seems to support the right of the state to bear arms (Rom 13:4c) and to collect customs and taxes (Rom 13:6-7). Overall, they would interpret the passage as a resolution reached by their Jewish subjects to support a foreign state, even if it is reached grudgingly by fitting such a foreign state into an idiosyncratic religious self-understanding.

Reading from the Bottom Up

When insiders, who are familiar with Paul's thoughts and whose social location would put them outside the power orbit of the ruling elite, read these same terms in the context of his writings, however, they could reach vastly different conclusions. The verb *hypotassein* ("to submit or subject") is used thirteen times outside Rom 13:1, 5. The five times the verb is used in the active, God is the subject (Rom 8:20; 1 Cor 15:27 [twice], 28; Phil 3:21). The middle or passive is used eight times (Rom 8:7, 20; 10:3; 1 Cor 14:32; 15:27, 28 [twice]; 16:16); all but three are used explicitly for submission to God. The fleshly mind is not subject to God's law (Rom 8:7); unbelieving Israel did not subject itself to God's righteousness (Rom 10:3); and, in the end time, all things have been placed in subjection to the Son, God's viceroy, after which the Son will submit himself to God the Father (1 Cor 15:27-28). In two other occurrences of the verb, submission to God is at least implied. In Rom 8:20, creation was subjected to futility, involuntarily by God who subjected it; in 1 Cor 14:32, prophets are asked to take responsibility for the manner in which they prophesy, for the spirits of the divinely endowed prophets are themselves ultimately subjects, presumably to God.[34]

The only exception to this use of the middle or passive is 1 Cor 16:16. Here Paul exhorts his Corinthian readers to subject themselves to the likes of Stephanas and his household, Paul's first converts in Achaia, who should command their respect because "they have devoted themselves" (*etaxan heautous,* 1 Cor 16:15) to the service of the saints. While the meaning of *tassein* with a reflexive pronoun as to "devote (oneself)" to a certain task is well attested,[35] its combination with *hypotassesthai* ("to submit oneself") here forms a close parallel to Rom 13:1. Both verses are set in direct speech, as an imperative in Rom 13:1 and as a hortatory in 1 Cor 16:16 (*parakalō* followed by *hina* ["I exhort that"]). Both counsel submission to mortals as opposed to God. But what profoundly binds the two passages together is the reason adduced why such submission is proper and legitimate: in the case of Stephanas and his household, because of their labor for the "holy ones," who are "holy" by virtue of their divine election by God; in the case of "the supreme authorities," because authority comes ultimately from God.

From this survey, a pattern of Paul's usage of *hypotassein* ("to submit or subject") emerges. Absolute submission is rendered only to God. Submission to human agents is legitimate and tolerated only when it is based on or traced to a prior submission to God.[36] That is why in Rom 13:1, Paul follows his opening imperative immediately with a theological statement: that all authority comes from God. Hence, those who subject themselves to God do so from a reasoned position. They act not from fear or blind faith, but through a will informed by an evaluation of the source of authority. Such a view is likely behind the contrast between fear and conscience as motivation for submission (Rom 13:5).[37] The implication is that submission is warranted if, and only if, God, the only true legitimation for authority, stands behind the local officials.

If this is the theological structure recognizable to those in the know, they would readily make a distinction between the plural usage of *exousiai* ("authorities") in Rom 13:1a and the singular *exousia* ("authority") of Rom 13:1b, 2a, and 3b. Ceding that *exousiai hyperechousai* ("governing authorities") of Rom 13:1a refers to local officials and magistrates, they would follow the word play to the singular *exousia* of Rom 13:1b, which describes God as the true source of the officials' superiority and the reason behind the exhortation. Romans 13:1c furnishes the material connection between the officials and God's authority: The former are foot soldiers commanded and ordered by God (*hypo theou tetagmenai eisin*). As such, they serve at the pleasure of God. The singular *exousia* of Rom 13:2a would be seen in like fashion: Anyone who refuses "to submit oneself" (*antitassesthai*) to the authority—that is, any authority, not just that of the local magistrates—"has already opposed (*anthestēken*) the order of God." The perfect tense of *anthestēken* has merited relatively scant attention among commentators.[38] The verb is used in the Septuagint to denote futile resistance against overwhelmingly superior strength or against God,[39] and is here used as a near synonym of *antitassesthai* ("to oppose oneself, to resist"). The combination of the perfect verb *anthestēken* and perfect participle *hoi anthestēkotes* in Rom 13:2a-b could therefore be construed as: Opposition resistance to any authority—provided that authority is ordered by God—is actually based on a prior act of opposing the ordinance ordered by God.[40] Likewise in Rom 13:3, when the rulers carry out their function of rewarding good deeds and meting out punishments for bad, they are discharging their duty within an order ordained by God. It thus reinforces again the observation that insiders would view earthly authority as ultimately traceable to the absolute authority of God.

Public and Hidden Scripts

It is sharply ironic, not to mention subversive, that a passage ostensibly exhorting its readers to submit themselves to local magistrates at the end places these official under the umbrella authority of God—that is, the God of Jesus and the patriarchs, not Zeus or Apollo. Bruno Blumenfeld captures the mood of this co-optation by the underclass perfectly:

> Paul's deftness in manipulating the system by working against its self-negating proclivities is so successful as to camouflage his own wit when castigating its representatives. Throughout Rom. 13:1-7, the irony is veiled (to incomprehension) as a political stereotype. "Fear the governing officials" may sound as an irreproachable advice to the authorities' ear, but these are, unbeknown to themselves, slaves to God as well.[41]

The position expressed here is similar to mine,[42] if by "incomprehension" Blumenfeld means opacity and dissemblance to those in positions of civil power, outsiders to the Jesus movement. To insiders whose only recourse is coded resistance, Paul's intents are transparent. According to them, Paul misleads the dominant class of readers on purpose by using functional, administrative terms and categories that the early Jesus movement has already radically redefined. This results in a reading of the text at two levels. One, intended for public consumption, is meant to be pursued within the calculating logic of the dominant class. The other, the actual discourse between Paul and his intended readers, the underclass in Roman society, is carried out in a language spoken in the Jesus movement. James C. Scott calls these two levels the public and hidden scripts of political discourse.[43]

In any unbalanced relationship between a dominant ruling elite and its subordinates, discourses are constructed on two levels. There is the public script that dictates the rules and choreographs the interaction between the masters and their subjects, but it is written by the powerful to reflect their values and legitimate their rule. In that regard, the public script is at heart "the *self*-portrait of dominant elites as they would have seen themselves."[44] It is little more than self-flattery. As a matter of survival, the subjects under their colonial masters must feign obedience by playing along, ostensibly following the public script onstage, all the while writing their own script of the same events offstage. Their script must be hidden from the ruling elite, but this "hidden script contains what the oppressed say to each other and think about their rulers."[45] The gulf that exists between the public and the hidden scripts is bridged by a third form of political discourse, what Scott calls "a politics of disguise and anonymity that takes place in public view but is designed to have a double meaning or to shield the identity of the actors." In such a discourse, in truth a coded discourse of resistance, "a partly sanitized, ambiguous and coded version of the hidden transcript is always present in the public discourse of subordinate groups."[46] This, I submit, is the nature of Paul's exhortation on civic government in Rom 13:1-7.

The interconnectedness of the public and hidden scripts is especially evident when we consider the two peculiar designations *theou diakonos* ("deacon of God") and *theou leitourgos* ("servant of God"; Rom 13:4 [two times], 6) used in conjunction with the government. References to "God" in association with the civil officials that seem to call them "servants of God" are designed to coddle the self-understanding of the governing elite. Seeing their own political power as divinely ordained would be a natural extension of the Hellenistic political philosophy, according to which the ruler is an "imitator and servant of God."[47] For Paul's intended readers within the Roman congregation, however, *theou diakonos* and *theou leitourgos* have special meanings. Ten times *diakonos* appears in the undisputed letters of Paul outside Rom 13:4, and each time it carries a semitechnical meaning of "servant" or "minister" within the burgeoning Jesus movement. Paul calls himself or his fellow missionary *diakonos* on behalf of the gospel or of the church (Phoebe, Rom 16:1; Apollos and himself, 1 Cor 3:5; himself, 2 Cor 3:6; unnamed fellow workers, 2 Cor 6:4, Phil 1:1). He twice calls Christ a *diakonos*—of the "circumcised" (Rom 15:8) and ironically of "sinners" (Gal 2:17). The former means that the work of Christ is done on behalf of Israel, and the latter is the conclusion of a *reductio ad absurdum* argument that shows the illogicality of imposing circumcision on the Galatians.[48] Even when he polemicizes against the Superapostles of the Corinthian congregation, he does not refrain from calling them *diakonoi* (2 Cor 11:15 [twice], 23), even if he does doubt their authenticity.

The title is often combined with a genitive. Paul calls Phoebe a *diakonos tēs ekklēsias* (Rom 16:1), which could mean either she works for the church or she is commissioned by it. Either way, the thought is that she deserves the respect that is accorded her by her association with the church. Paul calls himself a *diakonos* for the gospel (implied in 1 Cor 3:5) and of the new covenant (2 Cor 3:6) because of the divine grace that has been given him to enable his work on behalf of the gospel. It, therefore, appears that a genitive of things (church, righteousness) would point to the task for which service is required. Data also seem to indicate that a genitive of agent in Paul's usage refers to the master to whom the deacon belongs, and it is this category that forms the bone of contention between Paul and his opponents. He hotly contests the Superapostles' self-designation as *diakonoi* of Christ; he instead calls them *diakonoi* of Satan disguised as *diakonoi* of righteousness (2 Cor 11:15). He reserves the title *diakonos* of Christ for himself (2 Cor 11:23), for he reckons that his sufferings have earned him the title. When he calls himself a *diakonos* of God in 2 Cor 6:4, he enumerates the same mark of sufferings as proof of his diaconate. In this connection, *diakonos* comes close to his preferred term *doulos Christou Iēsou* ("slave of Christ Jesus"; Rom 1:1) or the contested title *apostolos* ("apostle").[49] In the usage of the emerging Jesus movement, *diakonos* is a recognized title and, as far as Paul is concerned, a hotly contested designation.

Uses of the word *leitourgos* ("servant" or literally "liturgist" in a priestly sense) are decidedly more sparing in Paul's writings and, consequently, less polemical. He calls Epaphroditus a *leitourgos*, as well as an *apostolos*, working on behalf of the Philippians to minister to Paul's needs (Phil 2:25). But he calls himself a *leitourgos* of Christ Jesus to the Gentiles, rendering to them a priestly service in the form of the gospel (Rom 15:16). Even though the use of the term is metaphorical, the choice of a cultic designation for himself here is clearly intentional, since he also describes, again metaphorically, the collection for the saints as a *prosphora* ("offering, sacrifice"), presumably to be offered to God. To one who is familiar with Paul's thought, therefore, a *leitourgos* is a priest of God, a title Paul would not hesitate to use on himself.

Coded Resistance

Given the special theological weight with which Paul has freighted *diakonos*, it would be highly unusual if he were to call government officials by the very title over which he has waged mortal battle with his detractors. We have seen earlier that the change from the plural *exousiai* to a singular signals a shift from government officials to a general supremacy of God's authority. The same shift can be detected in Rom 13:3-4, except it is more complex here and takes the form of a repeated pattern. These two verses form what Robert Stein calls "a practical reason" adduced in support of obedience to the state, the practical reason being the natural calculus of avoiding punishment and gaining honor.[50] This section begins with a statement in praise of the benevolence of rulers (*hoi archontes*), who, Paul declares publicly, are not a terror to good conducts, only to evil (Rom 13:3a). This public declaration is immediately followed by a coded statement, structured as a question: "Do you wish not to fear the authority?" (Rom 13:3b). The change from the plural "rulers" to the singular "authority" is precisely how Paul disguises his hidden script. His colonial censors would approve the question, especially after the positive Rom 13:3a, no doubt connecting the singular *exousia* of 13:3b to the plural *exousiai* of 13:1a, as do the vast majority of modern critics. That would, naturally, miss the monotheistic connotation behind "authority," a connotation that only members of the in-group could winkingly acknowledge to each other. The God of Jesus and the patriarchs alone holds supreme authority, whom *all*—especially rulers and officials—must fear. A rhetorical question that is posed to fellow subalterns, publicly before the watchful eyes of the colonizers, thus becomes an accusatory question posed in judgment of the lordly and the powerful.

The rest of the section builds on the opening couplet, drawing out consequences of and giving the rationale for doing good (Rom 13:3c-4a) and avoiding evil (Rom 13:4b-d). The basic pattern remains the same: Solid, practical good-citizen advice immediately followed by a coded message to be shared among insiders. "Do good and you will have praise from it [that is, the *exousia*]" (Rom 13:3c). Again, the colonizers will mislead themselves into thinking they are the arbiters of conducts and purveyors of benefaction, but Paul winks offstage and writes them into his hidden script as recipients of a divine judgment based on the authority of God. This public statement is supported by a rationale in Rom 13:4a, *theou gar diakonos estin soi eis to agathon* ("for it is for you a deacon of God for good"). The subject of the verb *esti* ("is") in this context is ambiguous.[51] The natural candidate is *exousia* of 13:3b, so that the line would read "for *the authority* is for you a deacon of God for good." But the subject can just as well be *theou diakonos*, in which case we have "for *the deacon of God* is for you for good" or "for there is a *deacon of God* for you for good." The former has grammar on its side and would be favored by the elite, since they would understand *exousia* as a self-designation and would think of themselves as divinely appointed "deacons" for the good of the underclass. Insiders, however, who take *exousia* to be the absolute authority of the monotheistic God, would favor leaving the subject unspecified, secure in the knowledge that *there is* a deacon of God who executes justice with fairness and alacrity.

Doing good brings up its correlative, doing evil (Rom 13:4b-d). True to form, it begins with a nod to the colonial power, even military power: "If you do evil, be fearful, for not in vain does it bear the sword" (Rom 13:4c-d). As virtually all commentators have noted, "bearing sword" points to the use of police action by the powerful to maintain control of their subjects.[52] This public statement is designed to dissemble its true intention, which is, again, balanced by a rationale founded on the theological premise of the existence of a "deacon of God" (Rom 13:4d). The powerful would readily identify themselves with this "deacon," but only the insiders could identify the true and absolute authority of God who alone can mete out punishment to all, even the colonial lords themselves.[53]

Conclusion

Over the years critics have fought over the meaning of Romans 13, but, in spite of numerous attempts to soften the embarrassingly compromising tone of the passage, the regnant approach remains that of Paul ceding to earthly rulers provisional authority—however temporary it might be before the end time—functioning, full-bodied authority nonetheless.[54] At most, critics grant that for Paul, "[the civil government] is a part of the natural moral order, of divine appointment, but lying outside the order of grace revealed in Christ."[55] This approach might, at first glance, seem like a sort of political realism, but it actually creates an unbearable tension with Paul's attitude towards the government elsewhere. It also has the effect of forcing Paul's words into a single meaning, not allowing him to disguise the true intents of his discourse in the face of hostile authorities.

This chapter proposes a solution by taking seriously Paul's own social and political location in Roman society and that of his directly addressed and indirectly addressed audiences. Full weight has been accorded to the power differential between the two audiences. To the power elite, those indirectly addressed by Paul, the passage reads and is heard like a concession to the supreme authority of the state, to which believers are counseled obedience and submission—grudgingly, perhaps, but real regardless. To them, Paul seems willing to go so far as to legitimate the state's functions—chief among them taxation and police control—by appealing to divine ordinance. However well they might understand Paul's Jewish thought, it would be impressive enough that, to them, Paul appears to have carved out a niche in his theological edifice for earthly government.

Such a theological argument cuts both ways, however. Roman Jesus-followers, insiders to Paul's rhetoric and theology and the audience directly addressed in the epistle, are more inclined to understand Paul's argument in traditional biblical and Hellenistic-Jewish terms. The God who tolerates, even ordains political structures of the world can just as easily overthrow them if they fail to live up to expectation. Paul's apocalypticism would radicalize divine judgment even further. Elsewhere he speaks of the powers and authorities of this world drawing to a close in light of the eschatological triumph of Christ (1 Cor 2:6-8; 15:24). Once grafted into Paul's apocalypticism, political structures are doomed to oblivion. Such a critical stance would be lost on outsiders unschooled in Jewish wisdom or apocalyptic thoughts. When addressing them, Paul dissembles and disguises his discourse as an exhortation to submission and obedience.

14. A Famine of the Word: A Stringfellowian Reflection on the American Church Today

Neil Elliott
Metropolitan State University
and United Theological Seminary

Famine in a Land of Plenty

Although church leaders frequently lament the secularization of American culture, Americans remain (on their own report) a thoroughly religious people: at least as religious a people as Israel in the eighth century B.C.E. Amos did not address a lack of piety, after all. A fervent Yahwism thrived around him, centered in sites like the shrine of Bethel that could, with the enthusiastic support of the monarchy, exercise what Norman Gottwald has called an "asserted monopoly over the voice of Yahweh."[1] The priest Amaziah expelled Amos from the shrine at Bethel out of concern to protect "a king's sanctuary, and . . . a temple of the kingdom" from the intrusive voice of the herdsman from Tekoa (*Amos* 7:13). It was an intense and pervasive religious devotion that made Bethel an inhospitable environment for prophecy.

Something similar is the case in our own day. It is an ominous paradox of contemporary life in the United States that while we live in a culture saturated with religion, with biblical rhetoric pervading both the so-called political and religious spheres of society,[2] we nevertheless experience something like what the prophet Amos described as "a famine . . . of hearing the words of the Lord" (*Amos* 8:11), not least in our churches. The abundant forms in which the sacred is produced as a ubiquitous market commodity in American Christianity[3] presents a dizzying field of distraction that both complicates and dissipates our best efforts at discernment of the common good. At a prosaic level, the ready availability of the Bible in English, in print and electronic formats, in bookstores, libraries, churches, and our own homes, results in an optical and auditory illusion that seduces us into imagining that the discernment of the prophetic word in Amos's day—or in ours—is as convenient as consulting the pages of any of the Bibles on our shelves. It is hard for us to imagine that the prophet's coreligionists might have found his message both alien and repugnant precisely because they accepted as self-evident the "asserted monopoly over the voice of Yahweh" on the part of the national religion. How much more difficult is it for us to imagine that, despite our own ready access to the words of Amos, the Second Isaiah, the apostle Paul, or John of Patmos—despite, indeed, our pious and studied recourse to those words in weekly liturgies—we are suffering a "famine of hearing the words of the Lord," and how much more difficult is it for us to experience the "asserted monopoly over the voice of Yahweh" in our own society as inimical to any genuine discernment of the sacred directionalities of life and justice.

Our present crisis goes much deeper than the banal overabundance of religion, however. There are other ways in which actually existing Christianity obscures the true dimensions of our crisis.

Just here, we must guard against the American habit of collapsing our talk about religion into matters of individual belief and piety. The primary question before us is not how intensely any of us feels motivated by sacred symbols, that is, how "religious" we are. The primary question must be *which* religion we participate in, with whatever measure of devotion. We must analyze how social pressures at work in our culture shape our awareness and perception of the sacred; only after such analysis will we be in a position to ask what the intensity of our religiosity signifies.

The qualification is important. By identifying a "famine of hearing the words of the Lord," I do not mean to plead that any of us should seek out self-evident divine revelations, or that our congregations should cultivate self-authenticating prophetic speech as a regular part of our worship services. We are all aware how routinely right-wing churches, and the televangelists who act as their field marshals, take recourse to the rhetoric of revelation: Their strategies and campaigns are inspired, we are regularly informed, by "words from the Lord."[4] It is tempting for those of us who perceive the religious right as a massive hijacking of Christian symbols[5] to want to fight fire with fire—to claim that the deep conviction and passionate commitment that *we* feel is our response to *true* revelation, *true* prophecy. But such moves inevitably reinscribe a decontextualized rhetoric of revelation that is structurally indistinguishable from that used by the religious right. By falling into such rhetoric, we obscure our own responsibility for the ways in which we invoke and represent the sacred.[6]

One of the most conspicuous phenomena on the American religious landscape today is the overtly theocratic program of the religious right. More importantly, however, American religion is constricted and contoured by the ideological and cultural forces of capitalism, militarism, and an ascendant American imperialism. These forces so distort the church's engagement with sacred symbols as to make critically engaged theological reflection an increasingly remote possibility. One result is evident in Mark Lewis Taylor's discussion of locales and practices where "the prophetic spirit" is evident and vibrant in our world: Taylor names various groups of marginalized persons engaged in imagining and working for a more just world, but does not identify churches among those locales—despite the fact (to name this paradox again) that churches are one of the primary sites where "the words of the Lord" are expressly invoked on a regular basis.[7]

Naming Our Reality

The material culture that surrounds and permeates American Christianity both precipitates a "famine of hearing the words of the Lord" and inures those experiencing that famine from conscious awareness of it.

Over the century and a half since Karl Marx (and others) described the dominant religious ideas of the industrial age as "the opiate of the people,"[8] sociologists of religion have documented the functional role assigned to religious institutions in Western societies: offering sacred legitimation for the social, economic, and political status quo by making existing power relationships seem natural, proper, and inevitable.[9] Political scientist Michael L. Budde describes the profound capacity of the electronic global culture industries today to shape and discipline our perceptions of one another, of the horizon of the possible, and of the common good, far beyond the present capacity (or will?) of churches to offer an alternative Christian formation of their own.[10] These industries have so effectively shaped the cultural agenda to serve the interests of corporate capitalism and the state that churches increasingly accept that agenda as their own, striving to demonstrate their relevance to the prevailing order by "baptizing" the economic and political self-interest of their mostly middle-class participants. Budde quotes sociologist of religion Robert Wuthnow, who observes that in many American churches "what religious faith does more clearly than anything else is to add a dollop of piety to the materialistic amalgam in which most of us live."[11] In this way, Budde observes, the church is offered, and routinely accepts, a role of "chaplaincy" to the dominant culture, "defining its mission as being useful to existing social arrangements and institutions":[12]

> A better fitting late-Constantinian job description one cannot imagine for the churches in the media age: be useful to the political order and its deified self-description ("democracy"); prove one's value as a "service" to autonomous individuals and families, whose priorities and preferences continue to be formed independently of the church and gospel; and acquiesce in the atrophy of Christian language and formation in favor of more "universal" and "public" ones drawn from market and nationalist ideology.[13]

To the extent that American churches serve societal structures and ideologies, their capacity to form persons in alternative identities and practices is diminished. Budde speaks of their "nearly complete, unabashed failure" to form and equip persons for discipleship to Jesus:[14]

> [Christianity] has had little discernible impact in making the Sermon on the Mount . . . remotely relevant in Christian life and lifestyles; it has provided no alternative sense of community capable of withstanding the absolutist claims of state, movement, and market; and it can offer nothing but an awkward, embarrassed silence in response to the scandal of Christians slaughtering Christians (not to mention everybody else) in "just" wars blessed by hierarchs on all sides in slavish obedience to presumably more important loyalties.

> The failures are so huge, the contradictions with the gospel so enormous, that they don't even register as subjects of concern

in the churches. When forced to confront our hypocrisy and our obedience to other sources of meaning, we wring our hands, lament the sinfulness of the human condition, and pray for a human solidarity that would terrify us if it ever came to pass. And the institutions of death grind on in our world, with good Christians serving them efficiently, responsibly, and in ways indistinguishable from those who reject the premise that Jesus of Nazareth incarnated God's way for his people on earth.[15]

This "failure" should not be construed simply as a sin of omission: The more appropriate theological category might be idolatry. The churches have proven remarkably serviceable on the ideological plane precisely by their acquiescence to an imperial theology. Historian of American religion Richard Hughes documents the history of American civil religion as the history of a set of "myths America lives by," including myths of the nation's sacred origins, its divine vocation, and the sacred innocence of the nation's spectacular exercises of military force.[16] Richard Horsley, who has labored to keep imperial power and pretense at the forefront of biblical and theological scholarship, observes that the religious dimension of American imperial nationalism "operates all the more effectively because it is defined and understood as secular in the official American liberal ideology, and therefore not separated off into its own institutional expression, as are officially defined 'religions.'"[17] In the wake of the attacks of September 11, 2001, a number of theologians have observed with alarm that the Bush administration's proclaimed "war on terror" relied upon mythic themes of national innocence ("they hate us for our freedom") and messianic grandiosity ("our responsibility to history is . . . to rid the world of evil") through the exercise of holy war. Although the "theology of empire" embodied in policy documents like the *National Security Strategy of the United States of America* (2002) is fundamentally incompatible with Christian theology, however, it has been the subject of explicit critique among theologians only rarely,[18] and in American pulpits more rarely still.

Among the reasons for this strange silence on the part of the churches is the informal quasi-establishment of Judaism and Christianity in the United States, and their corresponding domestication, since the 1950s. Cold War ideological purposes were served by contrasting Americans as a religious people, in a generalized and diffuse way (for example, by reference to the "Judeo-Christian heritage"), with "godless" Communism. So President Dwight Eisenhower is reported to have remarked that "our government makes no sense unless it is founded on a deeply felt religious faith—and I don't care what it is."[19] Daniel Lazare observes that American liberalism has championed freedom for "all forms of religious expression as long as they bolstered the national cause." The liberal confidence that "there was no faith that America could not successfully absorb and put to its own use" now faces a crisis, however, as it confronts a religion—Islam—"that not only refuses to believe that God is on America's side but, according to some of its leading spokespeople, sees [God] as positively hostile [to the United States]."[20] The putative conflict between global Islam and Western civilization is, in reality, a crisis within Western culture between the values of global capitalism and its exponent states, on one hand, and the capacity of sacred symbols—including those of Judaism and Christianity as well as Islam—to invoke responses that are anything other than "essentially benign" and supportive of "the national cause," on the other. We might expect that crisis to be felt more keenly in American churches than seems to be the case.[21]

A Propaganda Model

We must also take account of the elements of a "propaganda model" at work in U.S. American culture, constraining knowledge and affecting the "manufacture of consent" in the religious sphere as well as in the political. That language was given us by Noam Chomsky and Edward S. Herman's illuminating analysis of the "political economy of the mass media" in the United States;[22] I apply it here to understand the systemic role assigned to American churches as well. Adapted to the symbolic economy of the "production of the sacred," the elements of this propaganda model include:

- the consolidation of religious broadcasting, especially following the 1996 "free-market" deregulation of broadcast media, in the hands of a few powerful (and notoriously conservative) corporations like Clear Channel;
- the dependence of American churches and para-church organizations upon voluntary contributions, which makes them increasingly vulnerable to the preferences of congregants/consumers,[23] and puts

those organizations oriented to the needs of the poor and working classes at a disadvantage compared to those organizations oriented to the defense and sacralization of privatized wealth. Most recently, the Bush administration's "Faith-Based Initiative" has privatized both social service programs and our imagination of the horizon of collective responsibility, an affect that is arguably its true goal;[24]

- the statutory exemption from property taxes, which makes religious organizations acutely sensitive even to the appearance of taking a political stance lest they risk that status: This risk is usually operative only against expressions of dissent, as one would expect, given the propaganda model;[25]

- aggressive and systematic "flak" from sophisticated, well-funded organizations like the Institute for Religion and Democracy, which seeks to "reform" mainline American denominations by discrediting and stigmatizing their more moderate and progressive elements;

- a tacit "national religion" (that is, the regnant civil religion) that is univocally procapitalist, probusiness, and promilitarist.[26]

These elements together filter what may be said and done, known and thought under the guise of American religion. These filters are operative in the American mass media, where (for example) one could easily have missed the report that a majority of mainstream denominations publicly opposed both the so-called "first" and "second" wars in Iraq (though religious and foreign news services carried the story prominently). Or, again, in the self-policing carried on in local congregations as well: In the week before the U.S. (re)invasion of Iraq in March, 2003, I heard two Episcopal clergy declare, in separate conversations, that they would not speak against the war from the pulpit lest they be perceived as "Bush-bashing."

It would be difficult to find a clearer contemporary analogy for the "asserted monopoly over the voice of Yahweh" that Amos opposed.

The Legacy of William Stringfellow: Analysis and Hope

All of this was described decades ago by Episcopal lay theologian William Stringfellow, who observed that the church had become confined, for the most part, to the sanctuary and . . . assigned to either political silence or to banal acquiescence. Political authority in America has sanctioned this accommodation principally by the economic rewards it bestows upon the church. The tax privilege . . . has been a practically conclusive inhibition to the church's political intervention save where it consists of applause for the nation's cause. Furthermore, the tax preference or political subsidy the church has so long received has enabled . . . the accrual of enormous, if unseemly, wealth. . . . The church has gained so huge a propertied interest that its existence has become overwhelmingly committed to the management of property and the maintenance of the ecclesiastical fabric which that property affords.[27]

Stringfellow is the focus of a resurgent interest, not only in the Anglican Communion.[28] His insights into the American scene are at risk of being obscured, however, by an Anglican celebration of "incarnational faith" that finds Stringfellow's chief contribution in the discovery of "the everyday presence of God, which transfigures even the most ordinary events."[29] This misses the heart of Stringfellow's theology, the insight that drew from Karl Barth the comment that America should "listen to this man":[30] namely, the reality of the "principalities and powers" as potently destructive social forces in our world.[31]

Stringfellow's theology of the powers allowed him readily to identify aspects of "the demonic" at work in American public life:

Typically, each and every stratagem of the principalities seeks the death of the specific faculties of rational and moral comprehension that specially distinguish human beings from all other creatures. . . . Demonic aggression always aims at the immobilization or surrender or destruction of the mind and at the neutralization or abandonment or demoralization of the conscience.[32]

Stringfellow had in mind particularly "official falsehood and propaganda" concerning Vietnam, Watergate, "and practically anything else in which the same political principalities are implicated":

What is most significant in any of these examples is . . . the premise of the principalities that truth is nonexistent, that truth is a fiction, that there can be no thorough or fair or comprehensive or detached discovery and chronicle of events and that any handling of facts is ideologically or institutionally or otherwise tainted. The recent official aggressions against the media have been based upon this proposition.[33]

The same phenomenon is evident today, in a United States administration where officials speak with contempt of "the reality-based community,"[34] in a pattern of official contempt for truth that is aptly described as "cognitive torture,"[35] and in the woeful incapacity of a leading investigative journalist to see in a long record of official mendacity regarding the war in Iraq anything more culpable than a "state of denial."[36]

For Stringfellow, the incarnation of the Word meant "the active sovereignty of the Word of God in common history in this world here and now," or more succinctly, the abiding presence in history of "the Word militant."[37] The incarnation is fundamentally an eschatological reality. The "mystery" of incarnation as revealed in John 1 is that of crisis and of judgment. The "secret" of the First Advent, Stringfellow wrote, is disclosed only in the Second Advent, in which "Christ the Lord comes as judge of the world and the world's principalities and thrones, in vindication of his reign and of the sovereignty of the Word of God in history."[38] The church's celebration of the incarnation, then, should be a starkly political matter,[39] a particular moment in the ongoing confrontation between the church and the powers (as Richard Horsley has also repeatedly urged).[40]

This understanding of incarnation is profoundly biblical. The heart of the Johannine mystery is not the metaphysical paradox of later Neoplatonist Christology or (more contemporary) the reassuring awareness of the sacramentality of the everyday. It is the prophetic scandal of the Word of God, which had once burned in the bones of an ostracized Jeremiah (*Jer* 20:7-12), being realized in the flesh of another rejected Israelite, who "was in the world; but the world, though it owed its life to him, did not recognize him. He entered his own realm, and his own would not receive him" (John 1:10-11).[41] The incarnation carries forward the momentum of a history in which Wisdom was sent forth from God, seeking a home among human beings like a dove seeking a lighting place upon the earth, but finding none (*Sir* 24; 1 *Enoch* 42). The incarnation is the historical and social scandal of the Word of God confronting the merely pragmatic use of language by the powers, embodied in Pilate's banal rejoinder, "What is truth?" (John 18:38).

This understanding of the incarnation also has immediate and weighty consequences for the church. As Stringfellow already saw, we live in a culture awash in an imperial theology that projects the state as the holy nation, enjoying a divine vocation. If the church is, however, the community of resistance gathered around the Word that is not only incarnate in history, but militant in opposition to the powers in history, then the members of the church must practice a peculiar vigilance against the demonic stratagems of counterrationality and obfuscation.

Addressing the specific realities of the world order described in the *National Security Strategy of the United States*, Eugene McCarraher remarks that the proper response on the part of the church must be "skepticism—unyielding, uncivil, and corrosive":

> With a harsh and dreadful love, we must disparage the martial and pecuniary faith that animates history's richest, most well-armed, and parochial superpower. . . . [U]nembedded intellectuals must assault the winter palaces of embedded ideology, revitalize and enlarge the political community called church, and rekindle the political imagination called theology. Against the totems and sacraments of empire we must hurl the most intolerable and virtuous of insults.[42]

When even apologists for the neocolonialism of global capitalism candidly admit that the American way of life depends upon the coercive force of military supremacy, McCarraher urges "unembedded" Christians to a similar frankness:

> Let us be candid where embedded Christians employ euphemism or change the subject. Our government is a franchise of multinational capital; our political culture is a seller's market in knavery; our economy is a gargantuan galley of imperious

executives, harried workers, and stressed-out families; our culture is a cheerful mendacity.[43]

Over against the formative disciplines of imperial and corporate pedagogy, McCarraher calls on the church to "recover the theological idiom of Christian political intelligence and moral imagination":

> Just as the increasingly indistinguishable iconographies of corporate advertising and state propaganda form a species of spiritual formation, so we must learn to think again of our practices of common prayer, common study, and Eucharistic observance as a spiritual formation that is also pedagogy in moral and political thought.[44]

Such formative practices would, of course, set Christians on a collision course with the national religion, no less severe than that evoked by Amos's prophesying at Bethel. But such practices are necessary to the ongoing incarnation of the prophetic Word in an age of manufactured famine.

Stringfellow could hardly be characterized as an optimist, and presumably would be among the first to observe that our present situation offers no cause for optimism. Christian hope, however, is another matter, depending as it does upon the sovereignty of the Word in history. So, decades ago, Stringfellow expressed hope for the American churches:

> Among the conventional ecclesiastical principalities, there are, mercifully . . . occasional congregations and para-congregations, and there are laity and clergy and some few ecclesiastics, that stand—together with more ad hoc communities and happenings and people—within the continuity of the biblical witness. . . . [T]hese constitute an emergent confessing movement in the United States: spontaneous, episodic, radically ecumenical, irregular in polity, zealous in living, extemporaneous in action, new and renewed, conscientious, meek, poor. It is to these phenomena, far more profound and much more widespread than is commonly recognized, that a person must look to sight the exemplary church of Jesus Christ acting as harbinger of the

holy nation. It is in this confessing movement that [the vision of the heavenly Jerusalem] is verified, now, in America, right in the midst of the ruin of Babylon's churches.[45]

Ours is a time for the practice of such hope.

15. Communities Reading the Bible and Public Vision

Antoinette Clark Wire
San Francisco Theological Seminary
and the Graduate Theological Union

IT WASN'T ANYTHING I HAD PLANNED, or even something I saw as it happened. But looking back after retirement, I see now that reading scripture has made sense of my life. I mean by this not the obvious fact that I took studying and teaching the Bible as my profession, nor even that my way of reading the Bible has changed as I have grown, making the Bible the unifying groundwork for the multiple revolutions in my worldview. Rather, the many different specific communities in which I have been reading the Bible have made me the person I am, the person who could do what I have done. Granted that I am part of other communities with their different texts—artistic, legal, botanical—texts that for members of those communities may play a life-orienting role, but my scripture has been the Bible.

Whatever the scripture, I wager that public vision is never an individual achievement but always comes out of the common struggle of people to understand their traditions because they have to live and act from them. I make this case in terms of key communities in my own life, where reading the Bible as scripture has been for me the seedbed of public vision.

Though I limit my report here to my own experience, I want to recognize before I begin a framework that might make space for reading texts as scripture in a postmodern world. Wesley Kort in *"Take, Read": Scripture, Textuality, and Cultural Practice* argues that reading texts as scripture is not restricted to religious groups, or to devout classicists or Marxists, but has been a long-standing practice in Western culture.[1] Kort notes how Francis Bacon and John

Locke developed ways of reading nature as scripture alongside the Bible, and saw science as the study of universal patterns in creation. Kort goes on to trace how Georg W. F. Hegel, among others, turned attention to reading history as scripture, revealing the evolving work of the Creative Spirit. After Immanuel Kant's reorientation of Western thought on human knowing, Kort shows us that Samuel Coleridge, Matthew Arnold, and later the New Critics took the human creativity seen in literature as the primary cultural concentrate that evokes a scriptural reading. Yet in our time, Kort recognizes that postmodern thought has rejected the possibility of reading nature, history, or literature as normative. We make reference to texts, but we are not confident we can access objects to which texts refer. This means that the one who chooses how to read looms as all-powerful, and the issue for Kort has become: Is truth at the whim of the reader? What can put the reader in question?

In answer, Kort prefers the largely negative proposals of Maurice Blanchot and Julia Kristeva, who respectively see exit from the culture, and from the self that it produces, as the only ways not to be co-opted. For Blanchot and Kristeva these ways are often evoked by biblical stories and insights.[2] I find particular pointers toward a critical foothold in three other postmodern thinkers that Kort presents. Barbara Herrnstein Smith claims that values do arise in culture today, but only by a process of social exchange in which what benefits us is chosen, as in an economic market.[3] This social exchange requires the broadest participation and openness, a crucial factor in groups that I have experienced seeking to claim what they value from their traditions. Stanley Fish is another who rejects essential values, but he sees them being constructed by interpretive communities such as the literary and legal professions which hold certain beliefs and work to persuade others of their value.[4] Religious communities can also be understood in this way, which puts the onus on them to clarify their beliefs through intense interchange with their scriptures and, thereby, to draw others into interpreting experience in this way. Finally, Edith Wyschogrod takes the saint as the sole measure of value, the person who sets aside all cultural givens in devotion to the welfare of the other.[5] She suggests to me that such radical acts of self-abnegation, practiced within community, might construct a cross-cultural counterculture able to receive the whole world as the face of the other. In light of these theorists, I want to ask whether religious communities in a postmodern world can read scripture in a way that fosters such open exchange, persuasive interpretations, and readiness to focus on the face of the other as a foundation for self-critical practice today. Specifically, I look at my own garden-variety experience of communities reading the Bible and ask whether it has fostered a public vision that puts me and other readers into question.

My experience goes back to the days when American homes had Bible reading after breakfast. This was relatively quick and painless in my missionary family in China because the day's duties pressed on parents as well as servants. Sometimes the practice would languish for months. We girls were supposed to read carefully and participate, but our father, who had written a dissertation on the social teachings of John Calvin, usually had the answers all laid out before we thought of the questions. Yet I remember that my sister Mary and I once went to Mother after reading the story of Dives and Lazarus in Luke 16. We asked why we didn't share our space with the family who lived in a wooden crate down the street. The next day Mother made a diagram showing how we could not house all the people who lived under the pagoda, so God had given her and Dad the job of caring for the people over at the church. Maybe we would get a different job when we grew up. That was about the time when a visitor at dinner argued about American policy on China with my father, and I realized for the first time that he might be wrong, and that I would have to figure all this out for myself. That process had started already in our reading the Bible.

While in seminary at Yale, another student and I did our field work through the Wider City Parish in a housing project down the hill. After knocking on dozens of doors, we met a few people for weekly Bible study in a second-story kitchenette, taking turns around the table reading verses from Genesis. I discovered that many Americans could barely read, but that, when they got through the sentence with assistance from one another, it was everyone's victory. At the same time, the discussions were profound and contentious: What was God's image in humans? Was the creation all good? Were farm labor and childbirth pain really punishments? In this community the ancient text received great respect, but it could not stand over against what worked on the ground. Real answers were worked on, and our plan to introduce historical criticism was lost in the whirlwind. We learned by listening and bringing our own questions to the table.

After my children were in school, and I began graduate studies, I took part in a group of young women, called the Lydia Circle, in my husband's Los Angeles church. It took some time to rise above, or rather appear below, the stereotype of the pastor's saintly wife. Yet as women managing jobs and children, some of us on our own, we were not cowed by Paul when he counseled women to cover their heads and be silent in church. Much later, in my *Corinthian Women Prophets*, I found some resources for interpreting an author's rhetoric as a means of access to contending voices in the text.[6] At that earlier time, however, it was the welcome into the homes of other women under similar pressures, in this area off of Crenshaw Boulevard, that kept us working through the texts to claim the rights and responsibilities that we knew were given us. This was bold in our context, yet we did not see ourselves as the vanguard of something new so much as the generation that was able to speak out for the household of God that our mothers and grandmothers had been building all along.

Women like us were beginning to enroll in seminaries and demand women faculty, allowing me to teach for more than thirty years at San Francisco Seminary and the Graduate Theological Union. In this way I joined a group reading the Bible that included all those I taught, and those I taught with, in lay, ministerial, and doctoral programs. Often the work was perfunctory, as faculty sought to cover the bases, and students to get the units. But no one could presume business as usual when working with our community's scripture. We were dealing with a historical and literary text like any other, but at the moment when its claim on us became clear, the valence of the discussion could surge. I learned to gain time by asking, "And what do you think?" if someone had not beaten me to the question. We asked: Why are the gospels each different? How could a resurrection be historical? Who says the account of Paul's colleague Thecla is not scripture? I coplanned and cotaught courses with over twenty people, a serious challenge each time, and discussed interpretations of texts with hundreds of colleagues, some only in print.

Biblical scholarship, at its best, is a long and broad Bible study group. By this time there were voices like that of Elisabeth Schüssler Fiorenza to keep telling us we had an ethical responsibility to the whole society to expose how each text speaks to our world. As in the physical sciences, theoretical and methodological work is necessary for new applications to emerge, but when arcane labor bears no fruit, the tree is best cut down and thrown into the fire. I do see fruit today, but not enough, and increasingly the distribution system seems to be broken.

In the last twenty years, my husband and I have been part of a house church meeting Sunday evenings in an Oakland apartment, a shifting crew of a dozen or so people, from infants to elders. There are ministers and activists, engineers and health workers, students and those not defined by work, all interested in an hour's struggle with a Bible text read in terms of what accosts us on the street and in the news. From time to time we have rejected the patriarchal assumptions and violent images of the Bible and tried other books, but again and again we have come back to scripture, struggling to reclaim it and face our world with God's judgment and mercy. We grapple with Isaiah, a psalm or a gospel, or we revert to the lectionary texts to plow up and replant the sermons we heard in the morning. Each person's job and family and travels are our opportunities to foster constructive moves in a society under judgment, and, occasionally, we work as a team to organize a demonstration, plan a conference, or support another community. The work is never done, but it always matters, and when we are away from home, life is difficult without this circle.

We have met another group of scripture readers in China over the last two decades, as I have pursued several research projects and as we have twice taught for a year in universities and seminaries there. In the process of recording indigenous songs sung by Christians in small gatherings—often psalms or promises or instructions directly from the Bible—I have discovered new interpretations from their melodies and their voices. Other songs they sing retell in their own words Ruth's journey with Naomi, the trials of Mary, and Zacchaeus found in the tree. The act of singing itself confirms the values of filial piety, mother love, and respect for the despised. I did not see people tear into a text the way we North Americans do. That would not be considered respectful of what is ancient. But people will rise, one after another, in a weekday church service to exposit Israel's desert wanderings and their own. One afternoon, a gathering of about forty people in a small shop and adjoining bedroom heard a young man read a chapter of Proverbs while they, with their own Bibles opened, read each line after him, a long procedure interrupted by his disquisitions on the wisdom of the instructions. At the end, they pressed him to read it again; he agreed, and then we returned to work. These were country people, with little or no schooling, finally now learning to read. They were eager to learn the scripture and the practical wisdom and the characters in which it was written, not distinguishing between the three. Two blind women seemed to be memorizing the text, repeating it quietly over and over whenever the young man stopped to talk. When we speak of communities reading scripture we need to know that some of the most intent do not read, but hear, and it serves their purposes just as well.

How, then, do communities of all these kinds foster a public vision through reading scripture? Or do these people simply use the texts for their personal ends, so that, as Kort phrases it, the readers see what they want to see, and no one can put their readings in question? This would be the postmodern problem. Yet one could argue that I have lived in a premodern world where the biblical text is assumed to be authoritative and to provide a fixed north that orients the reader's compass. The fact is that I have found respect for the text and for those who went before us on this way. But this has served, in my experience, not to chart the course for us but, if anything, to provoke our questions, more in the manner that Blanchot reads Jacob at the Jabbok or Kristeva reads Paul's "What I want, I do not do," namely, to lure us into new and deeper questions. How is it that scripture frees rather than binds, opens rather than closes?

The bottom line is that no one can tell us what the text means. Everyone reads it out of his or her own experience, but because we are listening to each other, we hear options rather than formulas. We test out where we stand by speaking, and we share responsibility to figure it out, to take it this way or that way, or to leave it. This exchange of interpretations in an open forum is essential, as Barbara Herrnstein Smith argues, and the exchange may be the reason why, looking back at the groups that came to mind above, I have not included worshipping communities, conferences, or public lectures where one person, however profound, reads and interprets the Bible for others.

At the same time, people reading together in groups tend to persuade one another, and some common commitments, or at least shared conundrums, develop that characterize each group as an interpreting community. One leg of the table requires the others in order to do its own job, and when one person is missing, others may suggest how she would have read the text in order to get the full picture. Thus a kind of interpreting community develops, as Stanley Fish argues about professional communities, one whose members can operate as a whole to influence each other and to persuade other people when the need arises.

This public function is not accidental but comes, I expect, from the nature of the texts being read. In my experience the Bible has not focused readers on themselves, but on each other, just as Wyschogrod interprets the focus of the saint—this in spite of the Bible's recurrent chauvinism. Historically speaking, the biblical corpus belongs to the people of Israel as a whole with all its needs, and to Israel as "a light to the nations" with all that implies. This could be expected to draw individuals or groups reading the Bible, in whichever of its forms, into acts of responsibility for the welfare of the whole people of Israel and of all nations. Theologically speaking, the Bible is a human account of God's creation and God's deliverance of human beings in spite of our homicidal and suicidal proclivities. The face of the other, for biblical readers, is finally seen in the face of God, whose mercy and justice uphold the world.

This means that the starting point of public vision is not in the book-lined offices where intellectuals gaze into their crystal screens, but in communities where common reading of scripture and mutual persuasion is nurtured. Here people can talk out their texts and their worlds, gaining in knowledge, confidence, and practice in supporting each other. Out of this comes the chance that a way will be seen where there is no way, and that responsibility will be taken to mobilize others and build it.

I concede that there is a gap seldom breached today between people who read scripture together and people who carry out public policy. Religious people have largely abdicated public responsibility, and politicians mobilize such groups only to get their votes, not their input. But there are some intermediate people, those in the public policy offices of religious groups and those in grassroots organizing of candidates, who could be encouraged by strong volunteer and money-raising efforts to provide more bridges between sectors. This will hardly be necessary, however, unless religious people begin to take far more seriously the traditions passed down to them. The work cannot be left to professionals in religion or in the academy, though we do have particular responsibility. It is as participants in communities, as believers and citizens and families, that we need to ask ourselves if we are getting the nourishment we want from what we read and watch. Or could we dig deeper, by joining others to study the narratives that kept our ancestors going—alongside the best literature of our time—so that we are ready to act? It would mean switching from the "escape mode" to the "engage mode" of living. We now work to get ourselves in shape physically, why not communally and spiritually?

Notes

Introduction

1. Elisabeth Schüssler Fiorenza, "The Ethics of Biblical Interpretation: Decentering Biblical Scholarship," *Journal of Biblical Literature* 107 (1988): 3–18.

2. Krister Stendahl, "Ancient Scripture in the Modern World," in *Scripture in the Jewish and Christian Traditions: Authority, Interpretation, Relevance* (ed. Frederick E. Greenspahn; Nashville: Abingdon, 1982), 205. See the discussion in Elisabeth Schüssler Fiorenza, "Paul and the Politics of Interpretation," in *Paul and Politics: Ekklesia, Israel, Imperium, Interpretation: Essays in Honor of Krister Stendahl* (ed. Richard A. Horsley; Harrisburg, Pa.: Trinity, 2000), 40–57.

3. Richard A. Horsley, *The Liberation of Christmas: The Infancy Narratives in Social Context* (New York: Crossroad, 1989).

4. Richard A. Horsley, *Jesus and Empire: The Kingdom of God and the New World Disorder* (Minneapolis: Fortress Press, 2003), 145.

5. Horsley, "Introduction: Krister Stendahl's Challenge to Pauline Studies," in *Paul and Politics*, 1–16.

6. Richard A. Horsley and Neil Asher Silberman, *The Message and the Kingdom: How Jesus and Paul Ignited a Revolution and Transformed the Ancient World* (New York: Grosset/Putnam, 1997).

7. Richard A. Horsley, *Hearing the Whole Story: The Politics of Plot in Mark's Gospel* (Louisville, Ky.: Westminster John Knox, 2001).

8. Richard A. Horsley, *The Liberation of Christmas: The Infancy Narratives in Social Context* (New York: Crossroad, 1989).

9. Horsley, "Rhetoric and Empire—And 1 Corinthians," in *Paul and Politics*, 72–102. See also Richard A. Horsley, *1 Corinthians* (Nashville, Tenn.: Abingdon, 1998).

10. Horsley, *Jesus and Empire*, 5.

11. Ibid., 146.

12. Richard A. Horsley, ed., *Oral Performance, Popular Tradition, and Hidden Transcript in Q* (Atlanta: Society of Biblical Literature, 2006); and Richard A. Horsley, ed., *Hidden Transcripts and the Arts of Resistance: Applying the Work of James C. Scott to Jesus and Paul* (Atlanta: Society of Biblical Literature, 2004).

13. Richard A. Horsley, ed., *Christian Origins* (vol. 1 of *A People's History of Christianity*; Minneapolis: Fortress Press, 2005).

Chapter 1

1. Warren Carter, *The Roman Empire and the New Testament: An Essential Guide* (Nashville: Abingdon Press, 2006); idem, *Pontius Pilate: Portraits of a Roman Governor* (Collegeville, Minn.: Liturgical Press, 2003); idem, *Matthew and Empire: Initial Explorations* (Harrisburg, Pa.: Trinity Press International, 2001); idem, *Matthew and the Margins: A Sociopolitical and Religious Reading* (Maryknoll, N.Y.: Orbis Books, 2000).

2. Thomas Kennedy, "Patriotism and Empire," *Word & World* 25 (Spring 2005): 118–26, esp. 118. This edition of *Word & World* is titled "American Empire." Kennedy borrows the phrase "anxious about empire" from Wes Avram, ed., *Anxious about Empire: Theological Essays on the New Global Realities* (Grand Rapids, Mich.: Brazos, 2004).

3. Richard Horsley, *Religion and Empire: People, Power, and the Life of the Spirit* (Minneapolis: Fortress Press, 2003). It is a pleasure to honor Dick Horsley's scholarly work and guild leadership.

4. For example, Michael Hardt and Antonio Negri (*Empire* [Cambridge, Mass.: Harvard University Press, 2000]) emphasized the pervasiveness of empire in human interactions beyond political control asserted by one nation over others.

5. Michael Walzer, "Is There an American Empire?" *Dissent* (Fall 2003): 28, quoted by Gary M. Simpson in "Hope in the Face of Empire: Failed Patriotism, Civil International Publicity, and Patriotic Peacebuilding," *Word & World* 25 (Spring 2005): 127–38, esp. 128.

6. Jean Bethke Elshtain, "International Justice as Equal Regard and the Use of Force," in Avram, *Anxious about Empire*, 130, summarized by Simpson, "Hope in the Face of Empire," 128–29.

7. Michael Ignatieff, "American Empire: The Burden," *New York Times Magazine*, 5 January 2003: 24; quoted in Simpson, "Hope in the Face of Empire," 128–29.

8. Dennis Duling, "Empire: Theories, Methods, Models," in *The Gospel of Matthew in Its Roman Imperial Context*, ed. J. Riches and D. C. Sim (London: T&T Clark International, 2005), 49–74.

9. For example, Richard A. Horsley, *Jesus and the Spiral of Violence: Popular Jewish Resistance in Roman Palestine* (San Francisco: Harper & Row, 1987); Horsley, *Hearing the Whole Gospel: The Politics of Plot in Mark's Gospel* (Louisville, Ky.: Westminster John Knox Press, 2001); Horsley, *Jesus and Empire: The Kingdom of God and the New World Disorder* (Minneapolis: Fortress Press, 2002); Horsley, ed., *Paul and Politics: Ekklesia, Israel, Imperium, Interpretation: Essays in Honor of Krister Stendahl* (Harrisburg,

Pa.: Trinity Press International, 2000); Horsley, *Hidden Transcripts and the Arts of Resistance: Applying the Work of James C. Scott to Jesus and Paul*, Semeia Studies 48 (Atlanta: Society of Biblical Literature, 2004); Horsley, ed., *Paul and the Roman Imperial Order* (Harrisburg, Pa.: Trinity Press International, 2004); John Dominic Crossan and Jonathan L. Reed, *Excavating Jesus: Beneath the Stories, Behind the Texts* (New York: HarperSanFrancisco, 2001); Crossan and Reed, *In Search of Paul: How Jesus' Apostle Opposed Rome's Empire with God's Kingdom: A New Vision of Paul's Words and World* (New York: HarperSanFrancisco, 2004); Brian Walsh and Sylvia Keesmaat, *Colossians Remixed: Subverting the Empire* (Downers Grove, Ill.: InterVarsity Press, 2004); Wes Howard-Brook and Anthony Gwyther, *Unveiling Empire: Reading Revelation Then and Now* (Maryknoll, N.Y.: Orbis Books, 1999); Carter, *Matthew and Empire*; Carter, *Matthew and the Margins*.

10. It cannot be protested that Jesus was crucified for offending the Jerusalem religious leaders. This claim artificially and anachronistically isolates religious matters from political matters and ignores the common Roman policy of ruling its empire through alliances with local elites. Jesus' crucifixion is not primarily an ethnic struggle, Jews against Romans, but a societal divide between the elite ruling alliance, comprising Judeans and Romans, and the rest of society. See Carter, *Pontius Pilate*.

11. Italics mine. Leander Keck, "Derivation as Destiny: 'Of-ness' in Johannine Christology, Anthropology, and Soteriology," in *Exploring the Gospel of John: In Honor of D. Moody Smith*, ed. R. Alan Culpepper and C. Clifton Black (Louisville, Ky.: Westminster John Knox, 1996), 274–88.

12. J. Louis Martyn, *History and Theology in the Fourth Gospel*, 3d ed. (Nashville: Abingdon, 1968; Louisville, Ky.: Westminster John Knox, 2003); Wayne Meeks, "The Man from Heaven in Johannine Sectarianism," *Journal of Biblical Literature* 91 (1972): 44–72.

13. Daniel Boyarin, "The *Ioudaioi* in John and the Prehistory of 'Judaism,'" in *Pauline Conversations in Context: Essays in Honor of Calvin J. Roetzel*, ed. Janice Capel Anderson, Philip Sellew, and Claudia Setzer (London: Sheffield Academic Press, 2002), 216–39, esp. 218, 220.

14. Paul Trebilco, *Jewish Communities in Asia Minor*, Society for New Testament Studies Monograph Series 69 (Cambridge: Cambridge University Press, 1991); John M. G. Barclay, *Jews in the Mediterranean Diaspora: From Alexander to Trajan (323 BCE–117 CE)* (Edinburgh: T&T Clark, 1996); Tessa Rajak, *The Jewish Dialogue with Greece and Rome: Studies in Cultural and Social Interaction* (Leiden, Netherlands: Brill, 2001).

15. E. Mary Smallwood, *The Jews under Roman Rule: From Pompey to Diocletian*, 2d ed. (Leiden, Netherlands: Brill, 1976; Boston: Brill, 2001), 135–36; 344–45.

16. François Vouga, *Le Cadre Historique et l'Intention Théologique de Jean* (Paris: Beauchesne, 1977), 11; less strongly, Raymond Brown, *The Community of the Beloved Disciple* (New York: Paulist, 1979), 42–43.

17. Tessa Rajak, "Was There a Roman Charter for the Jews?" in *Jewish Dialogue*, 300–333, esp. 300–301; Trebilco, *Jewish Communities*, 8–12.

18. See note 14 above.

19. Dominique Cuss, *Imperial Cult and Honorary Terms in the New Testament* (Fribourg: Fribourg University Press, 1974), 39, 148, 152–54; B. A. Mastin, "The Imperial Cult and the Ascription of the Title *Theos* to Jesus (John XX.28)," *Studia Evangelica* 6 (1973): 352–65; Mastin, "A Neglected Feature of the Christology of the Fourth Gospel," *New Testament Studies* 22 (1975–76): 32–51, esp. 46.

20. For discussion, see Edwin Ramage, "Denigration of Predecessor under Claudius, Galba and Vespasian," *Historia* 32 (1983): 201–14, esp. 210, n. 3, who sees this denigration tradition culminating with Pliny's *Panegyric*; Brian W. Jones, *The Emperor Domitian* (London: Routledge, 1992); Leonard Thompson, *The Book of Revelation: Apocalypse and Empire* (Oxford: Oxford University Press, 1990), 95–115. For a restatement of the older view, see Timothy Peter Wiseman, "Domitian and the Dynamics of Terror in Classical Rome," *History Today* 46 (1996): 19–24; Marcus Wilson, "After the Silence: Tacitus, Suetonius, Juvenal," in *Flavian Rome: Culture, Image, Text*, ed. Anthony Boyle and William Dominik (Leiden, Netherlands: Brill, 2003), 523–42.

21. Irenaeus, *Against Heretics* 5.30.

22. J. Christian Wilson, "The Problem of the Domitianic Date of Revelation," *New Testament Studies* 39 (1993): 587–605.

23. Steven Friesen, *Imperial Cults and the Apocalypse of John: Reading Revelation in the Ruins* (New York: Oxford University Press, 2001), 25–131.

24. Text in Friesen, *Imperial Cults*, 44.

25. Compare Suetonius, *Domitian*, 13.2; Philostratus, *Life of Apollonius*, 8.4; Pliny, *Panegyricus*, 33.4, 52.6.

26. Richard Cassidy, *John's Gospel in New Perspective: Christology and the Realities of Roman Power* (Maryknoll, N.Y.: Orbis, 1992), ix, 17–26; Paul Anderson, *The Fourth Gospel and the Quest for Jesus: Modern Foundations Reconsidered*, Library of New Testament Studies (London/New York: T&T Clark, 2006), 41, 64–66, 195.

27. I employ this approach in Warren Carter, *John and Empire: Initial Explorations* (New York: T&T Clark, 2008).

28. Julia Kristeva, "The Bounded Text," in *Desire in Language: A Semiotic Approach to Literature and Art*, ed. L. Roudiez (New York: Columbia University Press, 1980), 36–63, esp. 36–37.

29. For example, Fernando Segovia, "The Gospel of John," in Fernando Segovia and R. S. Sugirtharajah, eds., *A Postcolonial Commentary on the New Testament Writings* (London/New York: T&T Clark, 2007), 156-93; James Scott, *Domination and the Arts of Resistance* (New Haven: Yale University Press, 1990); Janet Huskinson, ed., *Experiencing Rome: Culture, Identity, and Power in the Roman Empire* (London: Routledge, 2000); Helmut Koester, ed., *Ephesos Metropolis of Asia: An Interdisciplinary Approach to Its Archeology, Religion, and Culture* (Valley Forge: Trinity Press International, 1995). See also Carter, *John and Empire*.

30. Warren Carter, *John: Storyteller, Interpreter, Evangelist* (Peabody: Hendrickson, 2006).

31. Two useful resources include K. C. Hanson and Douglas E. Oakman, *Palestine in the Time of Jesus: Social Structures and Social Conflicts* (Minneapolis: Fortress Press, 1998); and Carter, *The Roman Empire and the New Testament*. The latter, comprising about 140 pages, could be read in sections and discussed by a group over consecutive weeks.

32. For discussion of each topic, see Carter, *John and Empire*.

33. Gerhard Lenski, *Power and Privilege: A Theory of Social Stratification* (Chapel Hill: University of North Carolina Press, 1984). For a good discussion, including a diagram, see Duling, "Empire: Theories," 53–73.

34. Kenan Erim, *Aphrodisias: City of Venus Aphrodite* (New York: Facts on File, 1986); Roland R. Smith, "The Imperial Reliefs from the Sebasteion at Aphrodisias," *The Journal of Roman Studies* 77 (1987): 88–138; Smith, "*Sacra Gentium*: The *Ethnē* from the Sebasteion at Aphrodisias," *Journal of Roman Studies* 78 (1988): 50–77.

35. Carter, *Matthew and Empire*, 20–34.

36. Carter, *Matthew and the Margins*, 413–18.

37. See, for example, the establishment of God's reign and purposes and feasting (Isa 25:5-10), abundant wine (Hos 14:1-7; Amos 9:13-14), and wedding/marriage (Hos 2:16-20; Isa 54:4-8).

38. Hanson and Oakman, *Palestine in the Time of Jesus*, 131-59; Carter, *Matthew and the Margins*, 418-21.

Chapter 2

1. Al Gore, *Earth in the Balance: Ecology and the Human Spirit*, paperback ed. (New York: Penguin Group, 1993 [1992]), 225.

2. I write from Tromso, Norway, on United Nations World Environment Day 2007, where a new report documenting the catastrophic effects of melting ice has been released: United Nations Environment Programme, *Global Outlook for Ice and Snow*, prepared by Pål Prestrud et. al, 2007, http://www.unep.org/geo/geo_ice/. I am grateful to Olav Fykse Tveit and Freddy Knutsen of the Church of Norway for their hospitality. I am grateful to Peter Perry, my research assistant, for bibliographic and editorial assistance with 2 Peter 3, and to the Louisville Institute, the Association of Theological Schools, and Thrivent for grant support for research.

3. *Working Group II Contribution to the Intergovernmental Panel on Climate Change Fourth Assessment Report: Climate Change 2007: Impacts, Adaptations and Vulnerabilities: Summary for Policymakers*. http://www.ipcc.ch/pdf/assessment-report/ ar4/wg2/ar4-wg2-spm.pdf.

4. In December 2006, *The Independent* reported obliteration of the island of Lohachara in India, once home to 10,000 people, where the Ganges and Brahmaputra Rivers empty into the Bay of Bengal ("Disappearing World: Global Warming Claims Tropical Island," *The Independent*, Dec. 24, 2006; see also "Sea's Rise in India Buries Islands and a Way of Life," *New York Times*, April 11, 2007). The Alaskan island of Shismaref, an Eskimo village with population of 600, has been so battered by storms as a consequence of the melting of sea ice that the entire population must be relocated ten miles inland at a cost of at least $180 million ("A Struggle to Stay Afloat," *Smithsonian Magazine*, April 2006).

5. James Hansen, "Why We Can't Wait," *The Nation*, May 7, 2007; see also "Warming Expert Sees 10-Year Window," MSNBC, September 14, 2006, http://www. msnbc.msn.com/id/14834318/. The second article reports on Hansen, who was speaking at a Climate Change Conference in Sacramento, California.

6. See Table SPM.4, "Estimated Global Macro-Economic Costs in 2030 for Least-Cost Trajectories Towards Different Long-Term Stabilization Levels," *Working Group III Contribution to the Intergovernmental Panel on Climate Change Fourth Assessment Report: Mitigation of Climate Change, Summary for Policymakers*, p. 12. The table projects the economic effects of three possible scenarios of different concentrations of carbon dioxide and equivalents: 445–535 parts per million (ppm); 535–590 ppm; and 590–710 ppm. http://www.ipcc.ch/pdf/assessment-report/ar4/wg3/ar4-wg3-spm.pdf.

7. The National Snow and Ice Data Center at the University of Colorado released evidence in May 2007 that the Arctic Sea ice is melting faster than computer models predicted, and the Arctic will probably be ice-free by 2020 rather than the expected 2050.

"This is the third time in the last few months that studies have suggested the IPCC's latest major global climate analysis, the Fourth Assessment Report, is too conservative" (Richard Black, "Arctic Melt Faster than Forecast," *BBC News*, May 3, 2007). Moreover, the Southern Ocean around Antarctica, a major carbon "sink," seems to have reached the limit of its ability to absorb carbon dioxide, even while rates of carbon emissions are growing faster than predicted by models (see Peter N. Spotts, "Global Carbon Emissions in Overdrive," *Christian Science Monitor*, May 22, 2007). Al Gore cited evidence of permafrost melting in Siberia at a rate five times faster than expected in testifying before the U.S. Senate Environment and Public Works Committee that "new evidence shows it may be worse than we thought" (U.S. Senate Environment and Public Works Committee, *Testimony of the Honorable Al Gore before the United States Senate Environment and Public Works Committee*, March 21, 2007, http://epw.senate.gov/public/index. cfm?FuseAction=Files.View&FileStore_id=e060b5ca-6df7-495d-afde-9bb98c9b4d41). Bristol University scientists cited data in May 2007 suggesting that global warming is making vegetation less able to absorb carbon (David Adam, "Ten-Year Warming Window Closing," *Sydney Morning Herald,* May 12, 2007).

8. The *Bulletin of the Atomic Scientists* created its Doomsday Clock to convey how close humanity is to catastrophic planetary destruction—the figurative "midnight." In January 2007 the Board of Directors of the *Bulletin of the Atomic Scientists* decided to move the minute hand from seven to five minutes to midnight, stating that "we stand at the brink of disaster." The last time the hands were closer to midnight was in 1984. See http://www.thebulletin.org/minutes-to-midnight/board-statements.html.

9. *IPCC Working Group III Summary for Policymakers*, Table SPM.5, p. 15.

10. See, for example, the testimony of Presiding Bishop Katharine Jefferts Schori and other religious leaders to the U.S. Senate Committee on Environment and Public Works, June 7, 2007. To read Bishop Jefferts Schori's speech, see *Episcopal Life Online*, "Presiding Bishop's Testimony to Senate on Global Warming, June 7, 2007," reported by the Episcopal News Service, http://www.episcopal-life.org/78703_86656_ENG_HTM.htm.

11. This article builds on previous work in which I have sought to reclaim the apocalyptic book of Revelation as a positive resource for ecological reflection by contrasting the Babylon/Rome vision of imperial injustice with the earth-renewing vision of New Jerusalem, and argued for an anti-imperial reading of the plagues of Revelation. See Barbara Rossing, "River of Life in God's New Jerusalem: An Eschatological Vision for Earth's Future," in *Christianity and Ecology*, ed. Rosemary Radford Ruether and Dieter Hessel (Cambridge, Mass.: Harvard Center for World Religions, 1999), 205–224;

Barbara Rossing, "Alas for the Earth: Lament and Resistance in Revelation 12," in *The Earth Story in the New Testament*, vol. 5, *The Earth Bible*, ed. Norman Habel and Shirley Wurst (Sheffield: Sheffield Academic Press, 2002), 180–92; Barbara Rossing, "For the Healing of the World: Reading Revelation Ecologically," in *From Every Tribe, Tongue, People, and Nation: The Book of Revelation in Intercultural Perspective*, ed. David Rhoads (Minneapolis: Fortress Press, 2005), 165–82.

12. Although *oikoumenē* is often translated "inhabited world" (see definitions 1, 3, and 4 in W. Bauer, F. W. Danker, W. F. Arndt and F. W. Gingrich, *A Greek-English Lexicon of the New Testament and Other Early Christian Literature* [3ᵈ· ed; Chicago, 1999 (BDAG)] and in H. G. Liddell, R. Scott, and H. S. Jones, *A Greek-English Lexicon* [9ᵗʰ ed. with revised supplement, Oxford, 1996]). I have argued that it is more accurately translated "empire" in the New Testament (see, by way of comparison, BDAG definition 2). See Barbara Rossing, "(Re)Claiming *Oikoumenē*? Empire, Ecumenism and the Discipleship of Equals," in *Walk in the Ways of Wisdom: Essays in Honor of Elisabeth Schüssler Fiorenza*, ed. Shelly Matthews, Cynthia Briggs Kittredge, and Melanie Johnson-DeBaufre (Harrisburg, Pa.: Trinity Press International, 2003), 74–87.

13. Translations of the biblical text are my own.

14. Rev 21:1, "The first heaven and the first earth had passed away," and 20:11, "Earth and sky fled away," can be read in a number of ways, but certainly not as evidence that God must destroy the first earth before the dawning of the new heavens and the new earth. I have suggested that the "first earth" that passes away is the earth that is captive to Roman imperial power, whereas the new earth of Rev 21:1 is envisioned as the earth free from Roman domination (see Rossing, "Alas for the Earth," 189).

15. See discussion in Bruce Metzger, *A Textual Commentary on the Greek New Testament* (New York: United Bible Societies, 1971), 706.

16. Some fundamentalist preachers applied the "dissolving" and "melting with fire" of 2 Peter 3:10 to the nuclear bombs dropped on Hiroshima and Nagasaki; see Paul Boyer, *When Time Shall Be No More: Prophecy Belief in Modern American Culture* (Cambridge, Mass.: Harvard University Press, 1992), 116–20.

17. Robert McClure and Lisa Stiffler, "Federal Way schools restrict Gore film: 'Inconvenient Truth' called too controversial," *Seattle Post-Intelligencer*, January 11, 2007, http://seattlepi.nwsource.com/local/299253_inconvenient11.html.

18. Jerry Falwell, "The Myth of Global Warming" (sermon, Thomas Road Baptist Church, Lynchburg, Va., February 25, 2007); see also Bob Allen, "Falwell Says Global Warming Tool of Satan," March 1, 2007, EthicsDaily.com, http://www.ethicsdaily.com/article_detail.cfm?AID=8596.

19. http://forums.wnd.com/index.php?fa=PAGE.view&pageId=22&forumPage=22.

20. Got Questions Ministries, "How Should a Christian View Global Warming?" http://www.gotquestions.org/global-warming.html.

21. For example, *Apoc. Pet.* 5 expands on the fiery imagery of 2 Peter 3, as does *2 Clem.* 16.3. See discussion of the origins and development of the cosmic conflagration tradition by Carsten Peter Thiede, "A Pagan Reader of 2 Peter: Cosmic Conflagration in 2 Peter 3 and the *Octavius* of Municius Felix," *Journal for the Study of the New Testament* 26 (1986): 79–96.

22. Gracia Grindal, "Hastening the Day," *The Christian Century* (November 20, 1996) 113:34.

23. In the Revised Common Lectionary, 2 Peter 3:8-15 is assigned for the Second Sunday of Advent in Year B. I urge preachers to take on this text and preach against the notion of a fiery destruction as being God's will for the earth.

24. Raymond Brown dates 2 Peter to 130 C.E., on the basis of its distance from the apostolic generation and its knowledge of an established collection of Paul's letters (*An Introduction to the New Testament*, Anchor Bible Reference Library [New York: Doubleday, 1997], 767); other scholars date it somewhat earlier. See, for example, John Elliott, "Peter, Second Epistle of," *Anchor Bible Dictionary* 5.282–87; Cynthia Briggs Kittredge, "2 Peter," in *Postcolonial Commentary on the New Testament Writings*, ed. Fernando Segovia and R. S. Sugirtharajah (New York: T & T Clark, 2007).

25. *First Enoch* 10–11 envisions the fallen Watchers being consumed by fire, but it is the destruction of the *wicked* by fire, not of the *world*. This is the case also for other biblical texts often cited as antecedents for the conflagration imagery of 2 Peter 3.

26. See for example Josephus *Antiquities of the Jews* 1.70-71. In Richard Bauckham's view (*Jude, 2 Peter*, Word Bible Commentary 50 [Waco, Tex.: Word, 1983], 300), the author of 2 Peter follows an unknown Jewish apocalyptic source for chapter three, from which he adopted the imagery. But Bauckham cites no evidence for this "Jewish notion of two universal judgments" (both flood and fire) prior to Josephus and Philo, both of whom may be influenced by Hellenistic tradition.

27. For the thesis that 2 Peter is arguing with Greco-Roman converts who are steeped in the Greek idea of *ekpyrōsis*, either through Epicureanism or, simply, Stoicism, see Tord Fornberg, *An Early Church in a Pluralistic Society: A Study of 2 Peter*, ConB NT 9 (Lund, Sweden: CWK Gleerup, 1977), 67, n. 7; Thiede, "A Pagan Reader of 2 Peter."

28. Justin Martyr, *First Apology* 1.20, 1.60; *Second Apology* 7: "We say there will be the conflagration, but not as the Stoics, according to their doctrine of all things being changed into one another."

29. Irenaeus, *Adv. Haer.* 1.7.1; Origen, *Contra Celsum* 4.11.79.

30. David Aune calls it "striking" that "a destruction of the cosmos by fire is not mentioned" in Rev 21:1 or anywhere else in Revelation. David Aune, *Revelation 17–22*, Word Biblical Commentary 52c (Nashville: Thomas Nelson, 1998), 1117.

31. See David M. Russell, *The "New Heavens and New Earth": Hope for the Creation in Jewish Apocalyptic and the New Testament*, Studies in Biblical Apocalyptic Literature 1 (Philadelphia: Visionary Press, 1996), 188.

32. Jerome Neyrey and others who examine the polemic of 2 Peter in the context of ancient debates between philosophical schools in the Greco-Roman world find that the attack upon those who deny divine judgment closely resembles the apology against Epicurean polemics against providence. See Jerome H. Neyrey, "The Form and Background of the Polemic in 2 Peter," *Journal of Biblical Literature*, 99(1980): 407–31.

33. See Raul Humberto Lugo Rodriguez, "Wait for the Day of God's Coming and Do What You Can to Hasten It . . . (2 Pet 3:12): The Non-Pauline Letters as Resistance Literature," in *Subversive Scriptures: Revolutionary Readings of the Christian Bible in Latin America*, trans. and ed. Leif Vaage (Valley Forge, Pa.: Trinity Press International, 1997), 202.

34. See J. N. D. Kelly, *A Commentary on the Epistles of Peter and Jude* (New York: Harper, 1969), 367; Bauckham, *Jude, 2 Peter*, 325.

35. Gale Z. Heide suggests that 2 Peter and 2 *Clement* might share the notion of a purging fire of judgment rather than an all-consuming fire, since 2 *Clem* 16:3 says that only *some* of the heavens (*tines tōn ouranōn*) will melt at the day of judgment. ("What is New about the New Heaven and the New Earth? A Theology of Creation from Revelation 21 and 2 Peter 3," *Journal of the Evangelical Theological Society* 40/1 (1997): 51, n. 42.

36. Ernst Käsemann, "An Apologia for Primitive Christian Eschatology," in *Essays on New Testament Themes* (Philadelphia: Fortress Press, 1982), 181.

37. Most scholars date Revelation to the mid-90s, although an earlier date may also be possible.

38. Elisabeth Schüssler Fiorenza, "The Phenomena of Early Christian Apocalyptic: Some Reflections on Method," in *Apocalypticism in the Mediterranean World and the Near East: Proceedings of the International Colloquium on Apocalypticism, Uppsala, 1979*, ed. David Hellholm (Tubingen: Mohr, 1989), 313.

39. John Dart, "Up against Caesar: Jesus and Paul versus the Empire," *The Christian Century* (February 8, 2005): 20.

40. See Claude Nicolet, *Space, Geography, and Politics in the Early Roman Empire* (Ann Arbor: University of Michigan Press, 1991). See also my "(Re)Claiming *Oikoumenē?*" for first-century Roman imperial texts.

41. Luke Timothy Johnson, *The Gospel of Luke*, Sacra Pagina 3 (Collegeville, Minn.: Liturgical Press, 1991); idem, *The Acts of the Apostles*, Sacra Pagina 5 (Collegeville, Minn.: Liturgical Press, 1992). Johnson translates *oikoumenē* as "empire" in Luke 2:1, 4:5 and Acts 11:28, 17:6, 24:5, but not in Luke 21:26 ("inhabited world"), Acts 17:31 ("world"), or Acts 19:27 ("inhabited world").

42. As a prelude to the exposé of Roman imperial power in chapter 13, Satan is called the "deceiver of the whole *oikoumenē*" (Rev 12:9). The fall of Babylon/Rome in Revelation 17–18 is preceded by a description of its own vassals, the "kings of the whole *oikoumenē*," assembling for battle (Rev 16:14).

43. Steven J. Friesen, *Imperial Cults and the Apocalypse of John* (New York: Oxford University Press, 2001), 158.

44. Other Jewish apocalypses such as 2 *Bar.* and 4 *Ezra* similarly depict a time between the destruction of the Roman Empire and the final judgment of humanity, although "their handling of the theme is much different" (Friesen, *Imperial Cults*, 160).

45. Pablo Richard, *Apocalypse: A People's Commentary on the Book of Revelation* (Maryknoll, N.Y.: Orbis, 1995), 157.

46. David M. Rhoads offers an important reading of the New Testament "as a manual for facing a possible end to the world," in order to learn from the behavior of early Christians how we might respond to the ecological crisis today. See "Who Will Speak for the Sparrow? Eco-Justice Criticism of the New Testament," in *Literary Encounters with the Reign of God*, ed. Sharon Ringe and H. C. Paul Kim, (New York: T & T Clark, 2004), 83–85.

47. Harry O. Maier, *Apocalypse Recalled: The Book of Revelation after Christendom* (Minneapolis: Fortress Press, 2002), 147.

48. *IPCC Working Group III Summary Report for Policymakers*, p. 25: "The range of stabilization levels assessed can be achieved by deployment of a portfolio of technologies that are currently available and those that are expected to be commercialized in coming decades."

49. Elisabeth Schüssler Fiorenza, *Revelation: Vision of a Just World* (Minneapolis: Fortress Press, 1991), 72.

50. Barbara Rossing, *The Rapture Exposed: The Message of Hope in the Book of Revelation* (New York: Basic Books, 2004), 85, 91.

51. Maier, *Apocalypse Recalled*, 130–31.

52. Richard, *Apocalypse: A People's Commentary*, 33.

53. Brian K. Blount, *Can I Get a Witness? Reading Revelation through African American Culture* (Louisville, Ky.: Westminster John Knox, 2005), 40.

54. See the United Nations Environment Program report *Global Outlook for Ice & Snow*, p. 125, "The increasing number of glacial and moraine lakes in Central Asian mountains is a matter of great concern." Examples of glacier lake outburst floods cited in the report include a 1998 flood in the Shahimardan Valley of Krgystan and Uzbekistan that killed over 100 people, and a 2002 flood in the Shakhdara Valley of the Tajik Pamir Mountains that killed 23 people.

Chapter 3

1. The *Kairos Document* was originally published in Braamfontein by the Kairos theologians. All references in this article are taken, for convenience, from the version published as documentation in *Journal of Theology for Southern Africa* 53 (1985): 61–81. It is available electronically also at http://www.sahistory.org.za/pages/library-resources/official%20docs/kairos-document.htm.

2. Interestingly, the website of the ruling African National Congress still posts a paper from 1990 of the Institute for Contextual Theology setting out the theology of the *Kairos Document* (http://www.anc.org.za/ancdocs/history/transition/kairos.html). The director of the ICT, the Rev. Frank Chikane, one of the original Kairos theologians, subsequently became official advisor to President Thabo Mbeki.

3. The concept of the church and the Bible as "sites of struggle" has also found a continuing currency among feminist theologians and exegetes, for example, Elisabeth Schüssler Fiorenza, *Sharing Her Word: Feminist Biblical Interpretation in Context* (Boston: Beacon Press, 1998), 160.

4. *Kairos Document*, 61.

5. Ibid., 63.

6. Piet Naudé, "Can We Still Hear Paul on the Agora? An Outsider Perspective on South African New Testament Scholarship," *Neotestamentica* 39/2 (2005): 339–358.

7. *Kairos Document*, 62.

8. Ibid., 74.

9. The South African Constitution, including the Bill of Rights, can be found in electronic form at http://www.info.gov.za/documents/constitution/1996/.

10. The statement made at this COSATU meeting on 25 May, 2007 was widely reported in the South African press. For convenience a report on the meeting including the speech of Zokwana can be found on the BBC archival website: http://news.bbc.co.uk/2/hi/africa/5016024.stm. It is interesting, however, that Zokwana ran together

the two issues of the secular state and the strategic appointment of a woman deputy president to replace Zuma who had been relieved of this post by the state president when he was accused of rape. At its most recent Congress, the ANC elected Zuma to replace Mbeki as head of the party and its candidate to run for national president in the country's next general election.

11. See *Weekly Mail and Guardian* reports of 10 May, 2006.

12. *Kairos Document*, 65–67.

13. Ibid., 67–73.

14. The churches were by no means in agreement on the issue of a secular state. The Anglican Church (Church of the Province of Southern Africa), for instance, quite specifically opted for the secular state (*Outlines of a Christian Response to the Constitutional Debate for a New South Africa* [Marshalltown: CPSA Publishing Committee, 1991]). Other churches, for instance the Catholic Bishops' Conference, were not convinced.

15. This idea is taken from the idea of the "shadow" in psychology. What a person attacks most vigorously is related to unresolved conflicts within their own personalities. Homophobia, for instance, on this model, would be related to a person's unresolved fears about their own sexuality. It would be a projection onto others of the conflict within the self.

16. Edward Said, *Orientalism* (New York: Pantheon; London: Routledge & Kegan Paul; Toronto: Random House, 1978). Said argues against essentialisms also in his major work of postcolonial literary theory: *Culture and Imperialism* (New York: Knopf-Random House, 1993).

17. Elsewhere I have used the terminology of "distantiation" or "explanation." See Jonathan A. Draper, "'For the Kingdom is inside of you and it is outside of you': Contextual Exegesis in South Africa," in *Text and Interpretation: New Approaches in the Criticism of the New Testament*, ed. P. J. Hartin and J. H. Petzer (Leiden, Netherlands: Brill, 1991), 235–57; "Old Scores and New Notes: Where and What is Contextual Exegesis in the New South Africa?" in *Towards an Agenda for Contextual Theology*, ed. M. Speckman (Pietermaritzburg, South Africa: Cluster Publications, 2001), 148–68; and "Reading the Bible as Conversation: A Theory and Methodology for Contextual Interpretation of the Bible in Africa," *Grace and Truth* 19/2 (2002): 12–24.

18. J. Severino Croatto, *Biblical Hermeneutics: Toward a Theory of Reading as the Production of Meaning* (Maryknoll, N.Y.: Orbis, 1987).

19. Jean Comaroff and John Comaroff, *Of Revelation and Revolution: Christianity, Colonialism and Consciousness in South Africa* (Chicago: University of Chicago Press, 1991).

20. Wilhelm Dilthey, *Selected Works*, vol. 4, *Hermeneutics and the Study of History*, ed. R. A. Makkreel and F. Rodi (Princeton, N.J.: Princeton University Press, 1996). Hans-Georg Gadamer, *Truth and Method*, 2nd English ed., trans. Joel Weinsheimer and Donald G. Marshall (London: Sheed & Ward, 1993), 383–491.

21. Paul Ricoeur, *Essays on Biblical Interpretation*, ed. L. S. Mudge (Philadelphia: Fortress Press, 1980), 15.

22. Karl Barth, preface to *The Epistle to the Romans*, trans. E. C. Hoskyns (New York: Oxford University Press, 1968).

23. Paul Ricoeur, *Interpretation Theory: Discourse and the Surplus on Meaning* (Fort Worth, Tex.: Texas Christian University Press, 1976); Paul Ricoeur, *Hermeneutics and the Human Sciences: Essays on Language, Action and Interpretation*, trans. and ed. J. B. Thompson (Cambridge: Cambridge University Press, 1981).

24. R. N. Bellah and others, *Habits of the Heart: Individualism and Commitment in American Life* (Berkeley: University of California Press, 1985).

25. This need was described by Peter Berger and Thomas Luckmann in their groundbreaking study, *The Social Construction of Reality: A Treatise in the Sociology of Knowledge* (Middlesex: Penguin, 1966), and by Berger in several subsequent studies (for example, *The Social Reality of Religion* [Harmondsworth: Penguin, 1973]).

26. J. P. Gee, *Social Linguistics and Literacies: Ideology in Discourses*, 2nd ed. (London: Taylor & Francis, 1996).

27. J. M. Foley, *The Singer of Tales in Performance: Voices in Performance and Text* (Bloomington, Ind.: Indiana University Press, 1995).

28. Jean and John Comaroff have shown this in their monumental examination of the interaction between missionaries and indigenous African people in *Of Revelation and Revolution*.

29. Berger and Luckmann, *The Social Construction of Reality*.

30. Clifford Geertz, *The Interpretation of Cultures* (New York: Basic Books, 1973).

31. Ricoeur, *Essays on Biblical Interpretation*, 102.

32. My translation. A recent text and translation can be found in the new translation by Bart Ehrman in the Loeb Classical Library edition of the *Apostolic Fathers*, vol. 1 (Cambridge, Mass.: Harvard University Press, 2003), 403–60.

Chapter 4

1. "The Inauguration – Looking Ahead: 'The Best Hope for Peace in Our World Is the Expansion of Freedom in All the World'" *New York Times*, January 21, 2005.

2. Orlando Patterson, *Freedom in the Making of Western Culture* (New York: Basic Books, 1991).

3. See especially Elisabeth Schüssler Fiorenza, *Wisdom Ways: Introducing Feminist Biblical Interpretation* (Maryknoll, N.Y.: Orbis, 2001), and *Rhetoric and Ethic: The Politics of Biblical Studies* (Minneapolis: Fortress Press, 1999).

4. Jeffrey Goldberg, "The Believer," *New Yorker* 82, no. 1 (February 13, 2006): 56–69.

5. President George W. Bush, "We Strive to Be a Compassionate, Decent, Hopeful Society" (State of the Union Message to Congress and the Nation, Washington D.C., February 1, 2006).

6. Ibid.

7. President George W. Bush, "We Must Pass Reforms That Solve the Financial Problems of Social Security" (State of the Union Message to Congress and the Nation, Washington D.C., February 3, 2005).

8. President George W. Bush, "The State of Our Union Is Strong; Our Cause in the World is Right" (State of the Union Message to Congress and the Nation, Washington D.C., January 24, 2007).

9. President Bush, "We Must Pass Reforms."

10. Ibid.

11. President George W. Bush, "State of the Union," (President's State of the Union Message to Congress and the Nation, Washington D.C., January 29, 2003)

12. George W. Bush, "Presidential Address to the Nation," October 7, 2001, in Bruce Lincoln, *Holy Terrors: Thinking about Religion after September 11* (Chicago and London: University of Chicago Press, 2003), 99–101, and available at http://www.whitehouse.gov/news/releases/2001/10/20011007-8.html.

13. President George W. Bush, "The Best Hope for Peace in Our World."

14. Ibid.

15. President George W. Bush, State of the Union Message to Congress and the Nation, Washington D.C., January 21, 2004.

16. President Bush, "We Strive to Be."

17. J.P. Louw and Eugene Albert Nida, *Greek-English Lexicon of the New Testament Based on Semantic Domains*, vol. 1 (New York: United Bible Societies, 1989), 474, 479.

18. Robert Jewett, *Romans: A Commentary*, Hermeneia (Minneapolis: Fortress Press, 2006), 377.

19. Ibid., 515.

20. Lincoln, *Holy Terrors*, 20.

21. Ibid., 20.

22. Ibid., 25.

23. Jewett, *Romans*, 422.

24. Jeffrey Goldberg, "The Believer," 56–69. See also Ryan Lizza, "Write Hand," *New Republic* 224, no. 21 (May 21, 2001): 14–16.

25. Goldberg, "The Believer," 60.

26. Ibid., 60.

27. Ibid., 64.

28. Ibid., 64.

29. "The Scribe," *Economist* 379, no. 8483 (June 24, 2006): 42.

Chapter 5

1. Full text of the poem can be found at www.amiribaraka.com/blew.html.

2. Translations of the biblical text are the author's, except where otherwise noted.

3. Richard Bauckham, "The Economic Critique of Rome in Revelation 18," in *Images of Empire*, ed. L. Alexander (Sheffield: JSOT Press, 1991), 79. For a detailed analysis of the list, see pages 58–79.

4. See Ernest Badian, *Roman Imperialism in the Late Republic* (Ithaca: Cornell University Press, 1968), 74–76.

5. See Michael W. Doyle, *Empires*, Cornell Studies in Comparative History (Ithaca: Cornell University Press, 1986), 86.

6. Maria Stewart, "An Address Delivered at the African Masonic Hall," in *Maria Stewart: America's First Black Woman Political Writer*, ed. Marilyn Richardson (Bloomington, Ind.: Indiana University Press, 1987), 63.

7. *Review of the Rev. U. C. Burnap's Sermon on Biblical Servitude* (Lowell: J. G. Pillsbury, 1844), 19.

8. *A Review of the Rev. Dr. Junkin's Synodical Speech . . . with an Outline of the Bible Argument against Slavery* (Cincinnati: Daily Atlas Office, 1844), 124.

9. The full text of Lincoln's second inaugural address is available at http://www.yale.edu/lawweb/avalon/presiden/inaug/lincoln2.htm (consulted 19 February, 2008).

10. W. B. Allen, interviewed by J. R. Jones, 29 June, 1937, in *The American Slave: A Composite Autobiography*, Contributions in Afro-American and African Studies 11 (originally published 1941; 19 vols.; Westport, Conn.: Greenwood, 1972), 12–13.

11. Jerry Eubanks, interviewed by J. R. Jones (no date), *The American Slave: A Composite Autobiography*, Supplement, Series 1, vol. 10: Mississippi Narratives, Part 5 (George P. Rawick, gen. ed.; Jan Hillegas, Ken Lawrence, eds.; Westport, Conn.: Greenwood, 1977), p. 687.

12. See Allen Callahan, *The Talking Book: African Americans and the Bible* (New Haven: Yale University Press, 2006), 193–202.

13. Brian Blount, *Can I Get a Witness? Reading Revelation through African American Culture* (Louisville, Ky.: Westminster John Knox, 2005), 117.

14. Cited in John Willie Roberts, *From Trickster to Badman: The Black Folk Hero in Slavery and Freedom* (Philadelphia: University of Pennsylvania Press, 1989), 153.

15. In R. Nathaniel Dett, ed., *Religious Folk-Songs of the Negro* (Hampton, Va.: Hampton Institute Press, 1927), 180–81, 146–47.

16. Thomas Wentworth Higginson, *Army Life in a Black Regiment* (1870; repr. New York: Collier Books, 1962), 48.

17. Dett, *Folk-Songs*, 158.

18. Ibid., 157.

19. From the spiritual, "I Got a Home in that Rock"; text available at http://www.negrospirituals.com/news-song/i_got_a_home_in_that_rock.htm (accessed on 19 February, 2008).

20. Theophilus Gould Steward, *The End of the World, or Clearing the Way for the Fullness of the Gentiles* (Philadelphia: A. M. E. Church Book Rooms, 1888), 135.

21. Ibid., 121–22.

22. Ibid., 122.

23. Ibid., 121.

24. Ibid., 122.

25. Ibid., 121.

26. Elijah Muhammad, *The Fall of America* (Chicago: Muhammad's Temple of Islam No. 2, 1973), 124.

27. Elijah Muhammad, *Message to the Blackman in America* (Chicago: Muhammad's Mosque of Islam No. 2, 1965), 88.

28. Muhammad, *The Fall of America*, 124.

29. Ibid., 124.

30. Ibid., 125–26.

31. Ibid., 130.

32. Ibid., 142.

33. Nathaniel Samuel Murrell, "Wresting the Message from the Messenger: The Rastafari as a Case Study in the Caribbean Indigenization of the Bible," in *African Americans and the Bible: Sacred Texts and Social Textures*, ed. Vincent Wimbush (New York: Continuum, 2000), 576, n. 54.

34. Ibid., 571.

35. Bob Marley and the Wailers, "Babylon System," *Survival*, LP recording © 1979 by Island Records, ILPS 9542.

36. Allen Callahan, "The Language of Apocalypse," *Harvard Theological Review* 88.4 (1995): 464.

37. See Laurence Breiner, "The English Bible in Jamaican Rastafarianism," *The Journal of Religious Thought* 42.2 (1985–86): 33.

38. Barry Chevannes, *Rastafari: Roots and Ideology* (Syracuse, N.Y.: Syracuse University Press, 1994), 230.

39. Murrell, "Wresting the Message," 576, note 54.

40. Haile Mikael Yenge Flagot Kezehemohonenow, "The Role of Rastafarians in the Caribbean," paper delivered at the Caribbean Symposium, Chaguaramas, Trinidad, November 1971, quoted in Murrell, "Wresting the Message," 570.

41. See Nathaniel Samuel Murrell, "Turning Hebrew Psalms to Reggae Rhythms: Rastas' Revolutionary Lamentations for Social Change," *CrossCurrents*, The Association for Religion and Intellectual Life, http://www.crosscurrents.org/murrell.htm.

42. Bob Marley, "Exodus," *Exodus* © 1977 by Island Records.

43. Murrell, "Wresting the Message," 576, note 54.

44. Chevannes, *Rastafari*, 208.

45. Ibid., 214.

46. David Katz, "Max Romeo—Chasing the Devil with Lyrics," Jammin Reggae Archives, http://niceup.com/writers/david_katz/chasing_the_devil.

47. Max Romeo, "Babylon's Burning," *Pray For Me: The Best Of Max Romeo 1967–1973* © 2000 by Trojan Records. The recording was originally released as a single on Upsetter Records in 1972.

48. Culture, "Babylon A Weep," *Trust Me* © 1997 by RAS Records.

49. Messian Dread, "Babylon" © 1988 Messian Dread, Reggae Lyrics Archive, http://hjem.get2net.dk/sbn/mdread/messian.htm#1 (wording slightly modified).

50. Messian Dread, "Jah Seh No," © 1989 Messian Dread, Reggae Lyrics Archive, http://hjem.get2net.dk/sbn/mdread/messian.htm#1.

51. Dwight N. Hopkins, *Heart and Head: Black Theology—Past, Present, and Future* (New York: Palgrave, 2002), 129.

Chapter 6

1. From *The Complete Poems of Emily Dickinson*, ed. Thomas H. Johnson (Boston: Little, Brown and Company, 1955), 558, poem 1277.

2. Corey Robin, *Fear: The History of a Political Idea* (New York: Oxford University Press, 2004).

3. Noted in Ibid., 1, 7.

4. This second person plural is addressed to the prophet's disciples. See Norman K. Gottwald, *All the Kingdoms of the Earth: Israelite Prophecy and International Relations in the Ancient Near East* (New York: Harper & Row, 1964), 156.

5. Emending the Masoretic Text "sanctuary" with Wildberger; see Hans Wildberger, *Isaiah 1–12. A Commentary* (Minneapolis: Fortress Press, 1991), 355–56.

6. Second singular imperative.

7. Author's translation, with reliance on Wildberger, *Isaiah 1–12*, 355–56.

8. Norman K. Gottwald, "The Politics of Armageddon—Apocalyptic Fantasies, Ancient and Modern," in *The Hebrew Bible in Its Social World and in Ours.* Atlanta: Scholars Press, 1993), 255–65.

9. William Shakespeare, *King Lear*, act 2, sc.4, lines 281–84.

Chapter 7

1. Max Weber, *The Protestant Ethic and the Spirit of Capitalism*, trans. Talcott Parsons (New York: Scribner's, 1958), 181.

2. Richard A. Horsley's published work is extensive, but for my purposes here I have referred only to his more general volumes. For this theme, the following are important: *Jesus and the Spiral of Violence: Popular Jewish Resistance in Roman Palestine* (San Francisco: Harper and Row, 1987); *Religion and Empire: People, Power, and the Life of the Spirit* (Minneapolis: Fortress Press, 2003); *Jesus and Empire: The Kingdom of God and the New World (Disorder* (Minneapolis: Fortress Press, 2003); *Christmas Unwrapped: Consumerism, Christ, and Culture*, ed. Richard Horsley and James Tracy (Harrisburg: Trinity Press International, 2001). Moreover, the three books edited by Horsley are valuable aids to understanding the theme of this essay: *Paul and Empire: Religion and Power in Roman Imperial Society* (Harrisburg: Trinity Press International, 1997); *Paul and Politics: Ekklesia, Israel, Imperium, Interpretation* (Harrisburg: Trinity Press International, 2000); and *Paul and the Roman Imperial Order* (Harrisburg: Trinity Press International, 2004).

3. See any of the works cited above, but especially Horsley, *Jesus and Empire*.

4. See, especially, Horsley, *Religion and Empire*.

5. See Hans-Georg Gadamer, *Truth and Method* (New York: Seabury Press, 1975).

6. Norman K. Gottwald, *The Tribes of Yahweh: A Sociology of the Religion of Liberated Israel, 1250–1050 B.C.E.* (Maryknoll, N.Y.: Orbis Books, 1979).

7. For theoretical material on the genealogy of "empire," I am relying heavily on Michael Hardt and Antonio Negri, *Empire* (Cambridge, Mass.: Harvard University Press, 2000). This analysis is continued in a post–9/11 context in Hardt and Negri, *Multitude: War and Democracy in the Age of Empire* (New York: The Penguin Press, 2004).

8. See the excerpts from S. R. F. Price, "Rituals and Power," and Paul Zanker, "The Power of Images," in Horsley, ed., *Paul and Empire*, 47–86, for concrete examples of how this functioned in the Roman Empire.

9. As one example out of many, see the essays in Horsley, *Paul and Politics*. Many of the same points are made in John Dominic Crossan's recent *God and Empire: Jesus against Rome, Then and Now* (San Francisco: HarperCollins, 2007).

10. Hardt and Negri, *Empire*, 229–34.

11. See the essays by David Ray Griffin, "America's Non-Accidental, Non-Benign Empire," John B. Cobb Jr., "Imperialism in American Economic Policy," and Richard Falk, "Slouching toward a Fascist World Order," in *The American Empire and the Commonwealth of God: A Political, Economic, Religious Statement*, ed. David Ray Griffin (Louisville, Ky.: Westminster John Knox, 2006), 1–66.

12. Mark Lewis Taylor has an extremely good discussion of the neoconservatives in *Religion, Politics and the Religious Right: Post-9/11 Powers and American Empire* (Minneapolis: Fortress Press, 2005), 62–95.

13. Taylor makes much the same point, but describes the neoconservatives as "secular revolutionary romanticists" who are paired uneasily with the religious right whom he dubs "religious revolutionary romanticists." Ibid., 47–62.

14. Ibid., 47–62.

15. The effects of this combination of oil, Christian fundamentalism, and debt are discussed in Kevin Phillips, *American Theocracy: The Peril and Politics of Radical Religion, Oil, and Borrowed Money in the 21st Century* (New York: Viking, 2006).

16. For an excellent critique of the Rapture and end-times theology, see Barbara R. Rossing, *The Rapture Exposed: The Message of Hope in the Book of Revelation* (Boulder, Colo.: Westview Press, 2004).

17. Horsley, *Religion and Empire*, 1–9. This is a theme throughout Horsley's work.

18. This is the basic theme of the essays in Horsley and Tracy, *Christmas Unwrapped*.

19. For the importance of patronage in the Roman Empire, see the essays by Peter Garnsey and Richard Saller, "Patronal Power Relations," and John K. Chow, "Patronage in Roman Corinth," in Horsley, ed., *Paul and Empire*, 96–125.

20. On "post-Westphalian" possibilities and perils, see the essays by Richard Falk, "Slouching toward a Fascist World Order," and "Renouncing Wars of Choice:

Toward a Geopolitics of Nonviolence," in Griffin, ed., *The American Empire and the Commonwealth of God*, 44–85.

21. On the principles of subsidiarity and global democracy see the essays by John B. Cobb Jr., "Democratizing the Economic Order," and David Ray Griffin, "Global Empire or Global Democracy: The Present Choice," in Ibid., 86–119.

22. Alfred North Whitehead, *Adventures of Ideas* (New York: The Free Press, 1967), 26.

23. Charles Hartshorne, *Omnipotence and Other Theological Mistakes* (Albany: State University of New York Press, 1984).

24. Alfred North Whitehead, *Process and Reality, Corrected Edition by Griffin and Sherburne* (New York: The Free Press, 1979), 342–51.

25. "The essence of Christianity is the appeal to the life of Christ as a revelation of the nature of God and of his agency in the world." Whitehead, *Adventures of Ideas*, 167.

26. This is the theme of David Ray Griffin's *Reenchantment without Religion: A Process Philosophy of Religion* (Ithaca: Cornell University Press, 2001).

Chapter 8

1. Gerald O. West, "Early Encounters with the Bible among the Batlhaping: Historical and Hermeneutical Signs," *Biblical Interpretation* 12 (2004): 251–81.

2. John Campbell, *Travels in South Africa: Undertaken at the Request of the Missionary Society* (London: Black, Parry & Co, 1815), 192.

3. Ibid., 192.

4. I. Schapera and John L. Comaroff, *The Tswana*, rev. ed. (London and New York: Kegan Paul International, 1991).

5. Jean Comaroff and John L. Comaroff, *Of Revelation and Revolution: Christianity, Colonialism and Consciousness in South Africa*, vol. 1 (Chicago: University of Chicago Press, 1991), 179; idem., *Of Revelation and Revolution: The Dialectics of Modernity on a South African Frontier*, vol. 2 (Chicago: University of Chicago Press, 1997).

6. Campbell, *Travels in South Africa*, 208.

7. Ibid., 208.

8. Ibid., 208.

9. Carol Ann Muller, *Rituals of Fertility and the Sacrifice of Desire: Nazarite Women's Performance in South Africa* (Chicago and London: The University of Chicago Press, 1999), 26.

10. Ibid., xix.

11. Elizabeth Gunner, *The Man of Heaven and the Beautiful Ones of God: Writings from Ibandla Lamanazaretha, a South African Church* (Leiden, Netherlands: Brill, 2002), 20–21.

12. Robert Papini, introduction to *The Catechism of the Nazarites and Related Writings*, ed. Robert Papini and Irving Hexham (Lewiston: The Edwin Mellen Press, 2002), xiii–xiv.

13. Irving Hexham and G. C. Oosthuizen, eds., *The Story of Isaiah Shembe: History and Traditions Centered on Ekuphakameni and Mount Nhlangakazi*, vol. 1 of *Sacred History and Traditions of the Amanazaretha* (Lewiston: The Edwin Mellen Press, 1996), 224.

14. Ibid., 224–25.

15. Ibid., 225.

16. Ibid., 225.

17. Ibid., 225.

18. Ibid., 225–28.

19. Gerald O. West and Bongi Zengele, "The Medicine of God's Word: What People Living with HIV and AIDS Want (and Get) from the Bible," *Journal of Theology for Southern Africa* 125 (2006): 51–63.

20. Takatso Mofokeng, "Black Christians, the Bible and Liberation," *Journal of Black Theology* 2 (1988): 37–38.

21. Ibid., 40.

22. Ibid., 40.

23. Ibid., 40.

24. Ibid., 40.

25. Itumeleng J. Mosala, *Biblical Hermeneutics and Black Theology in South Africa* (Grand Rapids: Eerdmans, 1989).

26. Tinyiko S. Maluleke, "Black Theology as Public Discourse," in *Constructing a Language of Religion in Public Life: Multi-Event 1999 Academic Workshop Papers*, ed. James R. Cochrane (Cape Town: University of Cape Town Press, 1998).

27. Tinyiko S. Maluleke, "Black and African Theologies in the New World Order: A Time to Drink from Our Own Wells," *Journal of Theology for Southern Africa* 96 (1996): 14.

28. Kairos theologians, *The Kairos Document: Challenge to the Church*, rev. 2ᵈ ed. (Braamfontein, South Africa: Skotaville, 1986).

29. Walter Brueggemann, "Trajectories in Old Testament Literature and the Sociology of Ancient Israel," in *The Bible and Liberation: Political and Social Hermeneutics*, ed. Norman K. Gottwald and Richard A. Horsley (Maryknoll, N.Y.: Orbis, 1993), 202.

30. Having signaled that 1985 would herald in a new era of dialogue and political transformation, the National Party reneged on this path and instead clamped down on any dissent, using the declaration of a State of Emergency to provide legitimation for massive state repression.

31. Albert Nolan, "Kairos Theology," in *Doing Theology in Context: South African Perspectives*, ed. John W. de Gruchy and Charles Villa-Vicencio (Cape Town: David Philip, 1994), 213.

32. Kairos theologians, *The Kairos Document*, 4.

33. Ibid., 18.

34. Sampie Terreblanche, *A History of Inequality in South Africa, 1652–2002* (Pietermaritzburg, South Africa: University of Natal Press, 2002).

35. See chapter 3, "Biblical Hermeneutics in a Secular Age: Reflections from South Africa Twenty Years after the *Kairos Document*" by Jonathan A. Draper, in this volume.

36. Kairos theologians, *The Kairos Document*, 16.

37. Gloria Kehilwe Plaatjie, "Toward a Post-Apartheid Black Feminist Reading of the Bible: A Case of Luke 2:36-38," in *Other Ways of Reading: African Women and the Bible*, ed. Musa W. Dube (Atlanta and Geneva: Society of Biblical Literature and WCC Publications, 2001).

38. Thabo Mbeki, *4th Annual Nelson Mandela Lecture by President Thabo Mbeki: University of Witwatersrand, 29 July 2006*, http://www.info.gov.za/speeches/2006/06073111151005.htm (accessed June 12, 2006).

39. Cedric Mayson, "Liberating Religion" (working paper, September 1, 2005). Used with permission.

40. Ibid.

41. Ibid.

42. Ibid.

43. In response to these comments of mine, Mayson argued in a personal communication that, according to his understanding, "the Bible is essentially about secular spirituality, not the religious spirituality usually propounded by the religious institutions."

44. Itumeleng J. Mosala, "The Use of the Bible in Black Theology," in *The Unquestionable Right to Be Free: Essays in Black Theology*, ed. Itumeleng J. Mosala and Buti Tlhagale (Johannesburg: Skotaville, 1986), 196.

45. This campaign argues that the state should provide a basic grant to each citizen each month, enabling the poorest of the poor to have a minimum amount with which to purchase basic foodstuffs and use public transport in their search for work. This basic grant would be taken in tax from those who are employed.

Chapter 9

1. For examples on Jesus, see Richard A. Horsley and John S. Hanson, *Bandits, Prophets, and Messiahs: Popular Movements in the Time of Jesus* (Minneapolis: Winston, 1985); Richard A. Horsley, *Archaeology, History, and Society in Galilee: The Social Context of Jesus and the Rabbis* (Valley Forge, Pa.: Trinity, 1996). For examples on Paul, see Richard A. Horsley, ed., *Paul and Empire: Religion and Power in Roman Imperial Society* (Harrisburg, Pa.: Trinity, 1997); Richard A. Horsley, *1 Corinthians* (Nashville: Abingdon, 1998). For example on the assemblies, see Richard A. Horsley and Jonathan A. Draper, *Whoever Hears You Hears Me: Prophets, Performance, and Tradition in Q* (Harrisburg, Pa.: Trinity, 1999); Richard A. Horsley, ed., *Christian Origins* (Minneapolis: Fortress Press, 2005). For examples on contemporary issues, see Richard A. Horsley and James Tracy, eds., *Christmas Unwrapped: Consumerism, Christ, and Culture* (Harrisburg, Pa.: Trinity, 2001).

2. Stephen L. Harris, *The New Testament: A Student's Introduction*, 4th ed. (San Francisco: McGraw Hill, 2002), 319.

3. Bart D. Ehrman, *The New Testament: A Historical Introduction to the Early Christian Writings*, 3[d] ed. (New York: Oxford University Press, 2004), 317–18; comments in square brackets are in the original.

4. Abraham J. Malherbe, *Social Aspects of Early Christianity* (Baton Rouge, La.: Louisiana State University Press, 1977), 86–87. The quote is also found on the same pages in the second edition (Philadelphia: Fortress Press, 1983).

5. Wayne A. Meeks, *The First Urban Christians: The Social World of the Apostle Paul*, 1st ed. (New Haven: Yale, 1983), 73.

6. "The people whose souls were moved by the mission of Paul and his faithful companions were—the overwhelming majority at least—men and women from the middle and lower classes. . . . On the other hand, Paul mentions by name certain fairly well-to-do Christians. Those who possessed rooms so large that 'house churches' could assemble there for edification . . . cannot have been poor. . . . It is noteworthy that several women whose names are honourably mentioned in connection with Paul's missionary labours, appear to have been possessed of means." Quote is from Adolf Deissmann, *Paul: A Study in Social and Religious History* (2[d] ed.; New York: Harper & Brothers, 1957 [1st ed., 1925]), 241–43. For more on this, see my "Poverty in Pauline Studies: Beyond the So-Called New Consensus," *Journal for the Study of the New Testament* 26 (2004): 323–61.

7. I found two scholars who mentioned only lower classes, but these comments are too brief to be precise: "Begun under a special sense of personal insufficiency . . . , Paul's

work among the mixed population of the great heathen city had proved exceptionally fruitful . . . , though among the humbler classes (1:26), and against strenuous opposition" (in Benjamin Wisner Bacon, *An Introduction to the New Testament* [New York: Macmillan, 1902], 81); and "The Corinthian believers, though they were probably few and humble in station, had divided into parties" (in Edgar J. Goodspeed, *The Story of the New Testament* [Chicago: University of Chicago Press, 1916], 14). In addition, Martin Dibelius asserted, "In the course of the second century Christianity penetrated into propertied and educated circles, into houses and families for whom books meant something, and where a philosophical argument carried weight," in *A Fresh Approach to the New Testament and Early Christian Literature* (Hertford: Ivor Nicholson and Watson, 1936), 17. Since the English title of his book labeled it as a "Fresh Approach," this is not evidence for a consensus opinion (German title: *Geschichte der urchristlichen Literatur*).

8. Adolf Jülicher, *An Introduction to the New Testament* (London: Smith, Elder, & Co., 1904), 79.

9. Otto Pfleiderer, *Primitive Christianity: Its Writings and Teachings in Their Historical Connections*, vol. 1 (New York: G. P. Putnam's Sons, 1906), 144.

10. Theodor Zahn, *Introduction to the New Testament*, 3 vols. (Great Britain, 1909; Grand Rapids: Kegel, 1953), 1: 273. Citations are to the Kegel edition.

11. Haven McClure, *The Contents of the New Testament: An Introductory Course* (New York: MacMillan, 1921), 143.

12. Philip Vollmer, *The Writings of the New Testament in Their Historical Setting: An Outline Guide for the Study of the New Testament* (New York: Fleming H. Revell, 1924), 148.

13. Willoughby C. Allen and L. W. Grensted, *Introduction to the Books of the New Testament* (Edinburgh: T&T Clark, 1936), 119.

14. Albert E. Barnett, *The New Testament: Its Making and Meaning*, 1st ed. (New York: Abingdon-Cokesbury, 1946), 49.

15. Alfred Wikenhauser, *New Testament Introduction* (Freiburg: Herder & Herder, 1958), 383.

16. J. Cambier, "The First Epistle to the Corinthians," in *Introduction to the New Testament*, ed. A. Robert and A. Feuillet (New York: Desclée, 1965), 413.

17. W. D. Davies, *Invitation to the New Testament: A Guide to Its Main Witnesses* (Garden City, N.Y.: Doubleday, 1966), 18.

18. Everett F. Harrison, *Introduction to the New Testament*, 2d ed. (Grand Rapids, Mich.: Eerdmans, 1971), 283.

19. Werner Georg Kümmel, *Introduction to the New Testament*, rev. ed. (Nashville: Abingdon, 1975), 271.

20. It is also surprising that for three decades Western scholars have been calling this a "recent" development, as though the conclusion were perpetually new. This rhetoric of recent emergence is difficult to explain, but it does fit into a pattern in Western New Testament scholarship during the final decades of the twentieth century. This was the same period that brought us the *new* quest for the historical Jesus and the *new* perspective on Pauline theology.

21. Here are but a few of the examples: Goodspeed, *The Story of the New Testament*, 14–16; James Moffatt, *An Introduction to the Literature of the New Testament*, 3ᵈ ed. (New York: Charles Scribner's Sons, 1918); Allen and Grensted, *Introduction to the Books of the New Testament*; Barnett, *The New Testament: Its Making and Meaning*. The practice of ignoring economic issues continued on later in the century as well. For examples, see Willi Marxsen, *Introduction to the New Testament* (Philadelphia: Fortress Press, 1968); Oscar Cullmann, *The New Testament: An Introduction for the General Reader* (Philadelphia: Westminster, 1968); Norman Perrin, *The New Testament: An Introduction. Proclamation and Parenesis, Myth and History* (New York: Harcourt Brace Jovanovich, 1974); Stevan L. Davies, *The New Testament: A Contemporary Introduction* (New York: Harper & Row, 1988).

22. For example, see Pfleiderer, *Primitive Christianity*, 150; and Albert E. Barnett, *The New Testament: Its Making and Meaning*, 49–50.

23. A. Tricot, "The Greco-Roman World," in *An Introduction to the New Testament*, ed. Robert and Feuillet, 14–15. This is a translation from *Nouveau Testament*, vol. 2, *Introduction à La Bible*, which first appeared in 1959.

24. Robert W. Crapps, Edgar V. McKnight and David A. Smith, *Introduction to the New Testament* (New York: The Ronald Press, 1968), 188–89. This theme carried on in some texts at least into the 1970s. "The first century of our era was the golden age of city life in the Roman Empire. City vied with city in the magnificence of public buildings, town halls, temples, theaters, baths, aqueducts. Rich men, some of whom had risen to high positions in the emperor's service, delighted to honor their native towns with munificent gifts. Their reward was to have statues of them set up, carefully recording all the offices they had held"; Ralph P. Martin, *New Testament Foundations: A Guide for Christian Students* (Grand Rapids, Mich.: Eerdmans, 1978), 24–25 (see also pp. 18–19).

25. Robert M. Grant, *A Historical Introduction to the New Testament* (New York: Harper & Row, 1963), 248.

26. Davies, *Invitation to the New Testament*, 18: "There was, then, in the first century a genuine well-being. This manifested itself superficially in Rome itself; in the provinces, it was marked by a sense of security. The one exception was Palestine where there was dire poverty. But the over-all picture does not suggest a peculiarly strong economic reason for the success of Christianity in the first century. Although the Christian Gospel did appeal to the poor, its appeal was not merely in terms of compensation for injustice but of a challenge to love even in the midst of injustice."

27. Two early writers in this phase still defined poverty as irrelevant due to economic prosperity in the Roman Empire even as they began to shift attention toward the possibility that a few individuals from the assemblies were wealthy; see Gerd Theissen, *The Social Setting of Pauline Christianity: Essays on Corinth* (Philadelphia: Fortress Press, 1982), 36; Wayne Meeks, *The First Urban Christians* (New Haven: Yale University Press, 1983), 43–44. A mild version of this perspective popped up again at the end of the century; see Stanley E. Porter and Lee Martin McDonald, *Early Christianity and Its Sacred Literature* (Peabody, Mass.: Hendrickson, 2000), 81.

28. For example, Perrin, *The New Testament*.

29. See Harrison, *Introduction*, 283, and Kümmel, *Introduction*, 271, quoted in text, p. 121.

30. Friesen, "Poverty in Pauline Studies," 334–35.

31. Ibid., 333.

32. For example, Pheme Perkins, *Reading the New Testament: An Introduction*, 2^d ed. (New York: Paulist, 1988), 125–32.

33. There was one startling elaboration in this trend that devoted hundreds of pages to the description of social, cultural, and economic contexts for the early assemblies; see Helmut Koester's *Introduction to the New Testament*, 2 vols. (Philadelphia: Fortress Press, 1982). The entire first volume is devoted to *History, Culture, and Religion of the Hellenistic Age*. The German original appeared in 1980. In this first volume, Koester charted a complicated development. He wrote that the first two centuries were a time when the masses put up with Roman rule because the situations of the urban populations had not yet degenerated to the point where opposition was desirable. That point came in the third century when disenfranchisement of the middle class and of some aristocrats led to an alignment of interest with the impoverished masses (see pages 333–35). Koester's extensive coverage and his conclusions, however, have not become standard in New Testament studies.

34. Ehrman, *The New Testament*, 303–6, 316–19; Dennis E. Smith, "The New Testament and Its World," in *Chalice Introduction to the New Testament*, ed. Dennis

E. Smith (St. Louis, Mo.: Chalice, 2004), 21–22; David deSilva, *An Introduction to the New Testament: Contexts, Methods & Ministry Formation* (Downers Grove, Ill.: Intervarsity, 2004), 562–70.

35. Justin J. Meggitt, *Paul, Poverty and Survival* (Edinburgh: T&T Clark, 1998); Dale B. Martin, "Review Essay: Justin J. Meggitt, *Paul, Poverty and Survival*," *JSNT* 24 (2001): 51–64; Gerd Theissen, "The Social Structure of Pauline Communities: Some Critical Remarks on J. J. Meggitt, *Paul, Poverty and Survival*," *JSNT* 24 (2001): 65–84; and Justin J. Meggitt, "Response to Martin and Theissen," *JSNT* 24 (2001): 85–94.

36. Steven J. Friesen, "Injustice or God's Will? Explanations of Poverty in Proto-Christian Communities," in *Christian Origins*, ed. Richard Horsley, 240–60; and idem, "Poverty in Pauline Studies," 323–61. John Barclay, "Poverty in Pauline Studies: A Response to Steven Friesen," *JSNT* 26 (2004): 363–36; Peter Oakes, "Constructing Poverty Scales for Graeco-Roman Society: A Response to Steven Friesen's 'Poverty in Pauline Studies,'" *JSNT* 26 (2004): 367–71.

37. Louis Menand, "The Marketplace of Ideas," *American Council of Learned Societies Occasional Paper* 49 (New York: ACLS, 2001); http://www.acls.org/op49.htm (accessed May 28, 2007).

38. Richard Ohmann, *Politics of Knowledge: The Commercialization of the University, the Professions, & Print Culture* (Middletown, Conn.: Wesleyan University Press, 2003), 86.

39. Ibid., 32–33, 92–93.

40. Ibid., 140–42.

Chapter 10

1. See Cornel West, *The American Evasion of Philosophy: A Genealogy of Pragmatism* (Madison: University of Wisconsin, 1989), 1–41. As the essay will indicate, the title emanates from Emerson's 1844 "On Emancipation in the British West Indies" speech. See the speech in Ralph Waldo Emerson, *Selected Essays, Lectures, and Poems*, ed. Robert D. Richardson Jr. (New York: Bantam, 1990), 311–37. On Emerson as the first U.S. public intellectual, see Lawrence Buell, *Emerson* (Cambridge, Mass.: Belknap, 2003), 9. On Emerson's protest letter to President Van Buren, see Buell, *Emerson*, 244. Emerson may also be classified as a romanticist, but—if so—Cornel West's adumbration of three waves of romanticism, with Emerson and Karl Marx belonging to the second, while Jefferson and Rousseau belonged to the first, is heuristic. See West, *The American Evasion*, 216.

2. On these acts, see Cornel West, *Democracy Matters: Winning the Fight against American Imperialism* (New York: Penguin, 2004), 73. On page 73, West rightly

notes, though, that with these acts, "Emerson demonstrated a sincere, yet cautious, commitment to activism." In agreement, see Ibid., 242–60.

3. Emerson, *Selected Essays*, 312–14, 322–25. Historians, avers Buell (*Emerson*, 251), see the speech as the "watershed" moment that moved Emerson from intellectual activism to social activism, for, thereafter, he threw himself into abolitionist causes, and all the more so after the Compromise of 1850, which potentially would force northern states (including his beloved Massachusetts) to return fugitive slaves back to their enslavers. For more details on the speech, see Robert D. Richardson Jr., *Emerson: Mind on Fire, A Biography* (Berkeley: University of California, 1995), 395–99.

4. Emerson, *Selected Essays*, 324.

5. For example, the late public intellectual Edward Said scrutinizes the whole institution of Orientalism and its supportive infrastructure of foundations and centers. Said exposed the connection between power and knowledge, that is, the ways in which Western canonical cultural productions of knowledge (for example, Joseph Conrad's *Heart of Darkness*) were solidly tied to colonial structures of domination and subjugation. See Edward Said, *Orientalism* (New York: Vintage Books, 1978), 301–2.

6. Though critical biblical research in the West is a legacy of the Reformation and the Renaissance, it is the Enlightenment period out of which critical modern biblical criticism arose, particularly in the circles of the historicizing Deists and the studious, though fundamentally pragmatic Pietists. See Richard Pervo, *Profit with Delight: The Literary Genre of the Acts of the Apostles* (Philadelphia: Fortress Press, 1987), 12. The Protestant Reformation's *sola scriptura* doctrine gave impetus to the democratic study of scripture and to interest in the historical meaning of scripture. See William Baird, *History of New Testament Research* (Minneapolis: Fortress Press, 1992), xvi–xix. The Renaissance humanists provided the earliest and perhaps the crudest tools for biblical interpretation.

7. Mary Ann Tolbert, "The Politics and Poetics of Location," in *Reading from this Place: Social Location and Biblical Interpretation in the United States*, vol. 1, ed. Fernando F. Segovia and Mary Ann Tolbert (Minneapolis: Fortress Press, 1995), 314.

8. Richard Pervo and Mikeal Parsons have challenged the unity question on a number of fronts, insisting that it is possible to read the Gospel according to Luke as a complete text without considering the book of Acts as a prereading interpretive constraint (Mikeal Parsons and Richard Pervo, *Rethinking the Unity of Luke and Acts* [Minneapolis: Fortress Press, 1993]). Parsons's and Pervo's provocative study critiques the hyphenated "Luke-Acts" thesis, a thesis first brought into prominence, at least, with Cadbury's ground-breaking studies on Luke in the 1920s (Henry J. Cadbury, *The Making of Luke-Acts*

[New York: Macmillan Co., 1927], 8–11). Preferring to speak of Acts as a self-contained sequel to the Gospel according to Luke, the authors take to task the three assumed unities, namely, narrative unity, generic unity, and theological unity. Notwithstanding the merits of their critiques, most Lukan scholars (especially those with an audience-oriented perspective) still prefer to think of the two works as unified in terms of the impact of their cultural production. On the dominant view, see, for example, John Darr, "Irenic or Ironic? Another Look at Gamaliel before the Sanhedrin (Acts 5:33-42)," in *Literary Studies in Luke-Acts: Essays in Honor of Joseph B. Tyson*, ed. Richard P. Thompson and Thomas E. Phillips (Macon, Ga.: Mercer University Press, 1998), 125, note 12.

9. The English word "imperialism" first appears in an English dictionary in 1603 and most prominently in the nineteenth century, and is, thus, a modern word. A short list of modern examples of imperialism would include the Austro-Hungarian empire, the Ottoman empire, the Czarist Russian empire, the British empire, the French empire, the Dutch empire, the Belgian empire, the German empire, and the U.S. empire. See Cornel West, *Democracy Matters*, 54. Yet, imperialism actually "has characterized people as far back as history reaches." Mason Hammond, "Ancient Imperialism: Contemporary Justifications," *Harvard Studies in Classical Philology* 58 (1948): 105. Historical forces would include "the political, economic, and social domination" of one group by another while discursive forces include "the psychological domination of people through appeals to authority, based on the asserted superiority of one race, gender, class, or culture over another." See Kathleen O'Brien Wicker, "Teaching Feminist Biblical Studies in a Postcolonial Context" in *Searching the Scriptures: A Feminist Introduction*, vol. 1, ed. Elisabeth Schüssler Fiorenza (New York: Crossroad, 1993), 377.

10. On the interrelation of these two approaches, their recent impact on biblical studies, and their critique of empire, see Fernando F. Segovia, "Postcolonial and Diasporic Criticism in Biblical Studies: Focus, Parameters, Relevance," *Studies in World Christianity* 5 (1999): 177–95. With Segovia ("Postcolonial and Diasporic Criticism," 180–82), I read "postcolonial" not as meaning "after colonization" but the exposure of colonization's "discourses of imposition" and of those "anti-discourses of opposition and resistance" that seek to question colonization at any period, whether in its historical-political forms or in neocolonial forms. Thus—whether it may be said to have originated out of Commonwealth Studies (and New Literatures) or may trace its origins to the works of W. E. B. Du Bois, many of the Harlem Renaissance artists, C. L. R. James, and Frantz Fanon—postcolonial studies, as mediated through the trio Said, Spivak, and Bhabha, has several concerns: 1) exposing the "complicity of Western culture"; 2) democratizing canons, cultures, and genres; 3) undermining disciplinary

boundaries and the assumed divide between texts and contexts; and 4) highlighting culture's mediation of power. See Bart Moore-Gilbert, *Postcolonial Theory: Contexts, Practices, Politics* (New York: Verso, 1997), 5, 8. As Bill Ashcroft, et al., assert, moreover, it refers to "all the culture affected by the imperial process from the moment of colonization to the present day. This is because there is a continuity of preoccupations throughout the historical process initiated by European imperial aggression." See *The Post-Colonial Studies Reader*, ed. Bill Ashcroft, Gareth Griffiths, Helen Tiffin (London: Routledge, 1995), xv. In agreement with Segovia is R. S. Sugirtharajah who traces the shift in terminology from so-called Third World, Non-Western, Minority Studies in the 1990s to the term *postcolonialism* which, despite its shortcomings as a term, seeks to highlight: 1) the historical physical presence of colonialism from the past to the present, 2) a practice of discursive force designed to analyze texts and societies to expose colonial designs, and 3) a stance of political and ideological force with the goal of using its analyses to intervene in the world against colonial designs of any kind. See R. S. Sugirtharajah, *Postcolonial Reconfigurations: An Alternative Way of Reading the Bible and Doing Theology* (St. Louis, Mo.: Chalice Press, 2003). With Segovia ("Postcolonial and Diasporic Criticism," 187), I also read *diasporic* as "the geographic dispersion or scattering from one's own land and people to somebody else's land and people."

11. On thicker (historical) descriptions, see Clifford Geertz, *The Interpretation of Culture* (London: Hutchinson, 1975), 3–30. Note Stephen Moore's review of recent methods in New Testament interpretation, the argument of which is that a focus on empire has received the attention both of those New Testament critics who do postcolonial criticism and those who examine empire without necessarily drawing on postcolonial theory. See Stephen D. Moore, "A Modest Manifesto for New Testament Literary Criticism: How to Interface with a Literary Studies Field that is Post-Literary, Post-Theoretical, and Post-Methodological," *Biblical Interpretation* 15 (2007): 1–25, esp. 15. Also, see Elisabeth Schüssler Fiorenza, *The Power of the Word: Scripture and the Rhetoric of Empire* (Minneapolis: Fortress Press, 2007). A perennial concern for Richard A. Horsley has been the recovery of submerged histories of communities oppressed by the Roman Empire. See, for example, Richard A. Horsley, *Sociology and the Jesus Movement* (New York: Continuum, 1994), 5; Idem, "Submerged Histories and Imperial Biblical Studies," in *The Postcolonial Bible*, ed. R. S. Sugirtharajah (Sheffield, England: Sheffield Academic, 1998), 152–73; Idem, "Feminist Scholarship and Postcolonial Criticism: Subverting Imperial Discourse and Reclaiming Submerged Histories," in *Walk in the Ways of Wisdom: Essays in Honor of Elisabeth Schüssler Fiorenza*, ed. Shelly Matthews, Cynthia Briggs Kittredge, and

Melanie Johnson-DeBaufre (Harrisburg, Pa.: Trinity Press International, 2003), 297–317.

12. For a work prompted by a desire to respond to empire today, see John Dominic Crossan, *God and Empire: Jesus Against Rome, Then and Now* (San Francisco: HarperSanFrancisco, 2007), 1–48.

13. Ron Liburd, "'Like . . . a House upon the Sand': African American Biblical Hermeneutics in Perspective," *The Journal of the Interdenominational Theological Center* 22 (1994): 79.

14. Abraham Smith, "'I Saw the Book Talk': A Cultural Studies Approach to the Ethics of an African American Biblical Hermeneutics," *Semeia* 77 (1997): 121–24.

15. Clarice Martin, "The Haustafeln (Household Codes) in African American Biblical Interpretation: 'Free Slaves' and 'Subordinate Women,'" in *Stony the Road We Trod: African American Biblical Interpretation*, ed. Cain Hope Felder (Minneapolis: Fortress Press, 1991), 206–21.

16. West, *The American Evasion*, 233.

17. Elisabeth Schüssler Fiorenza, *Jesus and the Politics of Interpretation* (New York: Continuum, 2000), 11.

18. Shawn Kelley, *Racializing Jesus: Race, Ideology and the Formation of Modern Biblical Scholarship* (New York: Routledge, 2002), 30. See, by way of comparison, *Jesus and the Politics of Interpretation*, 20–25, 89; R. S. Sugirtharajah, *Postcolonial Criticism and Biblical Interpretation* (Oxford: Oxford University, 2002), 26. Stuart Hall provides a practical definition of *discourses*: "Discourses are ways of referring to our constructing knowledge about a particular topic of practice: a cluster (or formation) of ideas, images and practices, which provide ways of talking about, forms of knowledge and conduct associated with a particular topic, social activity or institutional site in society. These discursive formations of, and our practices in relation to, a particular subject or site of social activity; what knowledge is considered useful, relevant and 'true' in that context; and what sorts of persons or 'subjects' embody its characteristics." See Stuart Hall, *Representation: Cultural Representations and Signifying Practices* (London: Sage Publications, 1997), 6. David Theo Goldberg avers that *dominant discourses* are the discursive webs "that in the social relations of power at some moment come to assume authority and confer status." See David Theo Goldberg, *Racist Culture: Philosophy and the Politics of Meaning* (Oxford: Blackwell, 1993), 9.

19. Up until 1815, at the end of the War of Liberation (against Napoleon, who was defeated at Waterloo), what we now know as Germany consisted of distinct, largely feudal and culturally provincial principalities, with the largest one being ancient

Prussia. These principalities had originally been a part of the Holy Roman Empire, but both the German Reformation and the Peace of Westphalia (which ended the Thirty Years' War, 1618–1648) had weakened the empire's political power. Eventually, the rise of Prussia, particularly under the Hohenzollern, along with the influence of Napoleon Bonaparte, led to the dissolution of the empire in 1806. Later, in 1815, Germany became a loose federation of states, and still later, in 1871, largely because of Prussian expansionism, Otto von Bismarck unified eighteen German territories into a single, federal state, just at the end of the Austro-Prussian War (1870–1871), with King William I becoming the state's first emperor (Mary Fulbrook, *A Concise History of Germany* [Cambridge: Cambridge University Press, 1990], 123–31. See, by way of comparison, Kelley, *Racializing Jesus*, 34). Accordingly, before the end of the Austro-Prussian War, "German intellectuals sought to discern the proper foundation for the emerging people" (*The Johns Hopkins Guide to Literary Theory and Criticism*, ed. Michael Groden and Martin Kreiswirth [Baltimore: Johns Hopkins University Press, 1993], 338). That is, Johann Gottlieb Fichte (1762–1814) and the Young Romantics (Clemen Brentano, Achim von Armin, Joseph von Goerres) laid the political ground for a united Germany (Maurice Cranston, *The Romantic Movement* [Oxford: Blackwell, 1994], 42), but Johann Gottfried von Herder's insistence that each culture had its own set of "virtues and values and should not be judged by the standards of other cultures" laid the cultural foundation for a united Germany (see, by way of comparison, Cranston, *The Romantic Movement*, 23). That is, Herder aestheticized nationalism (arguing that "the myth and culture of a particular *Volk* [people] emerge naturally from the racial spirit of that *Volk*"; see Kelley, *Racializing Jesus*, 35), and in so doing also racialized nationalism because he presupposed that the German *Volk* was culturally pure (though was "careful to separate his views from the emerging biological racism"; see Kelley, *Racializing Jesus*, 35). Within that German nationalistic context, Strauss's *Life of Jesus* emerged and Renan produced his *Life of Jesus* (1863), the latter of which produced the artificial categories of Semitic Jews and Aryan Jews while assigning Jesus to the latter (see Denise Kimber Buell, "Rethinking the Relevance of Race for Early Christian Self-Definition," *Harvard Theological Review* 94 [2001]: 449–78, esp. 454). For more on German nationalism and the Orientalism of late-nineteenth-century Protestant liberalism (out of which the original quest for the historical Jesus arose), see Susannah Heschel, "Revolt of the Colonized: Abraham Geiger's Wissenschaft des Judentums as a Challenge to Christian Hegemony in the Academy," *New German Critique* 77 (1999): 61–85. Predating Strauss, but little known in biblical scholarship, is Rammohun Roy's *Precepts*, a life of Jesus produced by an Indian Hindu in 1820. See R. S. Sugirtharajah,

Asian Biblical Hermeneutics and Postcolonialism: Contesting the Interpretations (Maryknoll, N.Y.: Orbis, 1998), 29–53.

20. Halvor Moxnes, "Renan's *Vie de Jésus* as Representation of the Orient," in *Jews, Antiquity, and the Nineteenth Century Imagination*, ed. Hayim Lapin and Dale B. Martin (Bethesda, Md.: University of Maryland Press, 2003), 88.

21. Ibid., 89.

22. Ibid., 89. As studies of archaeology attest, moreover, the evolution of that discipline was not a "natural" pursuit. Rather, the discipline developed to support "myths of origins," especially "during the nineteenth century, the heyday of nation-building in Europe." Philip L. Kohl, "Nationalism and Archaeology: On the Constructions of Nations and the Reconstructions of the Remote Past," *Annual Review of Anthropology* 27 (1998): 223–46, esp. 228.

23. Johannes Hempel, "Chronik vom Herausgeber," *Zeitschrift für alttestamentliche Wissenschaft* 18 (1942/43): 212. Quoted (with the English translation) in Susannah Heschel, "Quest for the Aryan Jesus," in *Jews, Antiquity, and the Nineteenth Century Imagination*, ed. Lapin and Martin, 76. Hempel, notes Heschel on page 76, was editor of *ZAW* "from 1927 until his death in 1964."

24. Heschel, "Quest for the Aryan Jesus," 70. Also, see her "Nazifying Christian Theology: Walter Grundmann and the Institute for the Study and Eradication of Jewish Influence on German Church Life," *Church History* 63 (1994): 587–605. It should be noted, moreover, that some of the so-called objective tools of New Testament scholarship are riddled with "anti-Semitic assumptions," as Maurice Casey has shown, for example, in the case of the *Theological Dictionary of the New Testament*. See Maurice Casey, "Some Anti-Semitic Assumptions in the 'Theological Dictionary of the New Testament,'" *Novum Testamentum* 41 (1999): 280–91.

25. See, for example, Smith, "I Saw the Book Talk," 124–26, upon which this section draws.

26. Wai-Chee Dimock, "Feminism, New Historicism, and the Reader," *American Literature* 63 (1991): 604–5; Emile Durkheim, *Professional Ethics and Civic Morals,* trans. Cornelia Brookfield (Glencoe, Ill.: Free, 1958); Talcott Parsons, "The Professions and Social Structure," in *Essays in Sociological Theory* (Glencoe, Ill.: Free, 1954), 34–39.

27. Mark Seltzer, *Henry James and the Art of Power* (Ithaca: Cornell University, 1984), 4.

28. I define biblical discourse as the discursive nexus of biblical diction, biblical worldviews, and interpretations of the Bible.

29. The designation *Luke* is used for convenience and does not indicate a perspective on the flesh-and-blood author of the gospel about whom there is not a scholarly consensus.

30. Mary Rose D'Angelo, "The ANER Question in Luke-Acts: Imperial Masculinity and the Deployment of Women in the Early Second Century," in *A Feminist Companion to Luke*, ed. Amy J. Levine with Marianne Blickenstaff (London: Sheffield, 2002), 45. Note, for example, the pairing of the oracles of Simeon and Anna, the former actually depicted while the latter is narrated (2:22-39). Also, note how the call of the twelve (6:12-19) is paired with the mention of women disciples who traveled with Jesus (8:1-3). In each case, moreover, the mention of the men or the women is linked to a healing summary directly before the presentation of a teaching section (the so-called Sermon on the Plain, 6:20-49; or the so-called Parable of the Sower and its interpretation, 8:4-26). On the matter of the frequency, see Turid Karlsen Seim, *The Double Message: Patterns of Gender in Luke and Acts* (Nashville: Abingdon, 1994). She writes (3): "It is a statistical fact, compared with the other New Testament writings, the gospel of Luke contains more material about women. As many as forty-two passages in Luke are concerned with women or with female motifs."

31. Philip F. Esler, *Community and Gospel in Luke-Acts: The Social and Political Motivations of Lucan Theology* (Cambridge: Cambridge University Press, 1987), 180–81.

32. Furthermore, in the so-called parable of the rich man and Lazarus (16:19-31), the stark contrast between the hunger straits of Lazarus and the ostentatious gorging of the rich man colors the latter as a hedonistic aristocrat. As well, the hedonism theme in the first part of the parable also mirrors the rich man's selfish concern for his own family in the second part of the parable. That the entire parable should be read together is adequately supported by Ron Hock, "Lazarus and Micyllus: Greco-Roman Backgrounds to Luke 16:19-31," *Journal of Biblical Literature* 106 (1987): 447–63. Also, compare the so-called parable of the rich fool (12:16-21). According to Abraham Malherbe, because the parable of the rich fool exposes a man consumed by excesses, particularly riches, the parable may well *speak to* the Lukan theme against riches and hedonism in general and *comment on* the parable of the sower in particular. That is, in the sower parable, the word falls among the thorns, with the result that the word is choked by the cares and "riches" (*ploutou*) and "pleasures" (*hēdonōn*) of life (8:14). See Abraham Malherbe, "The Christianization of a Topos (Luke 12:13–34)," *Novum Testamentum* 38 (1996): 132.

33. Luke's portrait of the early church as idyllic is often enhanced by contrasting images. Note 4:32–5:11, for example, which contrast Barnabas, on the one hand, and Ananias and Sapphira on the other. Accordingly, after selling either their lands (*chorion*) or houses, most members of the idyllic community (as with Barnabas) brought the proceeds to the apostles (4:34). To the contrary, Ananias and Sapphira conspired to

keep a part of the proceeds of the land (*choriou*) for themselves and to give the rest to the apostles (5:3). Note Robert Tannehill's discussion of the contrast between Barnabas and the married couple, Ananias and Sapphira. See *The Narrative Unity of Luke-Acts: A Literary Interpretation*, vol. 2 (Minneapolis: Fortress Press, 1986), 79.

34. John T. Carroll, "The Gospel of Luke," in *The New Testament Today*, ed. Mark Allan Powell (Louisville, Ky.: Westminster John Knox, 1999), 62. See, by way of comparison, Mark Allan Powell, *Fortress Introduction to the Gospels* (Minneapolis: Fortress Press, 1998), 93.

35. Carroll, "The Gospel of Luke," 60. By introducing the Hellenists (Greek-speaking Jews) in Acts 6, moreover, Luke seems to prepare the auditors for the movement away from Jerusalem. On this shift, see David Balch, "The Genre of Luke-Acts: Individual Biography, Adventure Novel, or Political History," *Southwest Journal of Theology* 33 (1990): 12. Saul's (Paul's) presence at the stoning of Stephen (7:58; 8:1a), one of the Hellenists, likely also contributes to the shift or is the first of many indicators that Paul will do his work both among the Israelites and the Gentiles (9:15; see, by way of comparison, 21:19; 26:17).

36. A patron or benefactor offered beneficence, clemency, and peace to others. See Powell, *Introduction to the Gospels*, 102–3. The patron-client system (a system of mediated social relations between patrons or benefactors and their clients) virtually obviated the conflict of different strata so that all were dependent on each other for greater fame or access to greater power. On the patron-client relationship, see Ramsay Macmullen, "Personal Power in the Roman Empire," *American Journal of Philology* 107 (1986): 521. On mediating brokers in Luke-Acts, see Halvor Moxnes, "Patron-Client Relations and the New Community in Luke-Acts," in *The Social World of Luke-Acts: Models for Interpretation*, ed. Jerome Neyrey (Peabody, Mass.: Hendrickson, 1991), 246. In his introductory description of John's adult ministry (3:1-6), Luke cites Isa 40:5 (*kai opsetai pasa sarx to sōtērion tou theou*, "and all flesh shall see the salvation of God"), thus interpreting John's ministry in the light of the deity's salvation to all. Jesus' adult ministry is framed literally from beginning to end by an emphasis on the deity's salvation to all. At the beginning of his ministry, Septuagintal texts or allusions indicate the inclusive character of Jesus' ministry. The Isaianic texts (see, by way of comparison, Luke 4:18-19) indicate a mission that will direct itself to a wide range of individuals—the poor, the captive, the blind, and the oppressed. And the allusions to the ministries of Elijah and Elisha, two prophets who aided foreign individuals (Luke 4:25-27), indicate a ministry that will extend itself to foreigners, both male and female. At the end of the gospel, moreover, Jesus' final narrated words become the basis for

the disciples' worldwide ministry, the narration of which will be taken up later in Acts: "Thus it is written, that the Messiah is to suffer and to rise from the dead on the third day, and that repentance and forgiveness of sins is to be proclaimed in his name to all nations, beginning from Jerusalem" (Luke 24:46-48).

37. Douglas Edwards, "Acts of the Apostles and the Graeco-Roman World: Narrative Communication in Social Context," in *1989 Annual SBL Seminar Papers*, ed. David Lull (Atlanta: Scholars, 1989), 362–77.

38. On the association of these ideals with Luke's construction of Paul, see John C. Lentz, *Luke's Portrait of Paul* (Cambridge: Cambridge University Press, 1993), 66.

39. Clarence E. Glad, *Paul and Philodemus: Adaptability in Epicurus and Early Christian Psychagogy* (Leiden, Netherlands: E. J. Brill, 1995), 137–52. See Seneca, *Moral Epistles*, 52.3–4.

40. Glad, *Paul and Philodemus*, 137–52.

41. Ibid., 162.

42. On John and the tyrant Herod, see John Darr, *Herod the Fox: Audience Criticism and Lukan Characterization* (Sheffield, England: Sheffield Academic Press, 1998). Note as well that the diction used to describe John (one who will help "turn" [*epistrephein*] hearts [1:17] and who commends "turning" or "repentance" [*metanoia*]) was often used to describe those who aided others in entering a philosophy. Abraham Malherbe has noted how the word *epistrephein* is used in philosophical circles as one of the key words describing conversion into a philosophy. Malherbe suggests further that another term, *metanoia* (repentance), was also used to describe entrance into a philosophy; in the latter instance, it should be noted that John the Baptist used this expression in his preaching in the wilderness (3:3, 8). See Abraham Malherbe, *Paul and the Thessalonians: The Philosophic Tradition of Pastoral Care* (Philadelphia: Fortress Press, 1987), 26, note 89. On *epistrephein*, see, by way of comparison, from Malherbe's list, Arrian, *Discourses of Epictetus*, 3.16.15; 22.39; 23.16, 37; 4.4, 7.

43. Glad, *Paul and Philodemus*, 162. On other texts that speak of the superior acumen of a twelve-year-old boy (for example, Cyrus and Epicurus), see Henk J. De Jonge, "Sonship, Wisdom, Infancy: Luke 2:41-51a," *New Testament Studies* 24 (1978): 354; Patricia Cox, *Biography in Late Antiquity: A Quest for the Holy Man* (Berkeley: University of California Press, 1983), 23. On the traditional Jewish expectation that the Messiah would be endowed by God with wisdom and understanding, see *1 En.* 49.3, *Pss. Sol.* 17, *T. Levi* 18.2.3; and esp. Isa 11:2.

44. On the exhibition of the righteousness of Jesus in refusing the devil's lures, see Luke Timothy Johnson, *The Gospel According to Luke*, Sacra Pagina 3, ed. Daniel

J. Harrington (Collegeville, Minn.: Liturgical Press, 1991), 76. On the endurance of sages and on sages as sons of God, tested by God, see Abraham Smith, *Comfort One Another: Reconstructing the Rhetoric and Audience of 1 Thessalonians* (Louisville, Ky.: Westminster John Knox, 1995), 126, nn. 50–55. See, by way of comparison, Christopher Bryan, *A Preface to Mark: Notes on the Gospel in Its Literary and Cultural Settings* (New York: Oxford University Press, 1993), 86. Also, see, by way of comparison, *Sir* 2:1, 4–5.

45. On the witty sayings of the sage Aesop, see Francisco Adrados, "The 'Life of Aesop' and the Origins of the Novel in Antiquity," *Quadoni Urbinate de Cultura Classica* 30 (1979): 99. Also, note that Jesus' sayings are designed either to demonstrate the protagonist's superior intelligence or to reveal the ulterior motives of others.

46. In the ancient world, habituation or the formation of habits of character came through constant practice of a philosophy's teachings and a constant pulling away from deeply entrenched preconversion beliefs and practices. In a part of the so-called Sermon on the Plain (6:20-38), Jesus seeks to get his learners to pull away from false propositions about life. In 6:39-49, Jesus illustrates how proper habituation comes— through constant practice of the teacher's instruction until one has formed "deep habits of character," or until one's heart is good and one's deeds match one's words. On the citation, see Stanley Stowers, "Paul on the Use and Abuse of Reason," *Greeks, Romans, and Christians: Essays in Honor of Abraham J. Malherbe*, ed. David L. Balch, Everett Ferguson, and Wayne A. Meeks (Minneapolis: Fortress Press, 1990), 277. Also, see, by way of comparison, Arrian, *Discourses of Epictetus*, 1:29–56; Dio Chrysostom, *Discourses*, 4.28–39. Eventually, Jesus' disciples gain a keen insight, but only after the resurrection when Jesus opens their minds and explains the Jewish Scriptures. With open minds and adequate perception (24:45), the disciples are able to offer Jesus the honor due him as God's messenger (that is, "they worshipped him," 24:52). They are now his prophetic successors. They now know keenly God's work in the world. Also, note that the expression "Physician, Heal yourself!" (Luke 4:23) trades on the ancient comparison between medicine and philosophy. See J. Nolland, "Classical and Rabbinic Parallels to 'Physician, Heal Yourself' (Luke 4:23)," *Novum Testamentum* 21 (1979): 193–209. On the Greco-Roman philosopher's use of a medical model, see Margaret Nussbaum, "Therapeutic Arguments: Epicurus and Aristotle," in *The Norms of Nature* (Cambridge: Cambridge University Press, 1986), 31–74, esp. 36. On Hellenistic medical discoveries as the cause for the philosophical interest in the medical model, see Julia E. Annas, *Hellenistic Philosophy of Mind* (Berkeley: University of California Press, 1994), 20. On philosophy as medicine, see Seneca, *Moral Epistles*, 78, 3–5.

47. This demeanor, as Greg Sterling has noted, would remind Luke's auditors of the *mors philosophi* (the death of a philosopher), particularly in the light of the Socratic traditions (as evinced, for example, through the "*teleutai, exitus illustrum virorum*, and the Jewish martyrological traditions"). Greg Sterling, "*Mors Philosophi*: The Death of Jesus in Luke," *Harvard Theological Review* 94 (2001): 383–402, esp. 395–400.

48. Abraham Malherbe, "'Not in a Corner': Early Christian Apologetic in Acts 26:26," *Second Century* 5 (1985): 197. Even the description of the church as one with "all things in common" and having "one soul" is drawn from the philosophical discourse on the ideal. Gregory Sterling, "'Athletes of Virtue': An Analysis of the Summaries in Acts (2:41-47; 4:32-35; 5:12-16)," *Journal of Biblical Literature* 113 (1994): 679–96. Sterling, page 694, asserts: "The presence of these proverbs [having "all things in common" and having "one soul"] suggests that readers should think of the community in philosophical terms."

49. Luke Timothy Johnson, *The Acts of the Apostles*, Sacra Pagina 4, ed. Daniel J. Harrington (Collegeville, Minn.: The Liturgical Press, 1992), 312.

50. Karl Olav Sandnes, "Paul and Socrates: The Aim of Paul's Areopagus Speech," *Journal for the Study of the New Testament* 50 (1993): 20.

51 Sterling, "*Mors Philosophi*," 400.

52. Lentz, *Luke's Portrait*, 62, follows the life of Paul in Acts and avers that Luke portrays Paul as one who incorporated the cardinal virtues of courage, justice, self-mastery, and wisdom. Note as well that Acts portrays Paul using the two lexical expressions most often associated with self-mastery: *enkrateia*, that is, self-control (Acts 24:25) and *sōphrosynē*, that is, restraint (Acts 26:25). On both expressions, see Helen North, *Sōphrosynē: Self-Knowledge and Self-Restraint in Greek Literature* (Ithaca: Cornell University Press, 1966).

53. Loveday Alexander, "'Foolishness to the Greeks': Jews and Christians in the Public Life of the Empire," in *Philosophy and Power in the Graeco-Roman World: Essays in Honour of Miriam Griffin*, ed. Gillian Clark and Tess Rajak (Oxford: Oxford University Press, 2002), 234–38, 43–249.

54. Seim, *The Double Message*, 9.

55. On the scramble, see Thomas Borstelmann, *The Cold War and the Color Line: American Race Relations in the Global Arena* (Cambridge, Mass.: Harvard University Press, 2001), 17.

56. On the "white man's burden" (the idea of bringing so-called civilization to the so-called barbarian nations), see Rod Bush, *We Are Not What We Seem: Black Nationalism and Class Struggle in the American Century* (New York: New York

University Press, 1999), 69–70; Norman F. Cantor, *The American Century: Varieties of Culture in Modern Times* (New York: HarperCollins, 1997), 20; Donnarae MacCann, *White Supremacy in Children's Literature* (New York: Routledge, 2001), 190–96.

57. As Victor Anderson has warned, a "hermeneutics of return" presupposes that one can find some "black" or "African" sources that will decree one's aesthetics or theology to be ontologically black and thus free of traces of whiteness or at least of its primary influence, methods, and categories. See Victor Anderson, *Beyond Ontological Blackness: An Essay on African American Religious and Cultural Criticism* (New York: Continuum, 1995). Anderson traces the term to Edward Said, *Culture and Imperialism* (New York: Vintage Books, 1994), xii–xiii.

58. bell hooks, *Black Looks: Race and Representation* (Boston: South End, 1992), 54–55.

59. On the term "double message," Lukan scholarship is indebted to Seim, *The Double Message*, 249. On Luke's reproduction of the past, see Abraham Smith, "'Hidden from Plain View': Postcolonial Interrogations, a Poetics of Location, and African American Biblical Scholarship," in *New Paradigms for Bible Study*, ed. Robert Fowler, Fernando Segovia, and Edith Blumhofer (Harrisburg, Pa.: Trinity Press International, 2004); Todd Penner and Caroline Vander Stichele, "Scripturing Gender in Acts: The Past and Present Power of *Imperium*," in *Mapping Gender in Ancient Religious Discourses*, ed. Todd Penner and Caroline Vander Stichele (Leiden, Netherlands: Brill, 2007), 231–66.

60. See, by way of comparison, D'Angelo, "The ANER Question," 50–51.

61. According to Seim, on the one hand, Luke portrays women as models who, having received benefactions, themselves become benefactors. See Seim, *The Double Message*, 92. On the other hand, Luke limits public roles to men. See Ibid., 253–56.

62. Ibid., 10.

63. As the caricature portraits in the so-called parable of the Pharisee and toll collector (18:9-14) make clear, however, Luke's narrative contrasts persons who trust in themselves and despise others (persons whom they deemed to be lower than them), on the one hand, and those who do not insist that they are righteous, on the other. On the caricature portraits of both the Pharisee and the toll collector in this parable, see David Neale, *None but the Sinners: Religious Categories in the Gospel of Luke* (Sheffield: JSOT Press, 1991), 167, 176.

64. Mitzi J. Smith, "Slavery in the Early Church," in *True to Our Native Land: An African American Commentary on the New Testament*, ed. Brian K. Blount, Clarice Martin, Cain Felder, and Emerson Powery (Minneapolis: Fortress Press, 2007), 16–18.

65. On the term "politics of respectability," I am indebted to Evelyn Brooks Higginbotham, "Rethinking Vernacular Culture: Black Religion and Race Records in the 1920s and 1930s," in *The House that Race Built*, ed. Wahneema Lubiano (New York: Vintage, 1998), 157–77.

66. Susan P. Mattern, *Rome and the Enemy: Imperial Strategy in the Principate* (Berkeley: University of California Press, 1999), 157.

67. Valerie Hope, "The City of Rome: Capital and Symbol," in *Experiencing Rome: Culture, Identity and Power in the Roman Empire*, ed. Janet Huskinson (London: Routledge, 2000), 83.

68. Ibid.," 83–85. Gary Gilbert, "The List of Nations in Acts 2: Roman Propaganda and the Lukan Response," *Journal of Biblical Literature* 121 (2002): 497–529.

69. Hope, "The City of Rome," 86.

70. Andrew Lintott, *Imperium Romanum: Politics and Administration* (London: Routledge, 1993), 175.

71. For example, that Augustus and his successors were deemed sons of the divinized Julius Caesar is well supported not only in Augustus's *Res Gestae* and in various inscriptions throughout the empire, but also in the numismatic evidence. Augustus took on the title *divi filius* (that is, "son of a god") in 42 B.C.E., a title appearing in Greek on coins found in Philippi and Ephesus and on inscriptions in Macedonia, Cyprus, and Rhosus. For the evidence, I am indebted to Adela Yarbro Collins, "Mark and His Readers: The Son of God among Greeks and Romans," *Harvard Theological Review* 93 (2000): 95, n. 50–52. Collins, on page 96, influenced by Price, correctly notes that the *divi filius* expression was always applied to a dead emperor, with the Greek expression (which was sometimes applied to living emperors) not necessarily being a direct translation of *divi filius* but rather an indication of the emperor as a figure deserving reverence and distinction. See Simon Price, "Gods and Emperors: The Greek Language of the Roman Imperial Cult," *Journal of Hellenic Studies* 104 (1984): 79–95. Likewise, coins from Rome also hailed Tiberius as *divi filius*. See Collins, 95, n. 53. On the provincial calendars that celebrated Augustus's birthday, see Lintott, *Imperium Romanum*, 182–83.

72. Lintott, *Imperium Romanum*, 177.

73. Richard A. Horsley, *Religion and Empire: People, Power, and the Life of the Spirit* (Minneapolis: Fortress Press, 2003), 99–103. On the provinces' own initiation of the cult, see Horsley, *Religion and Empire*, 101; Lintott, *Imperium Romanum*, 83–84.

74. Penner and vander Stichele, "Scripturing Gender in Acts," 233.

75. Albrecht Dihle, *Greek and Latin Literature of the Roman Empire: From Augustus to Justinian*, trans. Manfred Malzahn (London: Routledge, 1994), 32.

76. In Book I of the *Aeneid* (1.333-334), the god Jupiter comforts his daughter Venus with the following prophetic words about Aeneas's descendants: "On them [the Romans] I set no limits, space or time: I have granted them power, empire without end." On this translation, see Virgil, *The Aeneid*, tr. Robert Fagles, int. Bernard Knox (New York: Penguin, 2006). Dionysius of Halicarnassus gives a similar portrait of Rome as divinely ordained to rule the world. See John T. Squires, *The Plan of God in Luke-Acts* (Cambridge: Cambridge University Press, 1993), 41.

77. See Virgil, *Aeneid*, 1.342-355; 6.911-929 (Fagles's translation); Livy, *Ab Urbe Condita*, 1.1–2.6.

78. Musa W. Dube, *Postcolonial Feminist Interpretation of the Bible* (St. Louis, Mo: Chalice Press, 2000), 81.

79. See Penner and Vander Stichele ("Scripturing Gender in Acts," 233), who essentially read the propaganda of Livy and Ovid as I do.

80. On this reading, see Dube, *Postcolonial Feminist Interpretation*, 81, who writes, "It [*The Aeneid*] begins with the end of a battle described in *The Odyssey* between Greeks and Trojans, or Romans, and closely imitates its counterpart." It should be noted that the reconfiguration of the past was also a strategy used by earlier imperialists. For example, Herodotus wrote in "an age of imperialist expansion" when Athens, under Pericles, exerted a dominant role in Greek affairs. See G. Bowersock, "Herodotus, Alexander and Rome," *American Scholar* 58 (1989): 409. In order to justify Athens's imperialism, Herodotus looked to the past, to an earlier period, to the war between the Greeks and the Persians, a war in which the Athenians played a decisive role in securing the Greek victory over the Persians. For Herodotus, Athens's present prominence and right to dominate the Greek world may be traced back to this earlier period. Thus, Herodotus's tales of civilizations beyond the orbit of Athens resonated with Greeks who were "expanding and coming into contact with remote peoples" (Bowersock, "Herodotus," 409). Moreover, Herodotus's "artfully simple" detailing of famous figures and central cities beyond the pale of the Greeks is hardly a naïve construction (Bowersock, "Herodotus," 407). Rather, Herodotus's wonderland vogue tapped and justified the deepest strainings and obsessions of the early Greek expansionists.

81. Emma Dench, "Austerity, Excess, and Failure in Hellenistic and Imperial Italy," in *Parchments of Gender: Deciphering the Bodies of Antiquity*, ed. Maria Wyke (Oxford: Clarendon, 1998), 124. The contrast dates at least back to Aeschylus's *Persians*, in which Xerxes, the Persian king, is cast as a decadent and barbaric despot while the Greek military—in the interest of democracy—is drawn as virtuous (Dench, 125). Thucydides in the fourth century B.C.E., though, would take the same contrast to warn the Athenian

empire of the inherent danger of become tyrannical itself (Dench, 127). Later, in Hellenistic Italy, in Roman Republican times, and in Augustan Roman times, this rhetoric of contrast remained. On Aeschylus, as the beginning point for the "barbarian stereotype," see Pericles Georges, *Barbarian Asia and the Greek Experience: From the Archaic Period to the Age of Xenophon* (Baltimore: Johns Hopkins University Press, 1994), xv.

82. Dench, "Austerity, Excess, and Failure," 121.

83. Ibid., 121.

84. Ibid., 122. In her discussion of the Romans, Dench also notes that "accusations of [so-called] feminine vices such as decadence are most usually made by and against members of the Roman elite."

85. On this consolidation, see Douglas R. Edwards, *Religion and Power: Pagans, Jews, and Christians in the Greek East* (New York: Oxford University Press, 1996), 16.

86. Ibid., 12.

87. Whether a group wanted to enhance its chances of competition in the face of so many new cults or to foster its ethnic pride in the face of present domination, an appeal to antiquity was a standard course for securing public honor. On the importance of appeals to antiquity, see Ramsay Macmullen, *Paganism in the Roman Empire* (New Haven: Yale University Press, 1981), 2–4. With respect to the enhancement of a religion's competitive face, as Cotter (W. Cotter, "Prestige, Protection and Promise: A Proposal for the Apologetics of Q2," in *The Gospel Behind the Gospels: Current Studies on Q*, ed. Ronald A. Pier [Leiden, Netherlands: E. J. Brill, 1995], 122) has asserted, "At a time when the world was engulfed in new and exotic cults, the religions that could boast ancient roots had a surer hope of survival." See, by way of comparison, E. L. Bowie, "Greeks and Their Past in the Second Sophistic," in *Studies in Ancient Society*, ed. M. J. Finley (Boston: Routledge & Kegan Paul, 1974), 166–209.

88. Edwards, *Religion and Power*, 72–118.

89. According to Gerd Lüdemann, "Since Luke's census has failed to pass the test of historical verification, we can surprisingly identify an apologetic element in this report: Even Jesus' parents demonstrate their loyalty to the Roman state when they undertake the difficult journey from Nazareth to Bethlehem." See *Paul, Apostle to the Gentiles: Studies in Chronology*, trans. F. Stanley Jones (Philadelphia: Fortress Press, 1984), 18. Also, see H. R. Moehring, "The Census in Luke as an Apologetic Device," in *Studies in New Testament and Early Christian Literature*, ed. D. E. Aune (Leiden, Netherlands: E.J. Brill, 1972), 144–60.

90. Stanley Morrow, "*Parrhēsia* in the New Testament," *Catholic Biblical Quarterly* 44 (1982): 434. So powerful are the words of the cosmic powerbrokers that

the actions of opponents seem but par for the course. With almost nauseating accuracy, for example, the particular elements of Jesus' last passion prediction (18:31-33) come true. He is turned over to Gentiles (18:32; 23:1); he is mocked (18:32; 22:63; 23:11, 36), and he is flogged (18:32; 23:16, 22). Jesus' earlier prediction (9:44), moreover, sets up the thematic development of a negative *show of hands*. Between that prediction of his betrayal into the "hands of men" (*cheiras anthrōpōn*) and the reported speech of his prediction of deliverance into the "hands of evil men" (*cheiras anthrōpōn hamartōlōn*, 24:7), Luke speaks about "arresting hands," that is, provincial elites who attempted "to lay hands" (*epibalein . . . tas cheiras*, 22:53) on Jesus and eventually to deliver him to the governor (20:19-20). Jesus, himself, also speaks of a coming time when others will lay hands (*epibalousin . . . tas cheiras*) on the disciples and bring them before kings and governors (21:12-14), a prediction that is fulfilled in the Acts narrative when hands are laid upon (*epebalon autois tas cheiras*, Acts 4:3; 5:18; 21:27; see, by way of comparison, 12:1) the disciples or Paul or when Stephen is brought (*ēgagon*, 6:12) before the provincial council. The irony then is that Jesus' opponents have no idea that their hostile and forceful actions actually fulfill his prophecy. Thus, even if the opponents think they are in charge, Jesus' authority is revealed in the fulfillment of his prophecy. His opponents are not in charge. His words are in charge, as revealed by his control of the *show of hands*. Not to be missed, moreover, is the positive set of hands that Luke highlights (1:66; 23:46) in opposition to the negative hands (1:71, 74).

91. Edwards, *Religion and Power*, 72.

92. Ibid. 87. On the references to Josephus, also see ibid., 82, 86.

93. Loveday Alexander, *Acts in Its Ancient Literary Context: A Classicist Looks at the Acts of the Apostles* (New York: T&T Clark International, 2005), 111.

94. On "mental maps," see Edwards, *Religion and Power*, 72. For example, for the most part, Luke uses the term "Achaea" (18:12, 27; 19:21), a term "that the Greeks disliked . . . because the Romans used it as a reminder of the humiliation of the Achaean League." Alexander, *Acts in Its Ancient Literary Context*, 100, 112.

95. Lentz, *Luke's Portrait*, 67.

96. D'Angelo, "The ANER Question," 52.

97. Penner and Vander Stichele, "Scripturing Gender in Acts," 235. See, by way of comparison, Lentz, *Luke's Portrait*, 80.

98. On colonial mimicry, see Homi Bhabha, *Location of Cultures* (New York: Routledge, 1994), 86.

99. Lawrence M. Wills, "The Jewish Novellas," in *Greek Fiction: The Greek Novel in Context*, ed. J. R. Morgan and Richard Stoneman (London: Routledge, 1994), 224.

100. On the asymmetrical dichotomies and their use of light and dark imagery, see Samir Elbarbary, "*Heart of Darkness* and Late-Victorian Fascination with the Primitive and the Double," *Twentieth Century Literature* 39 (1993): 113–28; Patrick Brantlinger, "Victorians and Africans: The Genealogy of the Myth of the Dark Continent," *Critical Inquiry* 12 (1985): 166–203.

101. Gilbert, "The List of Nations in Acts 2," 497–529.

102. Lentz, *Luke's Portrait*, 66.

103. Here, I am thinking in part about the various missionary movements that were linked to imperialism. Presupposed by the architects of colonial regimes and their own mediating brokers was a superior/inferior distinction that then supposedly justified the "cosmopolitan beneficence" being offered by the colonizer. For more on this dichotomy, see Dube, *Postcolonial Feminist Interpretation*. In part, I am also thinking about the sad realities of contemporary offers of cosmopolitan beneficence. Both the aforementioned historical and contemporary forms of imperialism deserve adequate attention, and they are issues to be worked out in my subsequent publications though I cannot treat either here in the space allotted.

104. In *Bread, Not Stone: The Challenge of Feminist Biblical Interpretation*, Schüssler Fiorenza reconfigures hermeneutics to include four steps: 1) a hermeneutics of suspicion (a deconstructive phase), 2) a hermeneutics of historical remembrance (a recovery phase), 3) a critical-theological hermeneutics of proclamation (a desacralizing phase), and 4) a hermeneutics of creative actualization (a recasting phase). See Elisabeth Schüssler Fiorenza, *Bread, Not Stone: The Challenge of Feminist Biblical Interpretation* (Boston: Beacon Press, 1984).

Chapter 11

1. I use the term the "hermeneutic of the street" to signify the way ordinary, untrained readers of whatever context tend to read and interpret scripture. Unaware of the rules of modern exegesis, they often use scripture from anywhere they see connections in the Bible to interpret scripture, without any concern to limit interpretation to a particular biblical author. A detailed description of the reading approach of people on the margins in North America is beyond the scope of this article. In any case the hermeneutic of the street must be approached by the Bible scholar or "trained reader" with respect and sensitivity, so as to avoid disempowering people already timid about approaching anything written. I have dealt with this at length in my book *Reading the Bible with the Damned* (Louisville, Ky.: Westminster John Knox, 2005), 1–10, and in my article "Journeying with Moses towards True Solidarity: Shifting Social and Narrative Locations of the Oppressed and

Their Liberators in Exodus 2-3," in Gerald O. West, ed., *Reading Other-wise: Socially Engaged Biblical Scholars Reading with Their Local Communities*. Semeia Series 62 (Atlanta: Society of Biblical Literature, 2007).

2. Richard A. Horsley and Neil Asher Silberman, *The Message and the Kingdom: How Jesus and Paul Ignited a Revolution and Transformed the Ancient World*, (Minneapolis: Fortress Press, 1997).

3. See Ekblad, *Reading the Bible with the Damned*, 172–78. See also, *Stricken By God? Nonviolent Identification and the Victory of Christ*, ed. Brad Jersak and Michael Hardin (Abbotsford, British Columbia: Fresh Wind Press, 2007).

4. In certain manuscripts this verb occurs in Luke 1:42. See Pierre Bonnard's excellent treatment of this first cry in his commentary on Matthew, *L'Évangile Selon Saint Matthieu* (Geneva: Labor et Fides, 1992), 405–6.

5. Bonnard argues unconvincingly that the spirit that Jesus releases is simply the human spirit and could not be the Holy Spirit; see *L'Évangile Selon Saint Matthieu*, 407. In the Gospel according to Matthew, the spirit of God that comes upon Jesus at his baptism (Matt 3:16) is released at his death. In the Gospel according to John, we see the resurrected Jesus breathing on his disciples as his way of imparting the Holy Spirit to them (John 20:22).

6. Bonnard points out that there were actually two veils in the temple, an exterior veil that separated the temple from the court (Exod 26:36-37; 40:33), and a veil separating the holy place from the holy of holies (Exod 26:31-35, 40:21) that at times was sprinkled with the blood of victims. The veil referred to by Matthew could be either of these veils. If the text is referring to the first veil, access for the people, pagans included, to the presence of God would be suggested, thanks to Christ's sacrifice. If the text is referring to the second veil, Bonnard suggests that this would refer to the abolition of the priestly privilege occasioned by Christ the high priest, which is described in *Heb* 6:19; 10:20. Since Matthew does not distinguish these two veils, it seems possible to embrace both interpretations. Bonnard rightly points out that the text may well be emphasizing the destruction of the veil in a way that prefigures the destruction of the temple along the lines of Matt 27:40 (see also Matt 26:61; John 2:19), *L'Évangile Selon Saint Matthieu*, 407.

7. Brita Miko wrote this poem in response to this Bible study; used with the author's permission.

Chapter 12

1. See, by way of comparison, Richard A. Horsley, *Religion and Empire: People, Power, and the Life of the Spirit* (Minneapolis: Fortress Press, 2003); *Jesus and Empire:*

The Kingdom of God and the New World Disorder (Minneapolis: Fortress Press, 2002); *Paul and Empire: Religion and Power in Roman Imperial Society* (Harrisburg: Trinity Press International, 1997).

2. See Richard A. Horsley "Subverting Disciplines: The Possibilities and Limitations of Postcolonial Theory for New Testament Studies," in *Toward a New Heaven and a New Earth*, ed. Fernando Segovia (Maryknoll, N.Y.: Orbis, 2003), 90–105; Horsley, "Feminist Scholarship and Postcolonial Criticism: Subverting Imperial Discourse and Reclaiming Submerged Histories," in *Walk in the Ways of Wisdom*, ed. Shelly Matthews, Cynthia Briggs Kittredge, and Melanie Johnson DeBaufre (Harrisburg, Pa.: Trinity Press, 2003), 297–317.

3. The literature is extensive. See for instance Walter H. Capps, *The New Religious Right: Piety, Patriotism and Politics* (Columbia: University of South Carolina Press, 1990); Lawrence Grossberg, *We Gotta Get Out of This Place: Popular Conservatism and Postmodern Culture* (New York: Routledge, 1992); Sara Diamond, *Spiritual Warfare: The Politics of the Christian Right* (Boston; South End Press, 1989); James Hunter, *Culture Wars: The Struggle to Define America* (New York: Basic Books, 1991); Michael Barkun, *Religion and the Racist Right: The Origins of the Christian Identity Movement* (Chapel Hill: University of North Carolina Press, 1994); David Rose, ed., *The Emergence of David Duke and the Politics of Race* (Chapel Hill: University of North Carolina Press, 1992).

4. See my book, *Rhetoric and Ethic: The Politics of Biblical Studies* (Minneapolis: Fortress Press, 1999).

5. In order to indicate the brokenness and inadequacy of human language to name the Divine, I have switched in my book *Jesus: Miriam's Child, Sophia's Prophet: Critical Issues in Feminist Christology* (New York: Continuum, 1994) from the orthodox Jewish writing of G-d that I had adopted in *But She Said* and *Discipleship of Equals* to this spelling of G*d that seeks to avoid the conservative malestream association that the writing of G-d has for Jewish feminists.

6. For a more developed argument see my book *The Power of the Word: Scripture and the Rhetoric of Empire* (Minneapolis: Fortress Press, 2007).

7. Adriana Hernández, *Pedagogy, Democracy, and Feminism: Rethinking the Public Sphere* (New York: State University of New York Press, 1997), 31.

8. In order to lift into consciousness the linguistic violence of so-called generic male-centered language, I use the term "wo/men" and not "men" in an inclusive way. I suggest that whenever you hear "wo/men" you understand it in the generic sense. Wo/men includes men, s/he includes he, and fe/male includes male. Feminist studies of language have elaborated that Western, kyriocentric (that is, master, lord, father,

male-centered) language systems understand language as both generic and as gender specific. Wo/men always must think at least twice, if not three times, and adjudicate whether we are meant or not by so-called generic terms such as "men, humans, Americans, or citizens." To use "wo/men" as an inclusive generic term invites men in the audience to learn how to "think twice" and to experience what it means not to be addressed explicitly. Since wo/men always must arbitrate whether we are meant or not, I consider it a good spiritual exercise for men to acquire the same sophistication. Men must learn how to engage in the same hermeneutical process of "thinking twice" and of asking whether they are meant when I speak of wo/men. Since, according to the philosopher Wittgenstein, the limits of our language are the limits of our world, such a change of language patterns is a very important step toward the realization of a new feminist consciousness.

9. Hernández, *Pedagogy, Democracy, and Feminism,* 32

10. I use Christian Testament instead of New Testament in order to avoid the supersessionist anti-Jewish implications of the designations Old and New Testament.

11. See my book *The Book of Revelation: Justice and Judgment* (Philadelphia: Fortress Press, 1985; 2ᵈ ed. with new epilogue, 1998).

12. See, for example, Wes Avram, ed., *Anxious about Empire: Theological Essays about the New Global Realities* (Grand Rapids, Mich.: Brazon Press, 2004); David Ray Griffin, John B. Cobb Jr., Richard A. Falk, and Catherine Keller, *The American Empire and the Commonwealth of God* (Louisville, Ky.: Westminster John Knox, 2006); *Religion and Empire.*

13. See R. S. Sugirtharajah, ed., rev. 3ᵈ ed., *Voices from the Margins: Interpreting the Bible in the Third World* (Maryknoll, N.Y.: Orbis Books, 2006), 3–6.

14. Andrew J. Bacevich, *American Empire: The Realities & Consequences of American Diplomacy* (Cambridge, Mass.: Harvard University Press, 2002), 1–7.

15. Kim Yong-Bok, "Asian Quest for Jesus in the Global Empire," *Madang* 1/2(2004): 2.

16. See Jan Nederveen Pieterse, ed., *Christianity and Hegemony* (Oxford: Berg, 1992), 11–31; see also Paul E. Sigmund, "Christian Democracy, Liberation Theology, the Catholic Right and Democracy in Latin America," in *Christianity and Democracy in Global Context,* ed. John Witte Jr. (Boulder: Westview Press, 1993), 187–207.

17. Rose Wu, "Poverty, AIDS and the Struggle of Women to Live," *In God's Image* 24/3 (2005): 11, 12.

18. Nancy Hartsock, *Money, Sex, and Power: Towards a Feminist Historical Materialism* (New York: Longman, 1983), 12.

19. For this distinction see the works of Michael Hardt and Antonio Negri (*Empire* [Cambridge, Mass.: Harvard University Press, 2000]), who ascribe it to Spinoza.

20. Thomas E. Wartenberg, *The Forms of Power: From Domination to Transformation* (Philadelphia: Temple University Press, 1990), 5; See also Steven Lukes, ed., *Power: Readings in Social and Political Theory* (New York: New York University Press, 1986); Franco Crespi, *Social Action and Power* (Cambridge, Mass.: Blackwell, 1992); Michael Kelly, ed., *Critique and Power: Recasting the Foucault/Habermas Debate* (Cambridge: MIT Press, 1995).

21. For the development of biblical scholarship in the U.S., see my articles "Rethinking the Educational Practices of Biblical Doctoral Studies," *Teaching Theology and Religion* 6 (April 2003): 65–75; "Disciplinary Matters: A Critical Rhetoric and Ethic of Inquiry," in *Rhetoric, Ethic, and Moral Persuasion in Biblical Discourse: Essays from the 2002 Heidelberg Papers*, ed. Tom H. Olbricht and Anders Eriksson (New York: T&T Clark International, 2005), 9–32; "The Power of the Word: Charting Critical Global Feminist Biblical Studies," in *Feminist New Testament Studies: Global and Future Perspectives*, ed. Kathleen O'Brien Wicker, Althea Spencer Miller and Musa W. Dube (New York: Palgrave MacMillan, 2005), 43–62.

22. bell hooks, *Teaching Community: A Pedagogy of Hope* (New York: Routledge, 2003), 183.

23. See my book *Wisdom Ways: Introducing Feminist Biblical Interpretation* (Maryknoll, N.Y.: Orbis, 2001).

24. Alicia Suskin Ostriker, *Feminist Revision and the Bible* (Cambridge, Mass.: Blackwell, 1993), 122–23.

Chapter 13

1. Literature on the topic is enormous, but see the brief discussion and up-to-date bibliography of Robert Jewett, *Romans*, Hermeneia (Minneapolis: Fortress Press, 2006), 785–87. An inadequate sampling of options might include representatives of political submission and quietism: Bruce Winter, *Seek the Welfare of the City: Christians as Benefactors and Citizens* (Grand Rapids, Mich.: Eerdmans, 1994), 2–5; James D. G. Dunn, "Romans 13:1-7—A Charter for Political Quietism?" *Ex Auditu* 2 (1986): 55–68. Missiological approach: Jewett, *Romans,* 786; Philip H. Tower, "Romans 13:1-7 and Paul's Missiological Perspective: A Call to Political Quietism or Transformation?" in *Romans and the People of God: Essays in Honor of Gordon D. Fee on the Occasion of His 65th Birthday,* ed. S. K. Soderlund and N. T. Wright (Grand Rapids, Mich.: Eerdmans, 1999), 149–69. Engagement of society: Neil Elliott, "Romans 13:1-7 in the Context of

Imperial Propaganda," in *Paul and Empire: Religion and Power in Roman Imperial Society*, ed. R. Horsley (Harrisburg, Pa.: Trinity Press International, 1997), 184–204.

2 On submission to unjust rule, see Chrysostom, *Homilies on Romans* 23; on separation between church and state, see Augustine, *On Romans* 72; P. F. Landes, ed., *Augustine on Romans* (Chico: Scholars Press, 1982), 41–43.

3. So Neil Elliott, "Romans 13:1-7," 186: "The pagan world is characterized as hostile and shameful [within the eschatological context of Romans 12–13] *except* for the governing authorities as they are presented in 13:1-7, who are benevolent and to be regarded with 'honor' (*timē*, 13:7)" (emphasis his). See, by way of comparison, also Victor P. Furnish, *The Moral Teaching of Paul* (Nashville: Abingdon, 1979), 117, who calls Romans 13 a "monumental contradiction" in Paul's thought.

4. All translations are mine except where noted.

5. So, for example, James Kallas, "Romans 13:1-7: An Interpolation," *New Testament Studies* 11 (1964–1965): 365–74. (See Jewett, *Romans*, 783, n. 17, for full list.) This is no longer considered a serious option in recent years.

6. The phrase "imperial situation" is that of Richard A. Horsley (*Jesus and the Spiral of Violence* [San Francisco: Harper and Row, 1987], esp. 1–19), to whom this chapter is dedicated. He has been a friend and a mentor to me and many other junior colleagues all these years. It is my privilege to contribute this essay in his honor.

7. So Neil Elliott, *Liberating Paul: The Justice of God and the Politics of the Apostle* (Maryknoll, N.Y.: Orbis, 1994), 214–26; Elliott, "Paul and the Politics of Empire: Problems and Prospects," in *Paul and Politics: Ekklesia, Israel, Imperium, Interpretation*, ed. R. A. Horsley (Harrisburg, Pa.: Trinity Press International, 2000), 17–39; Dieter Georgi, *Theocracy in Paul's Praxis and Theology* (Minneapolis: Fortress Press, 1991), 81–104.

8. This two-level approach to Romans 13 is inspired by my former colleague William R. Herzog, "Dissembling, A Weapon of the Weak: The Case of Christ and Caesar in Mark 12:13–17 and Romans 13:1-7," *Perspectives in Religious Studies* 21 (1994): 339–60.

9. H. G. Liddell, Robert Scott, and H. S. Jones, *A Greek-English Lexicon* (rev. ed.; Oxford: Clarendon Press, 1996), 599; W. Bauer, W. F. Arndt, F. W. Gingrich, and F. W. Danker, *A Greek-English Lexicon of the New Testament and Other Early Christian Literature* (3ᵈ ed.; Chicago: University of Chicago Press, 2000), 352–54.

10. See references in W. Foerster, "*exestin*, etc.," *Theological Dictionary of the New Testament* 2:562–63; G. Delling, "*tassō*, etc.," *Theological Dictionary of the New Testament* 8:29.

11. Foerster, *"exestin,"* 563. James D. G. Dunn, *Romans 9–16*, Word Bible Commentary (Dallas: Word Books, 1988), 759, suggests that Paul's concern throughout the passage is governed by pragmatism, as a result of which he "speaks not of the state as such but of political and civic authority as it would actually bear upon his readers." Elsewhere Dunn calls this Paul's "political realism" ("Romans 13:1-7," 67). In contrast, Bruno Blumenfeld says in passing that this passage constitutes "a major Pauline political statement about government," but does not elaborate. *The Political Paul: Justice, Democracy and Kingship in a Hellenistic Framework*, JSNT Supplement 210 (Sheffield: Sheffield Academic Press, 2001), 391, n. 272.

12. Jewett, *Romans*, 787–88. See, especially, Adolf Strobel, "Zum Verständnis von Röm 13," *Zeitschrift für die neutestamentliche Wissenschaft* 47 (1956): 79–80, who detected a wide range of local and imperial offices behind the plural *exousiai*. Blumenfeld, *The Political Paul*, 389–90, and 390, n. 267, cites Josephus, *War* 2.350 in support.

13. So Isocates, *Oratio* 4.95; Aristotle, *Politics* 3.13, and so on. See G. Delling, *"hyperechō, hyperochē," Theological Dictionary of the New Testament* 8:523.

14. Jewett, *Romans*, 788.

15. See, by way of comparison, the juxtaposition of *hyperechein* with *basileus* ("king" or in the NRSV, "emperor") in 1 Pet 2:13. Since "king" is, in this case, compared to governors (v. 14), the participle *hoi hyperechontes* can justifiably be translated as "supreme"; so Delling, *"hyperechō,"* 524.

16. So Ernst Käsemann, *Romans* (Grand Rapids, Mich.: Eerdmans, 1980), 353–54, who calls it "one of the surest and most fruitful results" of discussion on Romans 13.

17. Blumenfeld, *Political Paul*, 391, suggests that *hoi archontes* translates the Latin *consul* and *praefectus*. Jewett, *Romans*, 792, appeals to 1 Cor 2:6 (one might add also v. 8) in support of a secular interpretation of *archontes*, but the context of 1 Corinthians 2, the only other place where the term appears, leaves ambiguous whether it refers to civil or angelic rulers. See Dunn, *Romans 9–16*, 763. More on this below.

18. Käsemann, *Romans,* 353.

19. So Plato, *Laws* 955c–d: *tous tē patridi diakonountas ti dōron chōris chrē diakonein* ("Those who serve the state must serve without gifts").

20. Hermann Beyer, *"diakoneō, etc.," Theological Dictionary of the New Testament* 2:82.

21. So H. Strathmann and R. Meyer, *"leitourgeō, etc.," Theological Dictionary of the New Testament* 4:231; Dunn, *Romans 9–16,* 764.

22 The translators of the Septuagint evidently used *diakonos* and *leitourgos* interchangeably. See Strathmann and Meyer, *"leitourgeō,"* 230–31, and 231 n. 8.

23. Jewett, *Romans*, 799. In n. 174, he cites H. Schlier who thought the use of the phrase on tax officials "paradoxical, grotesque."

24. Strathmann and Meyer, "*leitourgeō*," 216–18; Strobel, "Zum Verständnis," 86–87.

25. Paul's usage in Phil 2:25, however, may or may not fit this mode. It is unclear to what extent Paul attaches sacral significance to the service of Epaphroditus, especially since *leitourgos* is in parallel with *apostolos*; *pace* Joseph Fitzmyer, *Romans: A New Translation with Introduction and Commentary*, Anchor Bible 33 (New York: Doubleday, 1993), 669.

26. Delling, "*tassō*," 27; Liddell, Scott, and Jones, *Greek-English Lexicon*, 1759.

27. Jewett, *Romans*, 789.

28. Delling, "*tassō*," 29–30.

29. Ibid. 43.

30. Bauer, Arndt, Gingrich, and Danker, *Greek-English Lexicon*, 237.

31. A second century c.e. text explicitly opposes *diatagē* to *antitassesthai* (Vettius Valens, 9.11; cited in Delling, "*tassō*," 36). See the extensive discussion of whether *diatagē* is a technical term for government appointment in Jewett, *Romans*, 791.

32. See C. H. Dodd, *Epistle of Paul to the Romans* (London: Fontana Books, 1959), 210; Dunn, *Romans 9–16*, 762; Fitzmyer, *Romans*, 665.

33. For what Roman officials might have thought of divine appointment of their offices, see below.

34. For references to uses of *hypotassesthai* as due God alone, see James D. G. Dunn, *Romans 1–8*, Word Bible Commentary (Dallas: Word Books, 1988), 427.

35. Bauer, Arndt, Gingrich, and Danker, *Greek-English Lexicon*, 991, citing Xenophon, *Memorabilia Socratis* 2.1.11; and Plato, *Republic* 2.371c.

36. Stanley Porter, "Romans 13:1-7 as Pauline Political Rhetoric," *Filologia Neotestamentaria* 3 (1990): 115–37, esp. 121–22, stresses the voluntary nature of Paul's use of *hypotassō*, which would imply an ability to withhold submission. This survey shows, however, that Paul can speak of involuntary submission as well: for example, the decaying creation (Rom 8:20) or the fleshly thought that, in spite of itself, cannot submit itself to the law of God (Rom 8:7). The grounding for Paul's thought is probably Jewish monotheism independent of the human will. Nevertheless, Porter's application of his insights to the understanding of Romans 13 is essentially correct for reasons I will elaborate later.

37. Jewett, *Romans*, 788–89, agreeing with Porter, sees the middle or passive *hypotassesthai* as supporting an interpretation of "to submit voluntarily." See also

Dunn, *Romans 9–16*, 760; J. I. H. McDonald, "Romans 13.1–7: A Test Case for New Testament Interpretation," *New Testament Studies* 35 (1989): 543.

38. Jewett, *Romans*, 791, does discuss the perfect participle in the same verse.

39. See Dunn, *Romans 9–16*, 762, for references.

40. Herbert W. Smyth, *Greek Grammar* (Cambridge, Mass.: Harvard University Press, 1920), 435, calls it an "empiric perfect," which "[sets] forth a general truth expressly based on a fact of experience."

41. Blumenfeld, *Political Paul*, 391–92, n. 273.

42. Whether "Paul understood the political advantages of Christianity and used them to strengthen the Roman political system, which he admired and endorsed" (Blumenfeld, *Political Paul*, 391), however, remains to be seen.

43. See James C. Scott, *Weapons of the Weak: Everyday Forms of Peasant Resistance* (New Haven: Yale University Press, 1985); and Scott, *Domination and the Arts of Resistance: Hidden Transcripts* (New Haven: Yale University Press, 1990), *passim* but esp. 2–18. See, by way of comparison, also Herzog, "Dissembling," 341–42.

44. Scott, *Domination*, 18.

45. Herzog, "Dissembling," 341.

46. Scott, *Domination*, 18–19.

47. So Sthenidas, *On Kingship;* text and translation found in Blumenfeld, *Political Paul*, 254–55. Rulers as servants of God was a new *topos* among Hellenistic political writers, Jewish as well as Greek, according to Blumenfeld, who claims that Paul's statement that all political power comes from God can be found in Philo, Seneca, Aelius Aristide, and so on; see 391–92, nn. 272, 274, and 292–93.

48. Beyer, "*diakoneō*," 82.

49. Ibid., 89.

50. Robert H. Stein, "The Argument of Romans 13:1–7," *Novum Testamentum* 31 (1989): 332–36.

51. Herzog, "Dissembling," 356.

52. Fitzmyer, *Romans*, 668; Jewett, *Romans*, 795.

53. This switching back and forth between the public and hidden might seem implausibly confusing, but this is a sort of ideological "code switching," a linguistic term describing the effortless, even subconscious switching back and forth from one language to another common among adept multilingual speakers. One might hypothesize that is what Paul is doing here.

54. Representative are the remarks of Calvin Roetzel in response to my essay on Paul's anti-imperial stance. See Calvin J. Roetzel, "Response: How Anti-Imperial Was the

Collection and How Emancipatory Was Paul's Project?" in *Paul and Politics: Ekklesia, Israel, Imperium, Interpretation,* ed. R. A. Horsley (Harrisburg, Pa.: Trinity Press International, 2000), 228; and Sze-kar Wan, "Collection for the Saints as Anti-Colonial Act: Implications of Paul's Ethnic Reconstruction," in *Paul and Politics,* 191–215.

55. Dodd, *Romans,* 211.

Chapter 14

1. Norman Gottwald, *The Hebrew Bible: A Socio-Literary Introduction* (Minneapolis: Fortress Press, 1985), 306.

2. William Cavanaugh argues that the distinction of a "religious" sphere over against the "political" or "secular" sphere is false: "'A Fire Strong Enough to Consume the House': The Wars of Religion and the Rise of the State," *Modern Theology* 11:4 (Oct. 1995): 397–420; idem, *Torture and Eucharist: Theology, Politics, and the Body of Christ* (London: Blackwell, 1998), 4–11.

3. On the "production" of the sacred, see Robert Wuthnow, *Producing the Sacred: An Essay on Public Religion* (Urbana and Chicago: University of Illinois Press, 1994).

4. As an example, during the 2006 elections in Minnesota, Michelle Bachmann, an evangelical Christian running for U.S. Congress on the Republican ticket, revealed to a church audience that she had been convinced to run when she accepted her husband's encouragement as revelation from God ("Blogger's Video Pulls Back the Curtain on Bachmann," *Minneapolis Star Tribune,* Oct. 21, 2006). She was elected.

5. Protests of "hijacking" and calls for progressive Christians to "take back" their faith and/or their country are now common: Jim Wallis, *God's Politics: Why the Right Is Wrong and the Left Doesn't Get It* (San Francisco: HarperSanFrancisco, 2005); Dan Wakefield, *The Hijacking of Jesus: How the Religious Right Distorts Christianity and Promotes Prejudice and Hate* (Nation Books, 2006); Michael Lerner, *The Left Hand of God: Taking Back Our Country from the Religious Right* (San Francisco: HarperSanFrancisco, 2006); Robin Meyers, *Why the Christian Right Is Wrong: A Minister's Guide for Taking Back Your Faith, Your Flag, Your Future* (San Francisco: Jossey-Bass, 2006); Randall Balmer, *Thy Kingdom Come: How the Religious Right Distorts the Faith and Threatens America: An Evangelical's Lament* (New York: Basic Books, 2006).

6. Elisabeth Schüssler Fiorenza, *Rhetoric and Ethic: The Politics of Biblical Studies* (Minneapolis: Fortress Press, 1999).

7. Mark Lewis Taylor, *Religion, Politics, and the Christian Right: Post-9/11 Powers and American Empire* (Minneapolis: Fortress Press, 2005), chap. 7; William

Stringfellow makes a similar point in *An Ethic for Christians and Other Aliens in a Strange Land* (Dallas: Word, 1973), 118–22, excerpted in *A Keeper of the Word: Selected Writings of William Stringfellow*, ed. Bill Wylie-Kellermann (Grand Rapids: Eerdmans, 1994), 344–47.

8. Karl Marx and Friedrich Engels, "Towards the Criticism of Hegel's Philosophy of Right," trans. by Glenn Waas from *Historisch-Kritische Gesamtausgabe: Werke, Schriften, Briefe*, ed. D. Rjazanov, vol. 1, part 1: *Karl Marx Werke und Schriften bis Anfang 1844* (Berlin: Marx-Engels Verlag, 1929); excerpted in *Marxist Social Thought*, ed. Robert Freedman (New York: Harcourt Brace Johanovich, 1968), 230–31. The essay was originally published in the *Deutsch-Französischer Jahrbücher* in Paris in 1843; four years later, the Anglican socialist priest Charles Kingsley declared that the Anglican clergy had "used the Bible as if it were . . . an opium-dose for keeping beasts of burden patient while they were being overloaded—a mere book to keep the poor in order" (*Charles Kingsley: His Letters and Memories of His Life*, ed. Fanny Kingsley; 4th ed. [London: 1877], 156–57). Historian John C. Cort doubts that Kingsley could have been aware of Marx's use of the metaphor: *Christian Socialism: An Informal History* (Maryknoll: Orbis, 1988), 144.

9. Peter Berger, *The Sacred Canopy: Elements of a Sociological Theory of Religion* (New York: Anchor Books, 1967).

10. Michael L. Budde, *The (Magic) Kingdom of God: Christianity and Global Culture Industries* (Boulder: Westview, 1997).

11. Ibid., 145, citing Robert Wuthnow, "Pious Materialism," *Christian Century* (March 3, 1993): 240.

12. Budde, *(Magic) Kingdom of God*, 120.

13. Ibid., 124.

14. Michael L. Budde, "Pledging Allegiance: Reflections on Discipleship and the Church after Rwanda," in *The Church as Counterculture*, ed. Michael L. Budde and Robert W. Brimlow (Albany: State University of New York Press, 2000), 214.

15. Ibid., 214

16. Richard Hughes, *Myths America Lives By* (foreword by Robert H. Bellah; Chicago: University of Illinois Press, 2004); see Richard A. Horsley's historical sketch in *Jesus and Empire: The Kingdom of God and the New World Disorder* (Minneapolis: Fortress Press, 2003), 129–49.

17. Horsley, *Jesus and Empire*, 148 (emphasis added).

18. See Wes Avram, ed., *Anxious about Empire: Theological Essays on the New Global Realities*(Grand Rapids: Brazos, 2004). Several of the essays in this volume

address the theology of *The National Security Strategy of the United States of America* (Washington, D.C.: The White House, 2002). See also David Ray Griffin, John B. Cobb Jr., Richard A. Falk, and Catherine Keller, *The American Empire and the Commonwealth of God: A Political, Economic, and Religious Statement* (Louisville: Westminster John Knox, 2006); and Taylor, *Religion, Politics, and the Christian Right.*

19. The quotation is anecdotal; Daniel Lazare attributes it to a speech on Flag Day, 1954 ("The Gods Must Be Crazy," *The Nation*, Nov. 15, 2004). Eisenhower spoke often on the theme, declaring to a group of business and professional women in Detroit that "underlying all of our political institutions, indeed our entire system of government, is a deeply felt religious faith somewhere. It matters not exactly the form that faith takes . . ." (Oct. 17, 1960, accessed online at http://www.eisenhowermemorial. org/speeches/19601017%20Remarks%20in%20Detroit%20to%20a%20Group%20 of%20Business%20and%20Professional%20Women.htm on Jan. 4, 2008).

20. Lazare, "The Gods Must Be Crazy."

21. On the so-called "clash of civilizations" see Gilbert Achcar, *The Clash of Barbarisms: September 11 and the Making of the New World Disorder* (New York: Monthly Review Press, 2002); and Mahmood Mamdani, *Good Muslim, Bad Muslim: America, the Cold War, and the Roots of Terror* (New York: Pantheon, 2004).

22. See Edward S. Herman and Noam Chomsky, *Manufacturing Consent: The Political Economy of the Mass Media* (New York: Pantheon Books, 1988; with a new introduction by the authors, 2002), chapter 1.

23. One Minnesotan pastor saw hundreds of congregants leave his church during the 2006 election season after he protested the equation of Christianity with allegiance to the Republican party ("Call to Get Politics Out of Pulpit Puts Pastor in Spotlight," *Minneapolis Star Tribune*, Aug. 2, 2006).

24. Barbara Ehrenreich describes the "Faith-Based Initiative" as a "dangerous positive feedback loop" in which "the evangelical church-based welfare system is being fed by the deliberate destruction of the secular welfare state" ("The Faith Factor," *The Nation*, Nov. 29, 2004). That the program has been a cynical device for exploiting evangelical Christians has now been revealed by David Kuo's insider exposé *Tempting Faith: An Inside Story of Political Seduction* [New York: Free Press, 2006]).

25. The IRS continues its "investigation" into an Episcopal church from whose pulpit a priest remarked in 2004 that the Iraq war was the result of "sin"; meanwhile a neighboring church that boasted of delivering 80 percent of its membership to the Republican party went unchallenged (Steve Lopez, "The IRS Works in Mysterious Ways," *Los Angeles Times*, Sept. 24, 2006).

26. Originally writing in 1988, Herman and Chomsky described the "national religion" as "anti-communist": Since the fall of the Soviet Union and the Communist states of Eastern Europe, it is more appropriate to describe this aspect of the "national religion" as the near-absolute dominance of capitalist ideology.

27. William Stringfellow, *Conscience and Obedience* (Dallas: Word, 1977; reprinted Wipf & Stock, 2004), 102–5; in Wylie-Kellermann, ed., *A Keeper of the Word*, 127-29; see also Stringfellow's essay, "Does America Need a Barmen Declaration?" *Christianity and Crisis*, Dec. 24, 1973; in *A Keeper of the Word*, 266–72.

28. Personal and theological appreciations of Stringfellow's legacy are gathered in *Prophet of Justice, Prophet of Life: Essays on William Stringfellow*, ed. Robert Boak Slocum (New York: Church Publishing, 1997).

29. In an essay on "William Stringfellow's Sacramental Vision" (*Journal of Anglican Studies*, 2:2 [Dec. 2004]: 75–86), Wendy Dackson comments that most of what has been written about Stringfellow since his death in 1985 focuses on personal reminiscences (76)—a characterization I find belied by everything I have read about William Stringfellow since his death, most notably Wylie-Kellermann's splendid (and personal) anthology *A Keeper of the Word*. Dackson briefly describes Stringfellow's thought concerning "the church as a post-Christian nation" (84–85) but, remarkably, says not a word about the principalities and powers (on which see Walter Wink's trilogy, *Naming the Powers* and *Unmasking the Powers* [Philadelphia: Fortress Press, 1984 and 1986]; and *Engaging the Powers* [Minneapolis: Fortress Press, 1992]), or the "apocalyptic worldview" that "dominated his theology" (on which see Gary Commins, "Death and the Circus: The Theology of William Stringfellow," *Anglican Theological Review* 29:2 [1997]: 122–62).

30. On the occasion, a panel of theologians receiving Karl Barth at the University of Chicago Divinity School in 1962, see Bill Wylie-Kellermann, "'Listen to This Man': A Parable before the Powers," *Theology Today* 53:3 (1996). Wylie-Kellermann notes that although the comment was recorded, it does not appear in the University of Chicago Divinity School transcript of the event.

31. The 1979 *Book of Common Prayer* employs Stringfellowian language in the Baptismal renunciation of "the evil powers of this world which corrupt and destroy the creatures of God" (New York: Church Publishing, 1979, 302).

32. Stringfellow, *An Ethic*, 97, in *A Keeper of the Word*, 214.

33. Stringfellow, *An Ethic*, 99, in *A Keeper of the Word*, 216.

34. The term was used by an unnamed Bush administration official quoted by Ron Suskind, "Without a Doubt: Faith, Certainty, and the Presidency of George W. Bush," *New York Times Magazine*, Oct. 17, 2004.

35. Jonathan Schell, "Letter from Ground Zero: Cognitive Torture," *The Nation*, July 14, 2003.

36. Bob Woodward, *State of Denial: Bush at War, Part III* (New York: Simon & Schuster, 2006). Historian Juan Cole notes that the data Woodward gathers "do not point to denial or lack of realism. They point to lying and to deliberately spinning and misleading the U.S. public" ("Lies and Cover-Ups Are Not 'Being in Denial,'" commentary at http://www.juancole.com/2006/10/lies-and-cover-ups-are-not-being-in.html, accessed Oct. 1, 2007).

37. Stringfellow, "Christmas as Parody of the Gospel," *The Witness* (Dec. 1982), 10–12; in *A Keeper of the Word*, 388–93.

38. Stringfellow, *Conscience and Obedience*, 76–85; in *A Keeper of the Word*, 407–15.

39. See James E. Griffiss, "A Reluctant Anglican Prophet," in Slocum, ed., *Prophet of Justice, Prophet of Life*, 40–57.

40 Richard A. Horsley, *The Liberation of Christmas: The Infancy Narratives in Social Context* (New York: Crossroad, 1988).

41. Stringfellow, *Conscience and Obedience*, 77.

42. Eugene McCarraher, "'The Most Intolerable of Insults': Remarks to Christian Infidels in the American Empire," in Avram, ed., *Anxious about Empire*, 104.

43. Ibid., 111.

44. Ibid., 112–13.

45. Stringfellow's translation. Stringfellow, *An Ethic*, 118–22; in *A Keeper of the Word*, 344–37.

Chapter 15

1. Wesley Kort, *"Take, Read": Scripture, Textuality, and Cultural Practice* (University Park, Pa: Pennsylvania State University Press, 1996), 37–67.

2. Maurice Blanchot, *The Space of Literature*, trans. Ann Smock (Lincoln: University of Nebraska Press, 1982); idem, *The Infinite Conversation*, trans. Susan Hanson (Minneapolis: University of Minnesota Press, 1993); Julia Kristeva, *Powers of Horror: An Essay on Abjection*, trans. L. S. Roudiez (New York: Colombia University Press, 1982); idem, *Black Sun: Depression and Melancholia*, trans. L. S. Roudiez (New York: Colombia University Press, 1989); Kort, *"Take, Read,"* 97–117, esp. 103, 109–110, 114–15.

3. Barbara H. Smith, *Contingencies of Value: Alternative Perspectives for Critical Theory* (Cambridge, Mass.: Harvard University Press, 1988); Kort, *"Take, Read,"* 75–80.

4. Stanley Fish, *Is There a Text in This Class? The Authority of Interpretive Communities* (Cambridge, Mass.: Harvard University Press, 1980); idem, *Doing What Comes Naturally: Change, Rhetoric and the Practice of Theory in Literary and Legal Studies* (Durham, N.C.: Duke University Press, 1989); Kort, *"Take, Read,"* 80–85.

5. Edith Wyschogrod, *Saints and Postmodernism: Revisioning Moral Philosophy* (Chicago and London: University of Chicago Press, 1990); Kort, *"Take, Read,"* 88–92.

6. Antoinette Clark Wire, *The Corinthian Women Prophets: A Reconstruction through Paul's Rhetoric* (Minneapolis: Fortress Press, 1990).

Index of Names and Subjects